Prai

A MODERN GUIDE TO HEATHENRY

"This is the book of answers—the kind that will open you up to a road where the real questions begin. What is so fascinating about it is that it has the rare distinction of combining history, culture, divine inspiration, and hard academic and archeological facts—aspects that I personally have never seen combined in a work on this subject. This writer has a remarkable skill for not only unearthing ancient traditions and providing consistently factual bibliographical and historical sources for her statements, but she also breathes life and vision into these stories and teaches us if we listen intently enough, how to live our lives in accordance with the structures she unearths. The work is unapologetic and utterly honest. Anyone who takes heathenry, their practice, and their ethical and sacred work seriously would be handicapped without this work. *A Modern Guide to Heathenry* is an essential step towards understanding what it means to be a heathen and putting these beliefs into practice."

—Tatyana Vitta, gyðia of Freya

"Galina Krasskova's work, soundly rooted in careful scholarship and passionate devotion to the Gods, invites the reader into a deep and challenging exploration of the spiritual traditions of the Norse, Germanic, and Anglo-Saxon people. Fiercely discerning, Krasskova offers fresh and perceptive insights in this update of her classic introductory text."

—Susannah Ravenswing, Northern
Tradition shaman and spaekona

A MODERN GUIDE TO
HEATHENRY

Lore, Celebrations & Mysteries of the Northern Traditions

Galina Krasskova

Foreword by Edward P. Butler, PhD

WEISER BOOKS

This edition first published in 2019 by Weiser Books, an imprint of
Red Wheel/Weiser, LLC
With offices at:
65 Parker Street, Suite 7
Newburyport, MA 01950
www.redwheelweiser.com

ISBN: 978-1-57863-678-5
Library of Congress Cataloging-in-Publication Data
available upon request.

Cover design by Kathryn Sky-Peck
Cover images by iStock
Interior by Steve Amarillo / Urban Design LLC
Typeset in Adobe Garamond and Tim Rolands Odyssey

Printed in the United States of America
IBI
10 9 8 7 6 5 4 3 2 1

This book is dedicated to my mothers, Fuensanta Plaza (adopted) and Mary Ann Dabravalskas (née Hanna) (biological) and to my father, John Dabravalskas. I am, because you were, and I am grateful.

ACKNOWLEDGMENTS

Like any creative work, this book has been, in many ways, a collaborative effort. It could not have been written save for the unwavering support and inspiration of a number of people, both within the Heathen community and without. So many folks offered their support in the most unexpected of ways that they deserve recognition here.

First and foremost, I would like to thank three people who have nourished me spiritually and supported me in ways that leave me awed and grateful: K.C. Hulsman, Fuensanta Plaza, and H. Jeremiah Lewis. You've been pillars of sanity in a mad, chaotic, and frustrating world. I don't think I would even have had the wherewithal to begin this project but for your encouragement and support. Thank you.

Secondly, I'd like to thank those of the Starry Bull and Starry Bear traditions in which I work, most particularly my own Comitatus. I'd also like to thank MM and the terrible three, you all know why and of course my "boys," who've inspired me more than I can express.

I'm likewise grateful to my colleagues in the Medieval Studies department at Fordham University for their unwavering support and you, my readers, who let me know what you wanted to see in this book and whose support means so much.

Finally, last, but not by any means least, the editorial staff of Red Wheel/Weiser especially my editor Michael Pye. You have been a true pleasure to work with, and I am absolutely delighted with the chance to revise this, one of my earliest works. Any errors contained within this text are entirely my own.

CONTENTS

FOREWORD

A Modern Guide to Heathenry is a book that is at once accessible to the newcomer and yet written from a perspective of intense scholarly and devotional engagement. It is the determined work of an author who does not compromise on her vision of a Heathenry that can someday claim its place as one of the world's great living religious traditions. It not only expects this of the community, it demands it. Here, Galina Krasskova presents the Northern traditions as open to change and novelty, not in spite of, but precisely because of their secure grounding in a body of lore—but most of all, as an essential corollary of engagement with their living Gods.

The book reflects the significant growth of the Heathen community in numbers and complexity as well as Krasskova's own spiritual and intellectual journey, during which she has published prolifically works both popular and academic on Heathenry as well as on other topics pertaining to polytheism and the devotional life. She has a deep conviction concerning the importance of theological inquiry for every stage of Heathen practice; that it is never too soon for the new worshipper to integrate theological reflection into their devotional life; that the struggle to understand the nature of the Gods to the best of our human ability, as individuals and as spiritual communities alike, is a worthwhile endeavor; and that this process of reflection is never complete. This labor involves an engagement with the myths and rites that, catalyzed by the presence of the Gods Themselves, brings them to life in our spiritual Now, so that the entire sense of "tradition" is rendered dynamic, along with the role of the individual involved in practice. Krasskova also addresses the challenges faced by devotees of any polytheism in a culture where the voices of monotheism and of atheism are hegemonic and offers practical measures against the corrosive effect that the surrounding culture can have upon one's devotional work.

Krasskova's steadfast determination to put the Gods Themselves first in all things informs her presentation of the Norse pantheon. She distances herself from interpretations of the lore which would cast certain deities as "evil." This arises directly from her guiding principle that nothing should obstruct the possibility of any of the Gods receiving the devotion which They are due or the flexibility in interpreting that God's cosmic work which supports that engagement. This applies whether the interpretation is imparted to individuals or to communities collectively. In this respect, she is rigorously even-handed with regard to both the commitments that would tie certain individuals to certain Gods and those that would lead others to exclude those Gods from their own worship. The virtue of a polytheist community is precisely that these differences can be accommodated and all the Gods honored as befits Them in the system as a whole, but that no single tradition need worship all the Gods or worship Them all in the same fashion.

This book is a model, too, for the wider polytheist community beyond Heathenry, for how other polytheisms ought to present themselves to newcomers to their own traditions as well as to each other as fierce defenders of their traditions, but cognizant at the same time that tradition is never an end in itself, but rather a means of contact with the Gods, and as such always further perfectible. The necessity of recognizing this is more evident in the case of traditions which, like Heathenry, were historically sundered and had to be revived from materials inevitably incomplete and even corrupted. The Heathen lore, as such, cannot be treated as a sealed corpus either as to its contents or their interpretation. But in the necessity of reconstruction and reinterpretation there is a lesson, potentially, for the world's continuous polytheist traditions as well. Namely, that the reception of tradition is never complete, because the Gods remain engaged with the world and do not stand either solely at the beginning or at the end of history; we must continue, rather, to seek Them within it.

Edward P. Butler, PhD, author of
Essays on a Polytheistic Philosophy of Religion

PREFACE

I'm delighted to see the publication of this new edition of what was first issued as *Exploring the Northern Tradition*. This was my second book, first published in 2004, and my first attempt to fill what was then a gaping chasm in the literary world of Heathenry: the lack of good, solid books for newcomers and beginners. In the intervening years, Heathenry—all the many denominations that make up the Northern Tradition—has grown and grown, more than I ever could have foreseen. My own understanding of this body of traditions has grown too. Rereading my original text, I was gratified to see that while the lay of the land, as it were, within Heathenry may have changed a bit over the years, my own theological comprehension of this tradition has only deepened. Someone wrote me last year complaining that my writing and devotional life had changed, and I thought "Gods, I hope so!"

It is such an amazing time to be Heathen, to be a polytheist of any tradition. We are engaged in the restoration of our ancestral traditions, of rebuilding what was sundered so many generations ago. We are restoring to our Gods, our ancestors, and ourselves too (and all who will come after us) those ancient covenants that once bound our ancestors so strongly, in piety, devotion, and a comprehension of the sacred that we for all of our modern "enlightenment" have sadly lost. It's a powerful time to be a polytheist, and as you take your first faltering steps into this tradition, know that you're not alone. All over the world there are people doing the same thing, struggling to find their way, to root themselves once more in the beauty of these traditions.

Insofar as the contents of this volume go, I've added more material on devotional work, honoring the ancestors, and theological exegesis. If I could pinpoint the area in which my own understanding has grown the most, it would be in the importance of venerating our dead. It's not that I neglected this all those years ago, but I don't think that when I first wrote this book I realized how absolutely crucial it is. So I have expanded upon that and also added a few updated references in the bibliography.

Like any religion, Heathenry is rife with theological differences, ideological conflicts, and different attitudes on how to "do it right." I urge you not to allow the online community, or any controversies you might encounter, to scare you away. There are thousands of good, solid, deeply devout Heathens out there. It's just a matter of finding those with whom you resonate, in approach, practice, and piety. Don't compromise on your love and devotion for the Gods and the needs of your tradition. In the end, what's important is what happens in the secret fastness of our hearts, before our Gods, before our honored dead. Let us pray to make Them proud.

I hope this book will be a useful addition to your library. I hope it will benefit you who are seeking to learn more about the Norse Gods and the traditions that hold Their mysteries. May the Gods bless.

Galina Krasskova
Beacon, NY
June 27, 2018

INTRODUCTION

To most people, the word *heathen* is a pejorative, usually taken to indicate a godless or uncivilized person. If the listener is particularly enlightened, it may instead be understood to refer to one who does not worship the Abrahamic God, which is at least partially accurate. What most folks fail to realize is that, today, *Heathen* has also come to designate a unique and sacred identity for those who have returned to the worship of the pre-Christian Gods of Northern Europe. In fact, there is a growing religious movement, not only in America but across the world, of people who have chosen to honor the Gods and Goddesses of the pre-Christian Scandinavian, Germanic, and English world. They belong to a number of denominations in the modern rebirth of an ancient faith and call themselves Heathens. In the following chapters, we will examine why. Thousands and thousands of people are reconstructing the ancient rites, praying to the ancient Gods—Odin, Thor, Frigga, Freya, and Their kin—and remembering and honoring their ancestors in ways that reflect the wisdom and knowledge of this sacred tradition.

I became Heathen in 1996. By that time, I had been for a number of years a priest in the Fellowship of Isis, an eclectic Pagan organization dedicated to the promulgation and exploration of Goddess Spirituality.[1] I was an experienced ritual worker with a well-defined personal theology of practice. I never, ever, expected to end up Heathen. In the many years that I have been Heathen, I have seen my religious community grow and evolve, developing a strong cultural identity. I have watched as our spiritual focus deepened and as we began to examine our faith not only as religion but also as a folkway—a set of cultural and ethical parameters by which we were committed to living as we practiced our faith. One thing I have seen to be lacking, however, is an effective way to welcome newcomers into the tradition. Not only did I never expect to find myself drawn to Heathenry, in fact, I had a rather negative impression of it precisely because of the lack of friendly outreach. But there were many things about the religion that attracted me. First and foremost, I became Heathen because I fell in love with the God Woden (to use the Anglo-Saxon name for Odin.) Certainly, I appreciated the strong warrior ethic found in Heathenry, but for the most part, I was seduced by Woden. If not for that attachment and devotion, it would have taken me far longer to accept the identity of Heathen. This makes me unusual among Heathens, because the impetus that drew me to Heathenry was not lore, culture, or ethics. I came to Heathenry because of personal experience with a particular God, and I came with several years as a priest and pastoral counselor under my belt. Those experiences have continued to define my beliefs and practice.

There are two terms that anyone interested in Heathenry should be familiar with. The first is *lore*. Anyone with even passing familiarity with Asatru and Heathenry will hear the word *lore* used by practitioners—often accompanied by quotes from obscure Icelandic or Germanic texts. For the modern Heathen, much of the practical application of our sacred tradition is drawn from clues found in the Icelandic Sagas, the Poetic and Prose Eddas, Anglo-Saxon historical, legal, and medical texts, as well as modern archaeological, linguistic, and anthropological research. Studying these texts is very nearly a devotional experience for most Heathens, and this body of work is generally referred to as "the Lore." Heathens explore and debate these texts in much the same way a traditional Talmudic scholar might explore and debate the commentary on the Torah. In some cases, unfortunately, such debate has taken the place of personal devotion. In others, it naturally augments and supports devotion. But for anyone coming into Heathenry, a basic knowledge of *at least* the Eddas and Icelandic Sagas is essential. Such knowledge will go a long way toward ensuring a warm welcome from the community at large. Because we, as Heathens, are seeking to restore a spiritual and cultural tradition that was largely destroyed by the arrival and spread of Christianity across Europe, we draw upon clues found in the lore to ensure that our practices are as consistent with the practices of our ancestors as possible. While changes and additions are being made, given that we live in a drastically different time and place, they are done within a coherent historical and lore-based framework. This ensures that our modern religion remains attuned to the spirit of the original practice. While we don't know exactly how pre-Christian Heathens practiced, we can draw reasonable conclusions from what survived.

The second term one should be familiar with is *UPG*. UPG stands for "unverified personal gnosis." Within the Heathen community, this term is used for those experiences and spiritual epiphanies that, while very powerful on an individual level, are completely unverifiable through surviving Heathen lore. Acceptance of UPGs varies from community to community, with some granting far more credence to direct experience than others. One of the major divisions within Heathenry today concerns what should hold greater prominence: experience or doctrinal orthodoxy. As a priest, I've long believed that the two should walk hand in hand. Mysticism, that is, personal experience, is limited, if not useless, without the ability to conceptualize it. Lore provides the framework in which those direct experiences can be processed, understood, and communicated. At the same time, there comes a point at which the authority of lore must bow its head to the realities of experience or risk becoming a brittle parody of spirituality.

There are times when a given UPG is found so commonly across all segments of the community that it becomes accepted as modern lore. For instance, it is commonly accepted in modern

Heathenry that the *valknot*, a sacred symbol comprised of three interlocking triangles, is sacred to the God Odin.[2] Nowhere in the surviving lore is this stated. The valknot, however, is found carved on several runestones, in every case in association with sacrifice, warriors, and the valkyries—all things strongly associated with Odin in the lore. Modern Heathens, through personal experience with this God, have taken this to its reasonably logical conclusion and given Him the symbol. It would take a bold Heathen indeed to wear a valknot when he or she was *not* dedicated to Odin.[3] Another commonly accepted UPG is that the Goddess Freya likes offerings of strawberries. It's not written anywhere in the lore, but so many people have had this particular UPG in the Heathen community that it has gained overall acceptance.

Understanding the difference between these two terms and being able to accurately clarify when an experience is UPG and when it is soundly grounded in lore is a necessity within Heathenry. By and large, the Heathen community is fairly conservative. Change is accepted slowly and only after much consideration. In our efforts to maintain our cultural and religious integrity, UPG is occasionally greeted with skepticism. There is a deep aversion to Neo-Paganism and particularly to Eclectic Wicca among most Heathens. Heathenry is not a Neo-Pagan faith, nor does it bear any connection to Wicca. We do, however, have many converts coming from Wicca and generic Neo-Paganism, and there is something of a backlash within the community against any lingering Neo-Pagan influence. Most modern Heathens guard the integrity of their religious culture assiduously. This creates some problems for the newcomer, which I hope to address in this book.

Few of us were raised honoring the Gods and Goddesses. Most of us were raised in Christianity. For many raised in the fundamentalist denominations of the monotheist religions, coming to an awareness of and devotion to the Heathen Gods can be a terrifying experience, often fraught with guilt. Converting to any religion has its difficulties; converting to the worship of Gods one has traditionally been taught to think of as nonexistent or in many cases as evil can be all the more difficult.

There are few resources in the Heathen community to smooth such a transition. If the convert is very lucky, he or she will find a competent Heathen clergyperson who remembers the difficulties of her own early days in the religion. But often, that is simply not the case—there is no one available, there is no Heathen community where the new convert lives, or the only clergy available in the local Heathen community have given little thought to the subtleties of the conversion process and are untrained in pastoral counseling.[4] The online environment is harsh and often unfriendly to the newcomer who may know little of lore or Heathen social structure. The only books out there are either out-of-date or geared toward the New Age community rather than the Heathen. Often there is no family support during this time. It can be a frustrating experience.

One helpful thing to remember is that our spirituality did not evolve in a vacuum; it's not a matter of excising the lessons with which we were brought up, but of evolving and adding yet another layer to the tapestry of our sacred landscape. For instance, I was raised Catholic, and though I left the church when quite young, I still draw immense spiritual nourishment from the writings of the Rhine mystics, from C. S. Lewis, and from renegade modern mystic Matthew Fox.[5] It was from my Catholic grandmother that I first learned to value the spiritual and from the writings of the Rhine mystics, long-dead women of a religion I no longer practice, that I learned the importance of prayer and, more importantly, how to pray. None of us come to the Gods as blank slates.

Therefore, for one newly emerging into the Heathen faith, it's important to realize that it's okay to cull the beautiful devotional aspects of one's prior faith, if any. There's nothing wrong with that. It provides a bridge to the new, and this is a good thing. While purists may rage against anything smacking of syncretization, it is often a necessary and usually temporary step in one's spiritual journey.[6] Understand this and, if necessary, allow yourself the necessary transitional time. Moreover, there are commonalities to spiritual experience that transcend the barriers of denomination and religion. Great comfort and understanding can be achieved by the reading of shared experience—even if that experience occurs across religious lines. Find what nourishes you. Find those things that help you move forward toward greater awareness of the Gods. These are good and essential building blocks of faith.

This is actually something of a heretical idea in most Heathen circles, but the realities of conversion vary greatly from person to person; it is a simple fact that some may need the added comfort of that transitional time. The way in which we begin to allow ourselves to see the Gods is determined largely by the religion in which we were raised. Rather than fighting against that, it is far more effective to use it to one's advantage. Throughout the course of this book, I will provide suggestions and exercises to aid the newcomer to Heathenry not only in learning about our Gods and learning about lore, but in developing a strong personal discipline of devotion. Without that devotion, it is impossible to develop a strong faith and impossible for our traditions to grow.

In the following chapters, I will take you through everything you need to know to confidently enter into the Heathen community—from the history of Heathenry and its modern rebirth to our fundamental theological tenets. We will examine the ethics and values of modern Heathenry, the nature of our Gods and Goddesses, the fundamentals of Heathen rituals, and the building blocks of personal devotion. It is my sincere hope that this simple volume provides a thorough introduction to Heathenry, not only for the new convert but for anyone interested in learning about the modern resurgence of an ancient, indigenous faith.

CHAPTER I

THE EVOLUTION OF
MODERN HEATHENRY

There was a time when Northern Europe was completely Heathen. Of course, the term *Heathenry* wasn't used; that came later, with the imposition of Christianity and the need to give a derogatory name to the old religious beliefs that were not so easily discarded by the people. There was no specific name for the common faith practiced by the Germanic, Scandinavian, and English tribes, and none was needed. It was simply what they believed, what their ancestors before them had believed, and what had kept their communities strong and whole for generations. Fragments of their practices have come down to us in the Eddas, Sagas, histories, medical charms, and even Christian ecclesiastical writings. Theirs was not a single religion as modern theology might define it, but a collection of tribal religions with a common, cohesive, cosmological core. They shared a belief in the same Gods, though many regional variations on the divine names were known. They shared a common system of honoring those Gods, common ethics and values, and widespread veneration of their honored dead. At various times and in various regions, different Gods may have held local prominence, but the core beliefs were similar.

As early as 98 CE, the Roman historian Tacitus recorded the religious practices of the British Isles, noting that "their holy places are woods and groves, and they apply the names of Deities to that hidden presence which is seen only by the eye of reverence."[1] He examined at length the various governments of the Germanic tribes, their social customs, and the high regard in which they held their women. His is the only surviving record of the Goddess Nerthus, whose worship was once widespread throughout the North. Another important source of information was the eyewitness accounts of Arab travelers Ibn Fadlan and al-Tartushi. Given that the Germanic and Scandinavian traditions were primarily oral, we are forced to rely on these accounts of travelers, traders, and diplomats and on the writings of Christian historians and poets for most of what we know about their religious customs and beliefs, and most of that comes from the Viking Age, 800–1300 CE, a time of extensive interaction through trade, migration, and violent raiding. Viking trade routes spanned the continent of Europe, extending to what is now modern-day Russia and even as far as the Ottoman Empire.[2] At least one hundred years after the fall of the last Heathen temple in 1100, the Icelandic statesman and poet Snorri Sturluson committed to print the tales and sagas of the Gods and heroes. In other areas of Europe, most notably Lithuania, indigenous polytheism wasn't suppressed until the fifteenth century. Today, more and more people are returning to these polytheisms, working to restore and cultivate their traditions in the modern age.

Given the Vikings' extensive trade routes, the inevitable intermarriage with other cultures, the prevalence of Saami references in the context of Nordic magico-religious practices, the occasional reference in lore to folk who worshipped both Thor and Christ, and the ease with which early Christian healers combined

Heathen and Christian symbology in their healing charms, it's doubtful that there was any rigid Heathen orthodoxy. Recent scholarship confirms that Viking Age Europe was a world of cultural interconnection between Anglo-Saxon, Balto-Finnic, Celtic, Saami, and Norse cultures.[3] As with many polytheistic cultures, the initial attitude toward foreign Gods was quite likely not hostile. Any religion they came into contact with prior to the advent of Christianity would have been grounded in the specific cultures of its adherents, providing a logical continuity of cosmological understanding, and would have borne no imperative to dissolve and destroy other beliefs.

Unfortunately, this is precisely what occurred with Christianity. The arrival of Christianity in Northern Europe was inevitably followed by prohibitions against the practice of the indigenous faiths.[4] Some of the more zealous converted Christian kings, such as Norway's Olaf Tryggvason,[5] enforced those prohibitions with bloodthirsty zeal, torturing followers of the old Gods with a viciousness matched only by the later Spanish Inquisition. Christianity appeared in England with the arrival of Augustine of Canterbury, sent at Pope Gregory's behest in 597. In less than 200 years, England was thoroughly Christianized, though Heathen practices and customs apparently continued to coexist alongside the newfound faith. People did not readily give up their traditional beliefs and practices, and there is evidence easily into the eleventh century for a surviving Heathenry when King Canute, for instance, had to enact laws against these traditional practices.[6] Even into the nineteenth century, there are folk charms and practices that reference the Northern Gods.

The rest of Northern Europe fell to Christian conquest slowly but surely. Iceland converted in 1000,[7] when their lawspeaker, Thorgeirr Thorkelsson, was asked to mediate the growing dispute between Christian and Heathen factions. He withdrew "under the cloak"[8] for a day and a night and, when he emerged, settled in favor of the Christians. The last Heathen Temple, in Uppsala,

Sweden, was forcibly closed in 1100 after the defeat of King Sweyn "the Sacrificer." King Sweyn had taken the throne after his brother-in-law King Inge I was ousted for trying to impose Christianity upon the people. Inge later raised an army, killed Sweyn, and took back his throne, and Christianity became the state religion. This slow process of conversion was not without bloodshed on both sides as this example illustrates.

The conversion of Europe was finalized by historians and scholars who reinforced the idea of Christianity as a positive evolution of belief, regardless of the cultural and religious devastation of indigenous practices it left in its wake. Little attention has been given to pre-Christian Heathenry as a serious faith, and modern scholars remain equally dismissive of the rebirth of Heathenry, expressing biased, condescending, or antiquated views.[9]

Though some folk traditions remained alive in Scandinavian, English, and Germanic countries, the Nordic Gods were not openly worshipped again on any large scale until the 1970s. Some modern Heathens refer to the Heathens of pre-Christian Europe as "Arch-Heathens." Because they lived in a time when their faith and culture were able to develop not only without interference but also without conflict with the dominant cultural and social mores, it is thought that they had a clearer connection to the Gods—something that only this generation's children's children, raised Heathen, will have a chance to reclaim.

The rebirth of Heathenry began in late nineteenth-century Germany. German Romanticism saw a burgeoning interest in the tales and fables of the old Gods. The occult revival of the West, represented by Dion Fortune, Helena Blavatsky, and Aleister Crowley, had its German counterparts in Guido von List, Rudolf Steiner, and the Thule Society. Just as the occult revival in England led eventually to the birth of modern Wicca, so too might Heathenry have gone had World War II not intervened. Modern Heathens are often asked if their religion has anything to do with Nazism or racism. The answer is an unequivocal no. It is true that Nazi

Germany appropriated certain sacred Heathen symbols, such as the sun wheel (a symbol of the regenerative power of the sun found in nearly every Indo-European culture and even in Japan) and various runes. However, they were not Heathen, nor did Hitler and his Nazis ascribe to any Heathen practices or beliefs. In fact, Hitler several times expressed very negative views about followers of the old Gods, and in 1941, the head of his security police, Reinhardt Heydrich, banned a large number of spiritual and occult practices. Among the victims of this act were followers of Rudolf Steiner, Guido von List, and traditional Odinists (worshippers of the God Odin). Many were arrested. Their property was confiscated, and some were even sent to concentration camps such as Flossenberg and Dachau.[10] There will always be ignorant folk who attempt to misuse sacred symbols. Unfortunately there is a small percentage of racists who have attempted to latch on to Heathen principles in order to further their hate-filled agenda. However, the majority of modern Heathens find them deplorable and will have nothing to do with them.

World War II set the rebirth of Modern Heathenry back at least thirty years. It wasn't until the early 1970s that it truly began to emerge again. Groups in Iceland, the United States, and England and across Europe, independently of each other, began to worship the Norse Gods and reconstruct Heathen rituals and practices. Icelandic poet and farmer Sveinbjorn Beinteinsson and his friends formed the group Asatruarfelagid. In the U.S., Robert Stine and Stephen McNallon formed the Viking Brotherhood, later renamed the Asatru Folk Alliance. The Committee for the Restoration of the Odinic Rite was formed in the UK by John Yeowell and his associates.[11] The decades that followed saw immense growth in the Heathen community as well as schisms and splits. New groups, such as Thaet Angelseaxisce Ealdriht, devoted to the study and practice of Anglo-Saxon forms of Heathenry; Normanni Thiud, focusing on Norman Heathenry; and The Troth, an international networking organization, soon sprang up across the U.S. In 1973, Asatru[12] was named one of the official religions of Iceland, alongside the Lutheran Church. In 2003, the Lutheran Church in Denmark, which possesses ultimate religious authority in that country, granted official status to a Heathen religious group, which can now perform legal Heathen weddings.

Like any other religion, modern Heathenry is diverse, with many different denominations. While all modern Heathens share a common cosmological core, social structure and theological emphasis and approach can vary widely from group to group. Modern Heathenry can best be divided by where the groups draw their primary cultural inspiration. The major denominations draw upon Icelandic, Continental Germanic and Scandinavian, Anglo-Saxon, or Norman history, culture, language, and religion for their reconstructionist inspiration. Some focus on one particular culture, while others may rely on several or even all of the above.

Three terms that newcomers to the community will invariably hear are (1) Tribalist, (2) Universalist, and (3) Folkish. These aren't really denominations so much as a sociopolitical-religious spectrum into which various denominations of Heathenry and may fall. Within that spectrum, there are strict reconstructionists who restrict their practices to what can clearly and unarguably be referenced from the surviving lore. There are neo-Heathens who are more open to innovation and resources that are not lore-based, focusing on the modern evolution of Heathenry and asking what Heathenry would be like had we not endured 2,000 years of Christianity. There are also those Heathens who fall somewhere between the two, as well as those who believe that Heathenry, like Shinto or the Native American religions, is an indigenous religion and should be approached as such. Some Heathens may even fall into more than one category. Let's examine each, in turn, beginning with the one that falls in the middle of the spectrum.

Tribalism: Some groups are Tribalist—focused on rebuilding cohesive, interdependent communities structured around strict adherence to the Heathen thew of our ancestors. These denominations tend to have hierarchical social structures based on the comitatus model of the Anglo-Saxons and Normans and tend to be somewhat conservative. They are not inclusive generally, expecting a certain degree of commitment and demonstrated worth from new members. Among Tribalist Heathens, the family and community are the binding forces by which the individual Heathens govern their lives. Much focus is given to right action and right relationship, the accepted definition of frith being far more active and assertive than other denominations may expect. As with other denominations of Heathenry, honoring the Gods, blóting, and celebrating the holy tides are all considered extremely important. Religion, community, and culture are inseparable, being seen as necessary components of a well-balanced whole. The Tribal community is generally the primary means of self-definition for Tribalist Heathens.

Universalism: At the more liberal end of the spectrum, Universalist Heathens (a good example would be the majority of the Troth community) are generally far more tolerant of variations of thew and practice, with less concern for social organization or a centralized authority. They reject the hierarchical, theodish social structure and the need for a web of oaths (which we will discuss later). They generally appreciate diversity and are not focused on building insular Heathen communities, as their self-definition does not rest on the tribal unit but rather on the individual. Universalists are far more concerned with getting along with other Heathens and accommodating variations in practice than Tribalists. They are understanding, if not accepting, of Neo-Pagan influence; many Universalists even consider Heathenry to fall under the Neo-Pagan umbrella—a position most Folkish Heathens and Tribalists reject. More importance is ascribed to the commonalities between Heathens and commonalities of cosmological symbolism between cultures and religions than to cultural uniqueness. As with Tribalists, honoring the Gods, studying lore, and keeping the holy tides are all very important to Universalist practice.

Folkish Heathenry: At the more conservative end of the spectrum, we have Folkish Heathenry. Perhaps no other "denomination" causes such controversy as this one. When I first became Heathen in 1996, "Folkish" was interchangeable with "racist," denoting a person one step away from being a white supremacist. We now see a spectrum of belief and practice within the Folkish community. Basically, Folkish Heathens believe that, in order to practice Heathenry, one must either be of English/Germanic/Scandinavian descent or acculturated to such a community. For some, those who are not of European descent may become part of the community by adoption or blood-sib oath. For others, nothing less than English/Germanic/Scandinavian blood ancestry will suffice. Like Tribalists, they have a strong focus on building a Heathen community, and many Folkish Heathens are also Tribalist. Heathenry, however, is seen as an ancestral religion first and foremost; to appreciate it fully—to truly have a direct link to the Norse Gods—one must share in that ancestry. Most Folkish Heathens would not consider themselves racist but would simply not comprehend why someone of non-Germanic descent would choose to honor Germanic Gods and culture. Such a person would be encouraged to seek out and honor his or her own indigenous Gods. The Asatru Alliance is one example of a Folkish organization. This is where it becomes tricky: while some small percentage of Folkish Heathens may be racist, it does not follow that Folkism is automatically synonymous with racism. In most cases, it is not. The defining tenet of Folkish Heathenry is that Heathenry is seen, first and foremost, as an ancestral tradition.

Theodish Heathenry: Theodish Heathens are bound within a tribal structure by what is called a "web of oaths." Bonds are formed between individuals of varying social rank (and Theodish social structure is hierarchical) by means of sacred oaths, and this web of oaths holds the tribe together. So while all Theods are

Tribalist, one may be Tribalist without being Theodish. The difference is largely one of social structure and hierarchy.

Northern Tradition Paganism is much more open to magical and ecstatic practices and to nonlore-based ritual and inspiration. While I personally don't see anything in Northern Tradition Paganism that isn't specifically Heathen, those who claim this identity for themselves generally do so because more mainstream denominations are ambivalent about issues like shamanism, spirit work, and direct engagement with the Gods, especially the Jötnar, all of which form important foci of NT Paganism. It should be noted that there are Heathens who engage in all of these things, but having a more Tribalist orientation, hold firmly to the identity of "Heathen" rather than "NT Pagan." It's complicated.

Heathens do not meet in churches. Most gather in private homes or on private land. It is quite common for rites and celebrations to be held outdoors when weather permits. The most common name for a group of practicing Heathens is a *Kindred*. It may also be referred to as a *Mot*, if one is of Anglo-Saxon belief. Most of the kindreds and organizations out there fall somewhere along the spectrum of belief and practice mentioned above, and understanding and application of Heathen thews[13] will vary accordingly.

Now, denomination aside, being Heathen is about more than worshipping the Norse Gods and Goddesses, although that is and should be one's primary focus. Heathenry evolved as part of a cohesive culture. And while the natural evolution of that culture and religion was interrupted by some 1,600 years of Christianity, there are specific cultural, social, and linguistic patterns that are part and parcel of Heathenry. This is one of the things that differentiates indigenous traditions from Neo-Paganism and Wicca: they have a firm grounding in a specific culture, and with that culture comes a unique set of values, ethics, and a worldview and cosmology. And beyond simply honoring the Vanir or the Aesir, to truly be *Heathen* one must must also adopt and live by some version of Heathen values and worldview. Heathenry isn't just a belief in a specific set of Deities; it is a folkway—a way of living, thinking, and making choices consistent with Heathen lore and thew. That thew may differ from denomination to denomination, but a consistency of culture and cosmology unites them. And while most Heathens prefer to worship only the Norse Gods, I would go so far personally as to say it doesn't matter if a Heathen also honors non-Norse Deities in addition to the Norse, so long as the thews and values lie somewhere along the Heathen spectrum. There is historical precedent for this. When the Romans came North, they brought their Gods with them and often venerated local Gods as well, and when they left, Roman Gods had integrated into the fabric of the Northern culture to some degree. Religions don't evolve and exist in a vacuum, and polytheism had no expectation of exclusivity (though modern Heathens tend to be rather exclusive in mainstream circles). One honored the Gods of one's ancestors, one's community, one's city, and one's heart, too. Religion was about how to engage with the Gods and ancestors, establishing right practice and protocol, while ethics and values often came more from the community and philosophy than from religious practice. Thews and values impact the community at a greater level than what goes on in one's personal devotions, which are, when all is said and done, a rooftree issue.[14]

Interaction, education, and even sharing of rites and rituals between various denominations of Heathens, between Heathens and other indigenous religions, and between Heathens and Wiccans and Neo-Pagans have the potential to enhance all involved. There is much that we can all learn from each other. The line must be drawn, however, when such intercourse is approached not from a desire to share knowledge or from a position of mutual respect, but from a sense of entitlement and cultural misappropriation. While most Heathens are ever-willing to share the broadest aspects of practice and to explain Heathen lore, thew, and beliefs, many may be unwilling to openly discuss the more catalytic aspects of personal experience—specific sacred traditions such as the Heathen magico-religious practices of seiðr, spae, and runemal—with those outside of their faith. They are unique to Heathen culture. They assist in maintaining the community's might, worth, and strength, and some feel they should not be approached in detail, outside of specific Heathen cultural and cosmological paradigms. Most are very aware of what was lost with the coming of Christianity to Northern Europe and guard their newfound traditions assiduously.

Regardless of denomination, modern Heathens strive to reconstruct the practices of their ancestors, drawing on their lore for inspiration. Maintaining this sacred link to the past is a very important part of Heathen belief today. In many respects, it is the lifeblood of the faith. Mindfulness of that continuity and of the responsibility to forge yet another link in that never-ending chain forms the foundation of modern belief and practice.

Are Heathens Pagan or Polytheist or What?

The two words, *Pagan* and *Polytheist*, in my opinion, should be synonymous, but in today's communities, they're not. Polytheist means someone who believes in and venerates the Gods as individual, Holy Beings. Heathens are polytheists. The logical and necessary corollary then is the rightness of regular devotion and *cultus*. One would think this is self-explanatory. The meaning, after all, is embedded in the etymology of the word itself: πολύ (many) θέοι (Gods).

While the definition of Polytheist is self-explanatory, Pagan is more complicated. Some polytheists will use the term. But between about 2011 and 2014 there was a huge intercommunity explosion over it. There were growing attempts to A) allow for "Pagan" to include nontheists and atheists;[15] and B) force polytheistic traditions under the Neo-Pagan umbrella, which at its core was an attempt to force our traditions to open their boundaries to anyone and anything.[16]

The battle raged over blogs and newsgroups, and finally many leading polytheists (against my better judgment) decided to yield the term *Pagan*. So *Pagan* has become a catchall term that anyone can claim who has any connection to any God or Goddess, regardless of whether or not they believe Them to be real or mere archetypes or claim that all Deities are the same or are only interested in nature or making a political statement, the word entailing no core of any type of tradition or devotion. As a result, most devout polytheists I know, especially those who fought through this, won't use the term *Pagan* now. The Gods and Their devotion are at the heart of our practices. Of course, the moment we ceded the term *Pagan,* the non- and anti-theists started trying to claim Polytheist too, but so far we've successfully beaten them back.

It never ends, but there are those of us who will hold that line until we are all of us dust. Our Gods and traditions deserve that, at least, from us. I'd also add that part of the problem is that Polytheism involves traditions, which are relatively closed containers. Neo-Pagans often complain that this is elitist and amounts to policing devotion—unless we're talking about African Traditional Religions, say, in which case they are less likely to complain, because demanding open access to those might be construed as appropriative and racist.

So Pagan today can refer to someone practicing any of the many religions, which may or may not include devotion to any Gods, that grew out of occultism and the counterculture movements. It may also refer to those practicing and restoring Polytheistic traditions like Heathenry, Asatru, Kemetic orthodoxy, Hellenismos, Romuva, etc., but it is increasingly no longer the term of choice for these, especially in the US. But you will still find devout people using Pagan if they weren't particularly aware of the online arguments. Because of how spread out our communities are, we tend to hash out our identities online, but one should not think that the online world encompasses the whole of any tradition or practice. There are many devout Polytheists (and Pagans too) whose practice centers around hearth and home, land, community, and their Gods, and whose window into the greater world doesn't necessarily come through the internet. There are also Polytheists who obstinately refuse to cede the term Pagan and still use it. I like these folks. Newbies coming into our communities also tend not to be aware of these fault lines.

It's always worth querying when someone says "I'm Pagan," what they mean by that. The answers might surprise you.

CHAPTER 2

COSMOLOGY

Heathen cosmology is quite complex and rich in both symbolism and meaning. The majority of sacred stories are preserved in the Poetic Edda and Prose Edda, both dating from thirteeth-century Iceland. Remnants of the Heathen religion also survive in Anglo-Saxon histories and healing manuscripts, as well as the Icelandic Sagas. Current scholarship in the fields of archaeology, history, linguistics, and anthropology continues to increase knowledge of the pre-Christian world. This body of work comprises what modern Heathens refer to as "lore." It is from the lore that modern Heathens draw their inspiration for the reconstruction of their ancient faith. These stories are meant to be studied, explored, and meditated upon. They are not meant to substitute for personal gnosis; rather, they should enhance such things. The various stories may be interpreted on a variety of levels and provide insight into the nature of the Heathen Gods and one's own spiritual journey.

Modern Heathenry, like the Heathenry of old, is a polytheistic religion. This means that Heathens believe in individual Gods and Goddesses, each with an independent nature and personality.

Some modern Heathens believe that there is a common source to the Gods, rather like a tree with many individual branches. Other Heathens believe that each of the Gods is an individual entity and there is no common source. Regardless, the Gods are not seen as archetypal figures or aspects, but as living, evolving beings in Their own right. They may choose to interact with humanity both directly and indirectly, and there are many stories in lore of the Gods taking an active hand in human affairs. Some of these sacred stories, such as that of the creation of the world, may seem fanciful, but their complex symbolism points to the interconnectedness of all living things, their common origin at the hands of the Gods, and the cyclical nature of the world of which humanity is part.

According to the Eddas,[1] in the beginning, there existed a great chasm called Ginnungagap. Within this yawning void lay two worlds: Muspelheim, the world of raging fire, and Niflheim, the world of ice, fog, and stillness. Within Niflheim lay the well Hvergelmir, from which flowed ten primordial rivers. For eons, these worlds spun within the primal void of Ginnungagap in cosmic opposition to each other. Eventually, however, they began to draw closer and closer until they collided. From this, life burst into being and the process of cosmic evolution began.

From the primordial ooze created by the steam, ice, fog, and heat, there arose the first being: a proto-giant named Ymir. Ymir was born when the ice of Niflheim melted in the heat caused by the nearness of Muspelheim. Some scholars believe Ymir's name to be related to the Sanskrit word *yama*, meaning "twin," perhaps with the sense of "hybrid" or "hermaphrodite," and his dual nature is further shown in that he is the progenitor of both men and giants.[2] The giant race was descended from a man and woman brought to life from the sweat pooling in the sleeping Ymir's armpits, and from his legs came a son.

Ymir wasn't the only primal being to emerge from this cataclysmic meeting of ice and fire. Where the primordial streams in Niflheim congealed, Auðumla, a mighty cow, came forth. From her milk, Ymir drew his nourishment. Auðumla lived on salt, which she licked from the ice and brine of Niflheim. As Auðumla licked the salty brine—matter that was infused with the creative life force—a new being began to emerge. This was Buri. Unlike Ymir and his progeny, Buri was stately and handsome. Buri had a son named Bor, who married the giantess Bestla. (Like many creation stories, we do not know where these other giants came from if not from the body of Ymir.) From Bor and Bestla were born the first three Gods: Odin, Hoenir, and Loður. Sometimes They are called Odin, Vili, and Vé.

These three Gods slew Ymir. He was so vast a being that, when he was killed, the blood from the wound caused a great flood that killed all the giants, save for two: Bergelmir and his wife. From this couple, the race of Jötnar is descended. This ancient flood may help to explain the enmity with which the Jotun race often greets the Gods. From Ymir's body, the three Gods formed the foundations of the world. They shaped the land from his flesh, the seas and oceans from his blood, the mountains from his bones, and the various trees from his hair. Midgard, the world of men, was formed from his eyelashes, and his brains were fashioned into clouds. The race of dwarves (Duergar) was created when the Gods transformed the maggots that feasted on the remnants of Ymir's flesh into these new beings.

The Gods set the dome of heaven (by some accounts, crafted out of Ymir's skull) over all that was, and saw that it was supported at each corner by a sturdy dwarf. Each of these dwarves bore the name of one of the cardinal directions: Austri ("East"), Sudri ("South"), Vestri ("West"), and Nordri ("North"). Sparks flying out of Muspelheim were gathered up by the Gods and set high in the vault of heaven to glimmer and gleam as stars. The Gods took Night, a dusky giantess, and set her, along with her son, Day, in the heavens. Their individual passages across the sky set in motion the cycle of day and night. Night drives a great steed named Hrimfaxi, and the spittle from this horse's mouth as he flies across the sky, forms morning dew. Day follows after his mother with his steed, Skinfaxi. The radiance from Skinfaxi's mane casts a shining light over all the land, heralding the dawn. Night also had a daughter, Jorð. Jorð was the body of the living earth, a Goddess in Her own right, and eventually became the mother of the God Thor.

The Gods further set the sun and moon on their celestial courses. The moon is personified as a God named Mani, and the sun as the Goddess Sunna or Sol. As the God and Goddess ride across the sky, their carts are chased constantly and unceasingly by two giants who transformed into hungry wolves and wish to violently rid themselves of the order the Gods imposed. At Ragnarok, these wolves will capture the celestial carts and devour the sun and moon, leaving the world in darkness.

In the end, the Gods did not stop with the creation of just Midgard. They set in order nine worlds in all, which were connected by a gleaming rainbow bridge called Bifrost:

1. The pre-existing Muspelheim, the world of raging fire.

2. Niflheim, the other pre-existing world, of ice, cold, and stillness.

3. Asgard, the shining home of the Gods.

4. Vanaheim, the home of the Vanir-Gods.

5. Jotunheim, the stormy realm of the giants.

6. Swartalfheim, the home of the dark elves.

7. Lightalfheim, the world of the light elves.

8. Helheim, home of the dead.

9. Midgard, the world of men.

In addition to the Jötnar, there were other beings who interacted with the Gods as well. Light and dark elves each inhabited their own realm. In later Germanic folklore, they were associated strongly with nature spirits, Vaettir, and even the spirits of the dead. These beings may or may not be favorable to mankind, depending on the circumstances of interaction and the nature of the person involved.

Two symbols hold a place of utmost importance in Heathen cosmology: Yggdrasil, or the World Tree, and Urðabrunnr, the Well of Wyrd. The Tree itself is the supporting axis of the multiverse. It sustains life and being and supports the very fabric of existence. It is central to any understanding of the complexity and richness of Northern religion. Yggdrasil connects the worlds. It is the chief holy sanctuary of the Gods, their primary abode. There, by Urda's Well, the Gods pronounce judgment every single day. In the Griminismal (a tale in the Poetic Edda), Odin refers to Yggdrasil as "the best of Trees." Traditionally it is seen as a great ash tree with branches rising higher than the eye can see, with immense girth and large, thick roots. Conversely, some envision it as a yew tree, and still other sources consider it to be part of every type of tree that ever existed. Surprisingly, there is no indication that the Tree was created by the Gods. It, like the Nornir and the Well, is a thing outside of time and space.

Yggdrasil supports the web of fate, woven by the Nornir, three wise women who oversee the Well and use its sacred waters to nourish the Tree. This is very important, because the Tree that supports all that is and all that will be is under attack. Yggdrasil has three mighty taproots, each extending into one manifestation of the sacred well: one terminates in Niflheim, in the well Hvergelmir; one in Jotunheim, in Mimirsbrunnr, the well of the Jotun Mimir; and the final one in Urðabrunnr, the well of Fate. An ancient dragon, Nidhogg, gnaws at the root beneath Hvergelmir. If the Tree topples, so will the fabric of the multiverse. The Nornir prevent this however, by daily pouring healing waters from Urda's Well over the body of the Tree. This water, containing the resolution of all things past and the impetus for all things to come, restores the Tree, healing its wounds.

The Nornir, the three mighty women who sit at the foot of Yggdrasil, are, like the Tree itself, beings outside of time and space.

Even the Gods Themselves must bow to the fate the Nornir decree. The first and most ancient of the Nornir is called Urd (Urda, Urða, Urth, Wyrd). She governs all actions that have passed and that have become set fate. The second Norn is named Verdandi, and She embodies the actual process of fate being made. She is the here and now. The third and youngest of the Nornir is named Skuld, and She governs what is to come as a direct result of the choices of the past. The Nornir will be discussed in more detail later. For now, suffice it to say that these three powerful beings govern causality and consequence, setting it in an order and rhythm that even the Gods must obey. These threads of decision and obligation are woven into a vast web of intertwining threads that connects everything and everyone.

Urda's Well, a bubbling stream, is the place where all fate, memory, and being resolve. Eventually the essence and energy of all fate and all choices flow into Urda's Well. It contains the ancestral, primal memory of all that was and the potentiality of all that will come to pass. The Well itself is a sacred enclosure, and the force that fills it is of holy manifestation. It may be considered the source of all holiness, wholeness, and health. As such, its waters possess magic beyond even that of the Gods. The Well and the Tree define and determine the nature of Northern cosmological thought in that they are both beginning and terminus for every action taken not only by mankind but by the Gods as well.

Perhaps no other God is so strongly associated with Yggdrasil as Odin, the Allfather and foremost of the Gods. One of Odin's *heiti*, or sacred bynames, is Yggr: "The Terrible." The word *Yggdrasil* literally means "steed of Yggr." The World Tree was actually Odin's gallows; in search of power, Odin hung Himself on Yggdrasil, allowing it to carry Him beyond the realm of the living. He hung, wounded by His own hand, for nine days and nine nights until, in the midst of His agony, He was able to seize and win the runes. The runes are esoteric keys of transformative magic that allow him to enchant the mind, raise the dead, turn the tide of combat, strengthen warriors, incite fear, heal the wounded, and bind the forces of chaos. The Tree is a doorway, as well as the means to pass through it. Odin's ordeal on the Tree shows this and provides a cosmic paradigm for a powerful initiatory journey—one that has echoes in shamanic traditions in many European cultures. One may speculate that the Tree arose out of the proto-mire of Ginnungagap at the moment of the primal clash of worlds that brought about the creation of life, so that the Tree contains within itself that evolutionary drive, but there is no conclusive evidence in lore to support this theory.

After setting the worlds and multiverse in order, the three Gods—Odin, Hoenir, and Loður—decide to create humankind. They take an ash and an elm, both sacred trees, and transform them into the image of bodies, one male and one female. Odin gives them breath; Hoenir gives them consciousness and spirit; and Loður gives them blood, warmth, and actual life. Odin Himself walked among the first generations, teaching them right from wrong, establishing a system of ethics, and passing on to them the fundamental skills they would need to prosper. Later stories tell how a God (some say Heimdall, some say Odin), disguised as a man named Rig, traveled the earth, siring children and teaching them runes, rulership, wisdom, and lore. The important thing to remember is that humankind is kin of the Gods, first crafted by Their own hands, then imbued with Their own life force, and later descended directly from Them.

There are three mighty tribes of sacred beings: the Aesir (of which Odin, Hoenir, and Loður were the first), the Vanir, and the Jotun race. The Jötnar often intermarried with the other Gods, and many of them were thus elevated, though some denominations consider Them Gods in and of Themselves. Opinions will vary regarding the Jötnar and Their role, and whether or not to venerate Them is one of *the* major ideological fault lines across denominations today. Traditional scholarship ascribes the venues of warcraft, knowledge, order, and justice to the Aesir; fertility, love, prosperity, and abundance to the Vanir; and chaos, destruction, and change to the Jötnar. The Jötnar, at best, are greeted with ambivalence by a majority of modern Heathens and, at worst, actively despised. The relationship between the Aesir and the Vanir, however did not start out on a pleasant note either.

In another lay (tale) of the Poetic Edda, the Völuspá, the Seeress summoned to life by Odin speaks of the first war:

> *The first war in the world I well remember,*
> *When Gullveig was spitted on spear points*
> *And burned in the hall of the High God:*
> *Thrice burned, thrice reborn*
> *Often laid low, she lives yet.*
>
> *The gods hastened to their Hall of Judgement,*
> *Sat in council to decide whether*
> *To endure great loss in loud strife*
> *Or let both command men's worship.*
>
> *At the host Odin hurled his spear*
> *In the first world-battle; broken was the plankwall*
> *Of the God's fortress: the fierce Vanes*
> *Caused war to occur in the fields.* [3]

From this we see that the Vanir and the Aesir, two powerful tribes of Gods, began a war over who would be most honored and receive the sacrifices of humankind. The war began with the attempted slaying of Gullveig. Some modern Heathens view Gullveig as a hypostasis of the Goddess Freya, with the threefold burning being a type of initiation into power. Others believe She is the Seeress whom Odin commands to life in the Völuspá. Still others see Her as simply another Vanic Goddess in Her own right. Gullveig's name translates as "gold-intoxication" or "gold-inebriation" and it is believed that Her presence among the Aesir so disrupted the structure and the order of their society, by the inciting of greed and lust, that it was deemed necessary to kill her. It may also be that the type of magic possessed by the Vanir and embodied by Gullveig—a magic called *seiðr*, which involved illusion, mind control, and being filled with the intoxication of otherworldly forces—was seen as immensely dangerous by the Aesir. Odin Himself later mastered the wielding of this system of power.

At any rate, Gullveig was slain by being burned in the Hall of the Gods three times, and three times She rose from the flames. This was so great an insult to an emissary of the Vanir, that it brought the two tribes of Gods to the brink of war. War was officially declared by the casting of Odin's spear over the opposing force, a custom which continued to be a declaration of warfare in Norse society. The battle was long and vicious, but neither side was able to gain victory. Eventually a truce was declared and, as was not uncommon in Norse society, hostages were exchanged to cement a pact of peace. These hostages would be integrated into the opposing society as full members, serving as frith-weavers, or peace-weavers, and essentially making the two tribes kin.

The Vanir sent three of Their mightiest Gods, Frey, Freya, and Njorðr (we will learn about them in chapters 3 and 4), to the Aesir; the Aesir in return sent Odin's brother Hoenir and the wise Jotun Mimir, friend (and by some accounts, uncle) to Odin. Initially, this didn't work out so well. Hoenir, though wise, was slow of speech, and the Vanir initially thought that they had been sent someone lacking in wisdom. They observed how Hoenir often sought counsel with Mimir and, in anger, decapitated the Jotun, sending His head back to the Aesir. Though they were grieved by this turn of events, the war was not renewed. Eventually the two tribes of Gods integrated as kin, and Mimir's head was restored to life by Odin's magic.

Northern Cosmology is unique in that it contains the concept of "destiny of the Gods," or Ragnarok—a final battle in which the Gods will fight against the forces of entropy and destructive chaos led by Surt, the Lord of Muspelheim. Building up the army of

Asgard in preparation for Ragnarok is the driving motivation for Odin, and much of His seeking of knowledge is done with this ultimate goal in mind. The beginning of that final cataclysmic battle will be heralded by the sound of Heimdall's horn. The God Heimdall stands on Bifrost bridge, ever-watchful for the first signs of this impending doom.

During Ragnarok, the dead walk the earth, and chaos, oath-breaking, and violence will reign in the world of men:

Brothers will fight and kill each other,
Cousins will destroy kinship.
It is hard in the world, much whoredom,
An ax age, a sword age, shields are split,
A wind age, a wolf age, before the world falls;
No man will spare another. [4]

Yggdrasil finally falls prey to the gnawing of the dragon Nidhogg; Jötnar converge on Asgard, attacking the world of the Gods; and Loki is said to lead the forces from Jotunheim against the Gods. The sun and moon are finally captured and devoured by the wolves that chase them and many of the Gods fall in combat against Their foes: Odin is devoured by the wolf Fenris, and Frey is slain by Surt. Heimdall and Loki die locked in mortal combat against each other. Thor is killed by the foul breath of the world-serpent, and the very foundations of the multiverse crumble.

There is, however, rebirth after the destruction. The earth rises from the sundered sea, the children of the sun and moon take up their parents' mantle, and a man and a woman—Lif and Lifthrasir "Life" and "Stubborn Will to Live"—survive the carnage and live to repopulate the earth. Many of the Gods actually survive; Hoenir lives, and a reference is made in the Eddas to His casting lots, which indicates that the sacred rites and rituals also survive. Balder returns from the land of the dead, as does His slayer, the blind God Höðr. Thor's sons, Magni and Modi, survive, as do Odin's sons Vidar and Váli. The world is renewed, and divine order reestablished.

It is not known how deeply the catastrophic imposition of Christianity affected beliefs about Ragnarok (or about Loki). Nor is it known whether or not the Gods are able to prevent or avert this cataclysmic battle. But the multiverse was created by a violent collision of opposing forces, and from that moment on, that battle against Ragnarok was inevitable. It completes a cycle begun by the Gods' slaughter of Ymir and ordering of the nine worlds. Whether or not the Gods actually die in the way that man would understand it is unclear. The question of whether or not a God *can* die is best left to other theologians. In a way, the coming of Christianity to Europe was a type of Ragnarok, but as within the sacred stories, the Gods survive and the religion is reborn.

This chapter has offered the most basic explanation of our creation story and cosmology. There's so much more involved here it is worth going back again and again to study and meditate upon these stories. For instance, let's return to the moment of creation and look a little more deeply at that primordial collision.

A myth concerning the creation of the world itself creates a world. It holds within it the wisdom and knowledge to allow the world, its sciences, arts, philosophies, its beauty, and our understanding and engagement with it to unfold. The structures of creation are reflected in the ritual cycle, in the way the unfolding cosmic order is translated into cultural comprehension. Heathen cosmogony is so richly textured, so beautifully profound, and has so much to offer those of us who practice within its structures.

Heathen cosmogony begins with a "big bang," although this is a very modern term and perhaps a bit too prosaic to describe the type of collision conveyed through our mythos.[5] Before the Gods come to be, there is violence, a grinding together, there is noise and sound, there is change and exchange—a maelstrom, but with purpose, the seed of unnumbered possibilities. Does it happen slowly or all at once in a huge crash? If we look at the

Gylfaginning, and examine the fragments of cosmogonic lore left to us, it would seem to point to a slow interaction over an extensive period of "time." But even so, certainly there would be that one tipping point giving birth to something new. What we do know is that something happens that forever changes the very fabric of Being, something irreversible. The world of ice and the world of fire collide, and from that explosion of oppositional forces the cosmos begins to unfold. This is our starting point.

To the degree there is a "before" of this big bang, there was the "void," Ginnungagap. But the void is not and was not mere empty space. It was instead potentiality for all that was to occur from that collision. Ginnungagap has a particularly fruitful etymology. The prefix *ginn-* means "holy might," as in *ginn-regin*, meaning the "Holy Powers" (the Gods), or *ginn-runa*, "the mighty runes." It implies something filled with potential, creativity, and power. We usually translate *Ginnungagap* as "Yawning Void," but I think a better translation might be "chasm or space full of holy wonder, creativity, and potentiality." There is power in that moment before oppositional forces meet.

That moment is a doorway, the initiation of materiality. And it tells us something about any and all true initiation: the crossing of a threshold, an irreversible change, a pattern locked into the fabric of existence from the beginning. Later, throughout our cosmological narrative, when the Gods take form and function and begin moving and acting in Their worlds and ours, we will see this same pattern play out again and again, but the paradigm is given to us right here, at that very moment the potentiality of the Gap is transmuted through primordial collision into a new state of being: raw material. Its very nature and substance have been changed. The Gap's potentiality is a kind of contemplation, a pre-creation, but in order for there to be progress, something had to happen. Potentiality had to be urged into transformative action.

Thinking about the Gap and its nature, questions inevitably arise. Was the Holy undifferentiated within the Gap? I would say no, since within the Gap, from the moment our narrative starts, we already have two worlds moving. We already have Muspelheim and Niflheim. There was already differentiation, a plurality of Holy Beings differentiating Themselves within the holy. And if we consider Muspelheim, for instance, as one of the cosmological "worlds," we have to grasp it not just at that first moment, but through the whole sacred history that follows and in which it sustains. And so too, we have the Gap. Why is the Gap holy? Is it holy in and of itself or simply as a container for that which *will be* holy, when distinctions have been drawn? The word *holy* comes from the Old English *halig* which means "hale, whole, and complete, entire unto itself." By that rubric alone, Ginnungagap may be construed as holy. It is the ultimate entirety of everything, before differentiation, before articulation, before . . . everything.

If we accept the Gap as holy, as a fundamental and largely unchanging axiom, then what changes in holiness when life begins as an explosion of oppositional forces? Complementary forces might be a better way of putting it (and you see it echoed throughout our theological narrative). Niflheim and Muspelheim don't just oppose, but complement each other, balance each other. Before I continue, I want to pause for a moment to note that while we are dealing with oppositional and complementary forces, we are not working within a binary system. While it may seem that we have only two players and the Gap itself at this point in our narrative, each of those contains a multitude.

In Muspelheim and in Niflheim alike there is a plethora of beings and forces and concepts and powers to contemplate, divergent worlds creating. Perhaps the two worlds are still in conversation, still in union, still colliding and fighting for dominance, a push-pull of creation unfolding, even as I write this. We think of creation as something that happened a long time ago, because we ourselves are tied to temporality, to the here and now. We experience time as a limitation whereas the Gods are beyond temporality, native to the rhythm of the cosmic unfolding. Creation isn't a onetime event. It's a process that continues to unfold, fire and ice still engaging. So while the worlds each partake of place and order on the Tree, they also continue on in the moment of that big bang. That sizzling fermentation, the moment of creation, is still happening right now. It has never stopped.

Within Ginnungagap, Muspelheim and Niflheim form an interlocking network of ecology and environment, of culture, society, and nations. Niflheim seems to be the older of the two worlds and exists in the "north" of the Gap (though without temporality and materiality, spatial location is relative). The etymology of *Niflheim* simply means "the dark world." The primary denizen of this world that we know of is the great dragon Nidhogg, which means "the one striking full of hatred." Völuspá 39 describes Nidhogg as one who drinks the blood of the dead and eats corpses. Decay, so necessary to our world, and its cousin fermentation, are transformative destruction. This is what Nidhogg personifies as a Holy Being: transformative destruction, wasting nothing, maintaining the whole. In the poetic form of the creation account that we have via the Edda, there is much talk about poison and venom within Niflheim. Those elements break down the substance of what is and then transmute it into something else.

In the "south" of the Gap (again, metaphorically speaking), there is the world of fire, the world *as* fire, Muspelheim. The etymology here is more troublesome. It most likely refers to the "end of the world," which it was, just as it was the beginning of the new. It ended the stasis that existed before the worlds met. It was the hot sparks of Muspelheim that ignited the fermentation, that led to the clash, that brought about the moment of creation. These two worlds, which each contain everything within themselves, met, and through their synergy a new and different world was brought into being.

The principal being associated with Muspelheim is the Lord of Fire, Surt. His name means "the Black One," ostensibly a reference to the soot, smoke, and ash that comes as a byproduct of fire. Some sources[6] associate Him with volcanic activity, and this makes sense: lava is the lifeblood of the earth. It is unclear whether Surt is synonymous with the Muspel, or whether this is yet another Holy Being existing in Muspelheim. Fjolsvinnsmal[7] also references a female Fire Being named Sinmara. (The etymology of Her name is unclear.) It's interesting that we have a pair of beings in Muspelheim but only one, the dragon Nidhogg, mentioned in Niflheim. The gendered pairing may represent reproduction, while I choose to look at Nidhogg as the balance to that binary pairing, as the transformative, nonbinary term that also breathes its magic into creation. Dragons are serpents after all, serpent reptiles, and many reptiles can shift gender.

Fire embodies synthesis, pushing forward, evolution, expansion, adventure, heat, destruction, explosion, creativity, and ice embodies stability, integrity, solidity, ordered space, cold, lack of movement, stasis, structure, and silence. Creation is always a matter of the push and pull between these two forces. You see this mirrored in religious traditions too: the tension between those who want the tradition to be unchanging and those who want to bring forth change. It's from this grinding synergy, worked right into our creation story, that traditions, too, organically evolve.

In the world of Niflheim, there is the river Hvergelmir, which means "bubbling cauldron." Here our story becomes a bit more complicated. This is the primordial spring, the source of all the ancient rivers of the worlds, a collection of waters called "Elivagar." Simek regards these rivers as the proto-sea surrounding the world.[8] Fire expands the boundaries of creation while water from Niflheim nourishes it by means of eleven rivers: Svol (cool one), Gunnthro (thirst for blood/battle groove), Fjorm ("rushing"), Finbulthul ("mighty wind/speaker"), Slid (dangerously sharp), Hrid (stormy weather/tempest), Sylg ("devourer"), Ylg ("she-wolf"), Vid ("broad one"), Leipt ("lightning"), and Gjoll ("loud noise"). Note that the names for the most part do nothing to conceal the potential danger inherent in such primordial powers. The raw forces of creation must be mediated, first by the transition into material and temporal being and then by the Gods Themselves as they craft and transform the material building blocks into our cosmos. By themselves, they can be poison—too much, too fierce for mortality to hold. There must be mediation.[9]

Note the spatial orientation given for these two worlds within the Gap: fire leaps up, devouring and transforming, opening up all it touches, purifying it, consecrating it, while rivers rush downward. The eleven rivers flowed far from their source (where they flowed is not clear, perhaps into the Gap itself). The venom in them hardened to ice but because the rivers didn't stop their flow to accommodate the ice, there was a constant drizzle carrying more venom. This venom froze into rime and more ice and there was rain and roaring wind, the latter perhaps created by the moving musculature of the rivers. The longer this process continued, the more brine was created. This brine, a primal substance, a primordial ooze, gives rise to the first beings of the new world of synergy. Sparks and heat from the world of fire leap out into the world of ice, melting it, transforming the rime. In a moment of alchemy, potentiality moves from the Gap, through the threshold of fire and ice interacting, into the material world. Materiality comes alive in the form of the hermaphroditic proto-giant, Ymir.

The universe is a symphony unfolding. There is rhythm there. The initial big bang may be likened to a symphony warming up, playing the first somewhat dissonant note as all the musicians tune and align their instruments and then the music begins. Creation is not a quiet thing, it is not a meek, well-ordered event. It is a rush of power loosed into being. And then power, having taken form, becomes subject to wyrd. Power, having taken form, becomes potentially erratic and subject to chance. Wyrd becomes an active force with the birth of materiality and temporality. It too, begins its unfolding.

Synir Bors drápu Ymi jötun, en er hann féll, þá hljóp svá mikit blóð ór sárum hans, at með því drekkðu þeir allri ætt hrímþursa . . . (Gylfaginning 7)[10]

Moving on in the creation narrative, Odin, with his two brothers Vili and Vé, slay the first true being Ymir and from his corpse fashion not only the world of man, Midgard, but the scaffolding of the cosmos. From the very beginning, the Aesir defined the boundaries of worlds by violence. It's a compelling moment in our mythology. These three Gods (Odin, Vili/Hoenir, and Vé/Loður/Loki)[11] slaughtered, violently hacking to bits, Their eldest ancestor. The narrative in the Gylfaginning tells us this in only one or two lines and then moves on to the structure of the cosmos, why we have seasons, the movements of the sun and moon, and other cosmological features. However, this one moment defines our cosmology and repeats itself again and again throughout the corpus of our cosmological stories. It reenacts the dynamic of Muspelheim and Niflheim coming together in the moment of creation. Likewise, given that the entire scaffolding of our world and in fact all the worlds were created from Ymir, they partake of being through that primordial potentiality living on in and through them.

A bit of comparison might be useful here. In Genesis, Yahweh moves over the waters, creates, and sees that it is "good." Our Gods, however, look out across the primordial landscape of meta-creation and see potentiality, and then They bring that potentiality into concrete being by violently smashing the old paradigm. It is Ragnarok in anticipation: destruction in order to bring about renewal and restoration, to restart, reorient, re-create.[12] In Genesis, creation stops once Yahweh pronounces everything to be "good." In our creation story, it is forever ongoing and we are constantly participating in it.

At that moment when the three Brothers destroy Ymir, we have a moment of chaotic potential reshaped, brought into order by means of tripartite divine will made manifest through violent action. Odin with His brothers becomes an agent of choice confronting an infinite landscape of potential and by this act of conscious will, They elevate Themselves, separate Themselves from the other þursar and become Aesir.[13] They become divinity, making Themselves something more through the conscious enacting of Their will yoked to mindful forethought, yoked to an awareness of the inherent potential in chaos, and a ruthlessness to bring it into being.

This means, too, that chaos is important. Order cannot exist save in relationship. It must, by its very nature, be defined by its purpose: transforming chaos into something else. Quite often in contemporary Heathenry, chaos is viewed as inherently negative, in opposition to divine order. In reality, divine order is formed from chaos and cannot exist without it. That chaos is a necessary building block for all the work that the Gods then do. It is Their primary tool that allows itself to be transformed into anything that can be imagined and willed. It is chaos that gives order meaning.[14]

In this act, frenzy, will, and holiness—the etymological meanings of Odin, Vili, and Vé respectively—work together. The capacity to transform chaos into meaning is a sacred act, but will or frenzy unyoked to holiness (which for humans includes devotion, humility before the Gods, and piety) is dangerous and damaging. The three must work together for "good" to result, a divine homeostasis. Where that balance is lacking, destructive chaos ultimately ensues.[15]

Odin is the driving force behind this creation through destruction. Immediately before the slaughter of Ymir is discussed, Gylfaginning 6 notes that "ok þat er mín trúa, at sá Óðinn ok hans bræðr munu vera stýrandi himins ok jarðar."[16] Odin, mentioned first and specifically, is given sovereignty over everything that is created. His will to order holds the parsed bits of chaos together in a complex, functioning whole. This is why He cannot afford entropy and is constantly, throughout the mythic cycle, pursuing greater knowledge, greater power, greater ability to transform and transmute reality.

Our creation story contains within itself the underlying telos of our entire mythology. It is a complex and coherent system, reenacted again and again by our Gods and heroes. We can learn a lot about our Gods, Their natures, and the cohesive nature of our cosmology through ongoing examination of these stories.

You may be wondering, "So what? How is this important?" Those are good questions. First, this is the level of exegesis that we should aim for when we meditate on the lore. There's so much more there than we might think on first, second, or third reading. While the lore is not sacred in and of itself, it does contain tantalizing windows to the sacred and that's important. That is how theological awareness enriches a faith. Also, that moment of synergy, where two conflicting yet productive forces come together to create Being, echoes throughout our cosmology, repeated again and again in the interactions between our various Gods, and it's something that we too reenact every time we make the conscious decision to step into alignment with the Gods and Their will. Throughout the process of devotion, of reshaping and reforming our hearts and minds and spirits, we embed in our own spiritual lives that moment in which the order of the Gods was established. We participate in it as we meet our own devotional challenges. Lore is not static. It's not about memorizing stories in a book. It's about unlocking the mysteries contained in these tales that lead us into greater understanding and veneration of our Gods.

CHAPTER 3

THE GODDESSES

I n this and the following chapter, the various Deities will be explored both from the perspective of lore and from that of personal experience. Prayers and meditations will be provided to help the newcomer deepen his or her relationship to the Gods and Goddesses. It should be noted that everyone's experience with Them will differ, and one should avoid comparisons between how oneself and others may experience the same Deity. I have chosen to share some of my own personal experiences in this chapter, but readers should keep in mind that the Deities are individuals and Their relationship with each of us may differ just as our relationships with each other differ.

As noted previously, there are three tribes of holy and/or supernatural beings: the Aesir, Vanir, and Jötnar. The largest family of Gods was called the Aesir. (The word *Ás* means "God" in Old Norse.) The Goddesses numbered among this tribe were called *Asynjur*. In the Prose Edda, it is stated clearly that the Goddesses and Gods were of equal power. As a collective group, the various tribes of Gods are occasionally referred to as the *Reginn* or "Ordered Powers."

Frigga (Frige)

Shining Lady of Asgard, All-seeing, All-knowing,
at Your command worlds are born,
at Your nod and tender smile, life bursts into being.
Valiant Goddess, ruthless foe, cunning Queen,
Illuminate our wyrd.
Strengthen our hamingja.
Make us fruitful in all things, like the barley
*   and flax that is Your gift.*
Nourish our souls, God-Mother,
Pour forth from Your cornucopia of abundance
and in return we will give You our devotion,
*   our praise, our industry.*
Holy Mother of all life, foremost amongst the Asynjur,
bestow upon us Your wisdom.
Make our hearts fertile fields for Your bounty, and
on Your spindle of shimmering starlight,
weave for us a joyous fate.

As Odin is the Allfather, so Frigga is the Allmother, Lady of
Asgard. She is a great Seer, and it is said that She knows all fate but
speaks it not. She lives in a great hall in Asgard called Fensalir, and Her
chief companion among the other Goddesses is Her sister Fulla, who
guards Frigga's treasure chests. Additionally, eleven other Goddesses
serve as Her handmaidens and wise counselors. Though She does not
travel about the various worlds like Her husband, Frigga too takes a
strong interest in human affairs and, on at least one occasion, sent
her handmaiden Fulla to work Her will in the mortal world.

She is generally considered to be a Goddess of frith-weaving and
right order. In many respects, Frigga is a power broker. Many modern Heathens tend to see Frigga as a Goddess of the household, but
any pigeonholing of such a mighty being is, at best, ill-advised. In
considering Frigga as Goddess of the household, it is important to

look at what maintaining a harmonious home really entails. Do you want a home into which you can welcome your ancestors with pride (for within Heathenry, one's ancestors remain vital members of one's family)? Do you want a hearth that will reflect the bonds you have with those you love—a place to nurture heart and spirit in a way that far surpasses the simple provision of physical shelter? Such simple acts as cleansing one's personal space or creating a meal become acts of magic, the mindful crafting of a spiritual foundation and the cyclical renewal of reservoirs of wisdom and intent. These things then represent the unbending strength of ancestral knowledge flowing from one's own hands into everything and everyone touched. The home then reflects one's bond with the ancestors and willingness to contribute not only to the strength of loved ones but also to the line of knowledge that began with our foremothers. Frigga teaches us to make that connection. She also teaches us to reexamine female strength and power and shows us that femininity most definitely encompasses both virtues, for She is as formidable and fierce as any battle-tested warrior.

Frigga is also commonly seen as a Goddess of wisdom. The wisdom of Frigga is the wisdom of allowing one's wisdom and power to shine through in the small decisions, the smaller seemingly unimportant aspects of one's life, or the seemingly mundane. Establishing a home, for instance, becomes a thing of strength, reflecting devotion and connection to a line of knowledge and troth that will extend far beyond any one life. It becomes a thing of pride, reflecting one's love and openness to divine presence. And it becomes a declaration of duty to kindred and to the knowledge that what we do is not grounded in remote, arcane ritual but in the simplicity of our daily lives. In modern parlance, one might call Frigga the manager of Asgard, and as such, She is a Goddess of an almost military efficiency. She is the ultimate power broker.

On a purely temporal level, think about what the proper running of a household involves: financial management, healing skills, the strategic forethought of a master general, the intuitive spiritual awareness of a mystic, and vigilance and diligence against disruption on every possible level. It's a battle against entropy. And Frigga, as a divine power broker, teaches us how to best utilize our resources in every aspect of our lives to most efficiently win it. As power broker, Frigga is a Mistress of Wyrd and Queen of Asgard, with all that entails. Many modern Heathens see a strong connection between Her and the Nornir and associate Her spinning of cosmic threads with the maintaining of divine order.

My own personal experiences with Frigga have been most enlightening, and I will share them here. She is maternal, in a way, without being in the least motherly; Her presence has the most grounded and solid feeling of any Deity I have ever experienced. It is like the thick roots of some ancient yew stretching deeply enough into the earth that it will never be uprooted. Her presence is quiet; understated; strong, without being extroverted; firm, without any sense of what, in a mortal woman, would be self-aggrandizement. It is not the quiet of shy passivity at all, rather the concentrated knowledge of one's own skill and power. When Her presence is strong, it awakens in me the awareness of my own maternal lineage, of a powerful line of women stretching back into memory, and of experience patiently passed from mother to daughter through action and example. Over the years, Frigga has taught me how to accurately summon all of my resources to hand, of the necessity of domestic networking (a thing that would normally have occurred automatically through one's female relatives but that in today's society is fast becoming a forgotten art), and of assuming the position of leadership within the house—a position of accountability and responsibility for everyone and everything under one's roof.

With my love of the warrior arts, Frigga was kind enough to point out that the skillful warrior first puts herself beyond the possibility of defeat and only then looks for the opportunity of defeating her opponent.[1] That resilient clarity of purpose stems from having one's foundation firmly in order. The harmonious and swiftly functioning home is a reservoir of power that one can draw upon in times of stress and ever-increasing challenges. It is a place that should nurture the heart and fortify the spirit.

Under Frigga's guidance, creating a welcoming home has thus become synonymous with creating a welcoming heart and with keeping the metaphorical door open to any of the Gods or Goddesses. It is, again, that special quality of mindfulness, an awareness of one's interconnectedness to one's kindred and community, an awareness of the world around us. It involves a willing sharing of the journey and all the gifts found therein, even if that means occasionally causing conflict to spur one's growth.

Industriousness has become far more than simple plodding repetition of necessary tasks; it has become, to me, the process of constantly striving to develop one's gifts and the quality of excellence within one's self. It entails accepting the responsibility to do your life's work as Deity defines it, even if that means getting up and cleaning the kitchen! It is also the responsibility of being productive with one's knowledge and of taking pride in doing the smallest tasks well. There is something very contemplative in Frigga, yet it is a contemplation forged in swift action. When my hands are covered with Hers, guided by Her, even the most mundane task becomes a prayer, an act of reverence and thanks.

I have glimpsed vestiges of Frigga as Queen of Asgard, remote and awe-inspiring. I have certainly in my seiðr work glimpsed Her spinning strands as thick with magic as any that flow from the hands of the Nornir. As Odin is Allfather, I know that Frigga is Allmother. However, it is not in any such grand way or form that I have been most touched by Her. She chose to come in as wife and hearth-keeper and, by sweeping away those things that were most stunting my growth, opened my eyes to the preciousness of my Kindred, my home, and those I love. What I had once been so quick to disregard I now would defend with my life at blade's edge, if need be. I have come to see Frigga as defender of the home, in its broadest sense, and have often had cause to thank Her for Her unerring patience.

Meditation for Frigga

This is a mirror meditation. Have a small mirror into which you can gaze, perhaps resting in a circle of candles. There should also be a set of runes available. I have found that candlelight seems to act as a trigger for the unconscious mind. If you wish, you may set up an altar to Frigga or make offerings. Frigga shines in every woman and impacts the wyrd of every man. Everyone, male or female, has a connection to Frigga. She is the Allmother and can teach us much about strength and hallowing of the self. Gazing into the mirror, reflect on how Frigga manifests in you and which path of Her you most strongly allow to come through. Where do you block Her? What is your understanding of Her? What do you feel She most has to teach you? After 10–15 minutes of silent meditation, each person should draw a rune, which he or she will meditate on for the next seven nights. This is a gift from Frigga, a drop of Her wisdom.

Sif (Sibb)

I am the seed, lost in ignorance and fear.
Encompass me in the nurturing darkness
of Your rich soil. Let my roots drink deeply
from the nectar of wisdom that You offer.
Let me appreciate each day and hour of my journey,
each moment of my blossoming faith, for each step I take,
though difficult, brings me closer to You.
Let me treasure the time I must spend nurturing my awareness
of Your bounty and grace. Let me feel the gentle comfort
of Your patient guidance. I seek to grow in
   faith, in knowledge of You,
the lessons of the passage of time etched upon my toughening skin,

the tales of my survival by Your grace engraved
  upon each withering leaf
of the days and nights of my existence.
Teach me to craft, in gentle service, a home
within my heart that will be an honor to You.
Let me never hesitate to invite You
into the home that is my heart.

Sif hallows. Her husband, Thor, girds and wards hallowed space, and She sanctifies it within. She helps us maintain the holy. At least that is what I myself have learned from honoring Her, though it is not written in any body of surviving lore. My experience of Her has been that She makes things hale and whole. And that is no small gift; for the contemplative, it is perhaps the greatest gift of all. She helps us maintain integrity of spirit. She is a Goddess of both hallowing and harvest.

Sif is not mentioned much in the Eddas. When She does come up, it is usually as a corollary to Thor. She is known as the wife of Thor, mother of Their daughter Thruð ("strength"), and mother to the God Ullr (though Thor is not His father). One interesting mention of Her in the prologue to Snorri Sturluson's Poetic Edda refers to Her as a prophetess. She is also mentioned in various lays of the Edda: in the Skaldskaparmal, She is coveted, along with Freya, by the giant Hrungnir; in the Harbarddsljod, Odin accuses Sif of having a lover, which may of course simply have been to further harass Thor; Loki repeats this accusation in Lokasenna, naming himself as the erstwhile lover.

The most famous mention of Sif, however, involves Her long, beautiful, golden hair. Loki sneaks into her bedchamber one night and crops it off, infuriating Thor and shaming His wife. Of course the trickster replaces it with hair forged of real gold, the only way to escape a beating by Sif's irate husband. Many modern Heathens accept the idea that her hair represents the grain crop (particularly wheat) and that this story may be symbolic of the seasonal harvest:

the grain, so necessary for life, is cut and grows anew with the turning of the seasons.[2] Marion Ingham[3] points out that the few scholars who still support such nature symbolism point to the fact that it is virtually indispensable to have thunderstorms for the grain to ripen—it fixes the nitrogen. And Thor with His mighty hammer is associated with thunder. Sif is to the inner what Thor is to the outer: one who hallows and girds against that which would destroy our center.

It is difficult to get a complete picture of Sif's nature from the fragments surviving in our lore. In the Lokasenna, Loki was angered because He hadn't been invited to a feast of the Aesir, in breach of an oath by Odin that He would never accept drink at a feast unless it was also offered to His blood brother, Loki. In this instance, Sif appears as peacemaker, offering Loki a horn of mead and trying to still His anger. In fact, there is a strong connection between Sif and Loki in the surviving lore. He is the one that stole away her shining glory. I do not think that Her apparent grief over the loss of Her hair reflects simple vanity. Rather, I believe Her hair was an outward manifestation of Her inner power and strength. Loss of Her hair was, therefore, analogous to Thor's loss of His hammer. Everything surrounding Sif speaks of vital energy and strength: Her daughter's name; Her husband; Her sons; and even Thruðheim, "Home of Power," the dwelling wherein She lived. Therefore, the shearing of Her hair, the symbol of Her own strength, would be a metaphor for a loss of power. She added to the strength of Her hall. Germanic culture often ascribes to women a certain holy power. This is evident from our earliest lore, when Tacitus comments on the immense regard given to certain prophetesses such as Veleda. Sturluson does refer to Sif in similar terms, naming Her as a seeress. In this way, one might speculate that it was *worth* She brought to Thor's house.

Taking that a step further, Sif may be the perfect Goddess to work with when learning to maintain and increase our own worth. Given that She was able to gain remuneration for the offense done to Her, by working through others (Thor threatening Loki, who went to the dwarves, who crafted Her hair), She may also have much to teach us about making and maintaining alliances. Furthermore, as Her son Ullr is named by Sturluson as a good one to call upon in single combat, so perhaps is His mother a good one to call when seeking remuneration or wergild for one's hurts. In our lore, the Goddesses are reckoned equal to the Gods in power. This could be taken to imply that Sif is Thor's equal in power, which would make Her a mighty Goddess indeed.

Centering Meditation for Sif

(Note: The chakras are not a Norse or Anglo-Saxon concept, but I have found them very useful in meditations of this type.)

Find a comfortable position. Sit quietly and begin to focus on your breath. Feel it flowing through your body, flowing through each and every part of you. As you inhale, feel yourself being filled with living energy; let it flow through you. As you exhale, feel it cleansing you of any tension, any negativity. Inhale slowly, evenly . . . exhale, feeling the energy cleansing you. With each exhalation, feel yourself relaxing; feel yourself sinking deeper and deeper into the flow and pull of your breath.

As you breathe, begin to focus on your root chakra. This is located in the perineal area. It is the place of our strongest connection with the earth, the channel through which we take in raw, passionate, survival energy. It is our link to the source of life and to the center of the earth, the roiling fire of creation.

As you breathe, allow your consciousness to flow to the root chakra. With the gentle impetus of your breath, feel the root opening, filling with the lava, the churning, roiling energy that lies buried in the center of the earth. As you breathe, it becomes a burning, flaming orb of that chaotic life energy, one with the very core of the earth. With each exhalation, that fire burns brighter, hotter, connecting you in an unbreakable bond to the earth itself.

Now, allow your consciousness to move from the root, to the sacral chakra. This is located roughly three inches below the naval. This is not only the seat of sexuality, but of our body consciousness and our emotional boundaries. As you breathe, feel the energy of your breath moving from the fire of the root, that central burning life-core, to the steadiness of the dark, moist earth that surrounds it. As your root is filled with the roiling fire of the earth's core, so that fire is contained in the dark soil surrounding it, and that black earth fills the sacral chakra. As you breathe, feel its steady coolness pervading this chakra, connecting you even more strongly with the earth. As you breathe, feel that cool steadiness surrounding you, flowing through the sacral chakra.

Now, move your consciousness to your solar plexus, located at the bottom of the sternum. Feel the energy, the primal awareness, moving from the sacral chakra to the heat of the solar plexus. This is the seat of the will, the manifestation of the power first tasted at the root and nurtured at the sacral chakra. As you breathe, allow that life energy to fill the solar plexus. Feel the solar plexus expand, until your breath is like the hot wind across the deserts. The solar plexus is alive with desert sands, hot wind, focused breath. As you breathe, allow this chakra to pulse in time with your breathe, radiating with the power of sun, sand, and heat.

Now move your consciousness to your heart chakra. This is the seat of growth and compassion, loss, love, joy, and pain. As you breathe, feel this chakra come alive. See it bursting green and strong—grass shooting forth from the earth, trees, plants, shrubs . . . life and creation blossoming. As you breathe, envision your heart as an endless expanse of forest, mountain, grass, flowers, fields, and plants. It is a sacred sanctuary of life, creativity, and being. As you breathe, allow this chakra to pulse in time with that breath, radiant and whole.

Now, move your attention to your throat chakra. This is the place from which all communication flows. As you breathe, feel that chakra expand until it becomes the broad expanse of the oceans, ebbing and flowing with each exhalation. Feel its cool comfort, the confidence of the primal oceans. With every breath, the tides move and the chakra opens. With each breath, you are connected more and more strongly to the cool comfort of the waters.

Now, move your consciousness up to the third eye, between your brows. With each breath, this chakra expands and begins to shine and glow like the sun. As you breathe, that light grows brighter; the nurturing warmth of the sun blazes forth from your brow. With each breath, feel the warmth and light growing stronger; feel the chakra opening wider, connecting you to the heavens.

Now move your consciousness to your crown. This is your connection to Divinity. As you breathe, feel your awareness of this chakra open until within this chakra flows the expanse of the universe. A thousand galaxies pulse and dance within this chakra. With every breath, feel the energy flowing from the fiery core of the root, through your body, up to the crown, connecting you to the endless expanse of the heavens. As you inhale, draw energy up from that burning core, through your chakras. As you exhale, feel it bursting from the crown, illuminating and reaching up toward the heavens. Continue to breathe, resting secure in the subtle play of physical energy.

Now inhale, drawing energy from the heavens, in through the crown. As you exhale, allow it to flow through the third eye, throat, heart, solar plexus, sacral chakra, and down into the root, connecting you again strongly to the earth. Continue to breathe, focusing on allowing your energy to flow deeply into the earth, uniting you with its burning core, uniting you with the endless source of all life energy.

Now focus on your breath. Begin to inhale four counts, hold four counts. Exhale four counts, hold four counts. (Continue this until you are firmly grounded.)

Idunna/Iðun (Edgeongan)

Holy Idunna,
You see such promise in each tender seed.
Every vein of every leaf has been tenderly
drawn and creased by Your caring hands,
every petal of every living blossom
gently parted by Your deft fingers.
Would You then ignore the hearts of Your children?
We are scarred, and we are scared.
We push and we strive—wanting, needing,
rushing through the sacred moments of our lives.
We never see Your blessings; we never see the blessed
synchronicity with which You fill our lives.
Such care, such joyful simplicity, is so very foreign to us.
Teach us, Goddess, to treasure those things
You so lovingly place within us.
We miss so much in our mad, mad rush away from
all that is precious within ourselves.
Teach us, Goddess, to cherish the littlest blessings in our lives
So that when we finally pass from this world
We may pour forth these delicate jewels of memory
Into Your waiting hands.

Idunna is the Goddess who maintains the youth, vitality, and health of all the Gods. She does this by the gift of Her apples of immortality. Her name translates as "the Renewer," and that is precisely what She does. By some accounts (e.g., Oðins Korpgalder), She is strongly connected to Yggdrasil and its primal power. It is because of Her rejuvenating power that Loki was blackmailed into stealing Her away and delivering Her to the giant Thjazi. Of course, She was later rescued—by Loki, in fact—and returned to the Aesir, but this story gives hints of how deeply Her power was coveted by the Jötnar. It is interesting to note that the giants coveted Idunna, not Her apples. The apples were useless unless they were given directly from Her hands as the regenerating power lay in this Goddess Herself.

The very first image I ever had of Idunna was that of a medieval virgin caught in the Unicorn Tapestries, as indisputably bound and imprisoned as the unicorn she sought. For reasons that I am still unable to fathom, Idunna brought to mind images more befitting some troubadour serenading the courts of Aquitaine than proper Eddic lore. It was only once I truly began developing a relationship with Her that my preconceptions rapidly fell away. Now when I meditate on Idunna, my mind is flooded with images both exquisite and precise in their beauty but never, ever, passive. In Her, I see life and growth, endless and implacable. I see elemental union exploding in a vibrant tapestry of birth. I see a hand—sometimes delicate, sometimes ancient and withered—tracing the fragile veining of a single leaf, the fingers playing over the quivering green body, weaving it into life even as the Nornir weave the strands of our existence into being. I feel the sharp, aching poignancy of seasonal shift and change: one world withering to birth a new. For to me, Idunna is a Goddess of cycles and seasons, of ever-returning renewal and birth. Gentle in Her presence, She is everywhere, Her fingers caressing everything, urging life.

She connects what would not necessarily be united in our minds. I can easily envision Her deft fingers smoothing over the raw, knotted places on our life-skeins, gently coaxing those threads to bloom anew in unexpected ways. I believe there could be a very potent sexuality about Idunna, but I have not yet seen that aspect of Her nature. I catch glimpses of it in the urgency with which life is brought into being by Her hands. I have often experienced Idunna extending Her hand to the Goddess Hel, completing a cycle, creating union. As She brings life, so She honors and makes sacred death, the two being easily balanced in Her ever-serene hands. My student would say that Idunna gives to Hel, who gives to Idunna, who gives to Hel, and so forth, in never-ending cycle. Both nurture "deathing" and rebirthing. What Hel does below the surface (and that can be taken quite symbolically, as far as the spiritual journey and our unconscious resistance to growth is concerned), Idunna does above. Idunna is the surface of the earth, growing from the surface, reflecting all that Hel cherishes so deeply below in a very synergetic partnership.

Idunna is not a Goddess who surrenders easily to the pull of spiritual entropy and, though Her struggles may rest veiled under a disarming cloak of apparent passivity, I liken that aspect of Her divine nature to the state of *zanshin* so celebrated and sought by martial artists—that place of utter stillness and spiderlike awareness wherein everything is possible. I bring Idunna offerings of seeds, of all different types. Seeds are the quintessential symbol of initiation, for a seed symbolizes that knife-edge moment before concentrated potential bursts into being.

I would also call Her a Goddess of healing in that She has the ability to make sacred the most wounded parts of our spirits. She is a Goddess of the rhythms not only of evolution but of devotion. In whatever keeps one's spirit and heart pure, in whatever tends the gentle bud of hope, however delicate, there is Idunna. I find it interesting that Loki plays such an important role in the story of Her kidnapping for I would say that Idunna, like Loki, brings the gift of change, perhaps in a far gentler manner than the Sly One, but She brings it nonetheless. There is much in that connection between Loki and Idunna, however tenuous it may be by the standards of lore that begs further exploration.

Perhaps Her greatest gift is that of simplicity. I have come to believe that what She desires most of all is a mind and heart attuned to rhythms of devotion—attuned and therefore open to the planting of those spiritual seeds that are Her most cunning gift. *That* is Idunna, to me. That is the experience that I have been blessed to have at Her hands.

Frigga's Handmaidens

The next twelve Goddesses are numbered in the retinue of Frigga. Traditionally, They are considered Her handmaidens, but a word should be said about this appellation: it is in no way derogatory. Each of these twelve Goddesses is powerful and independent in Her own right. The term *handmaiden* merely indicates that She is a trusted companion of the Allmother, more closely connected to Her than other Asynjur.

Fulla

Wise Goddess, Fast Friend of Frigga,
I raise this horn to You.
Keeper of secrets, keeper of mysteries,
Overseer of all undiscovered wealth,
I praise You for Your wisdom.
Trusted companion of the Allmother,
Mighty Goddess in Your own right,
I hail You.
Bring forth the mysteries within my own soul.
Nourish the treasures within me.
Teach me to find the power within myself
and to hold fast to my own secret strength.
Speak not of my weaknesses as I struggle to overcome them,
as You speak not of the Allmother's plans.
Hail, Fulla, Goddess of stones.

Fulla is a very mysterious Goddess. She is mentioned specifically in the Merseburg Charms as Frigga's Sister. Her name means "bounty" or "plenty," and this may mean that She is a Goddess of hidden wisdom and hidden wealth, both actual and symbolic. She is said to be the Keeper of Frigga's treasure chest. This is no small duty. In Norse culture, the lady of the house kept the keys to the wealth of the house, managed all aspects of the homestead, and provided wise counsel to the men. Only the lady would have access or power to dispense the household wealth. To be entrusted with the wealth of the house was an immense responsibility and showed an incredible degree of trust on the part of Frigga.

It may be inferred that Fulla acted as Frigga's trusted counselor, for Sturluson notes in the Prose Edda that She shares the Allmother's secrets. Not only does She share Frigga's secrets, but She also often collaborates in Her plans. The Grimnismal tells that Frigga and Odin had each fostered a boy and wished to determine which one was the better man. Geirod was Odin's fosterling. It was Fulla who sent the message to King Geirod warning Him about Odin and turning His mind against the Allfather (who was planning to visit in disguise). When Odin arrived, disguised as an old wanderer, He was hung between two raging fires for eight days and nights by the king, an act that later resulted in Geirod's death. So it seems Fulla is as wise and cunning as Her sister.

Fulla is mentioned several more times in the lore. She is pictured as a lovely maiden with long, flowing hair held back by a band of gold. In poetic kenning, gold might be referred to as "Fulla's snood." There is a lovely prayer in the *Gisla saga Surssonar* offered by the hero shortly before his death:

> My Fulla, fair faced, the goddess of stones
>
> Who gladdens me much, shall hear of her friend
>
> Standing straight, unafraid in the rain of the spears.

Meditation Activity to Honor Fulla

This is a meditation rich in symbolism. The object is to create a reliquary box that may be used both for further meditations on Fulla and as a representation of Her wisdom on one's personal altar. Before this meditation rite begins, gather a pretty box, preferably one with lock and key, and a plethora of objects that represent things that are important to you in your life—things that you cherish, things that bring you closer to the Gods, things that nourish you emotionally and spiritually, things that strengthen your spirit.

Begin by setting up an altar to Fulla. This is a powerful way of calling on and connecting to a Deity (altar work will be discussed in more detail in a subsequent chapter). Anything that speaks of the sacred to you can go on a personal altar. Once your altar is complete, hallow the space and sit down in front of it. Light two candles and offer a prayer to Fulla. Then began laying out the objects that you have chosen to go into your treasure box. Quietly speak aloud what each object represents, why it is sacred to you, and why it deserves to be in your treasure box. When you are finished, think for a moment about those things that are missing from your box. Is there anything that you would like to add but felt you could not? If asked, Fulla can help a person examine his or her life, looking deeply beneath the surface. Offer the box to Her now and ask Her aid. Ask Her to help you explore the hidden parts of yourself, the talents, wisdom, and strength that remains suppressed and secret. Spend as long as you want sitting in the presence of this Goddess, and when you are ready, thank Her, blow out the candles, and declare the rite over.

Saga

> I hail Saga, Mistress of Sokkvabekk,
> Historian, Scop, Keeper of memory,
> Collector of stories, preserver of truths,
> Patroness of poets, sharp-tongued skald.
> I will praise You with horn of mead,
> with pen to page, with mindful thoughts
> of connections and consequence and blood-red threads.
> I will think upon You when I hail my dead, when I
>   raise them to life with tales of their deeds.
> I will hold You in my heart when I craft by
>   action the story of my own life.
> I will ask that You remember, when no others do, those
>   moments of quiet epiphanies which ask no celebration,

those moments of awareness so often
unremarked by Your younger kin.
Let not my words pass into the void, You whose
words are cunning and wise.
Give them power, that they may adhere to the fabric
of my wyrd as ink to the pristine page.
Let them stand with the weight of stone.
I hail Saga, Companion of Odin;
I hail Saga, ever-wise.

Saga's name comes from the Old Norse word *segja*, "to speak or to tell," and is related to the word for an epic tale. She is the historian of the Aesir, the collector of ancestral tales (perhaps one may infer from this that She is the genealogist of the Gods), the poet, skald, and memory keeper. Saga resides in a great hall named *Sokkvabekk* ("treasure bank" or "sunken bank") and is the frequent drinking companion of Odin.

In my own experiences with Saga, I have known Her as a Goddess who sets the patterns of one's life in order. She is an excellent Goddess for researchers, librarians, historians, and storytellers to call upon. I personally have connected to Her most strongly as a writer, particularly when it comes to bringing old tales to light. As a skald, or poet, Saga wields immense power. Skalds were held in very high esteem in Germanic culture, their skill with words being likened to a powerful type of magic. Personally, I have always found Saga very forthright and willing to speak Her mind, but also very genial. Because She is a historian, there is a strong ancestral element to Her work and a good way to honor Her may be to begin the ongoing project of researching and recording one's genealogy. Certainly She may be of aid in learning to honor one's ancestors properly. Recording family history, family stories, researching one's genealogy are all good activities in which to ask Her blessing. Keeping a daily journal makes a lovely meditation activity for Her as well.

Eir

I will hail Eir, the Divine Physician. Fortunate
*   are those commended to Her care.*
She is wise and mighty, and the weal of Her
*   hands strengthens the wounded.*
Her works are filled with a ruthless compassion, and to all
*   things She brings the gift of fierce contemplation.*
I will praise this Mighty Goddess,
Whose touch upon our beings is like the fingers of a master gardener
closing around a tiny seed and plunging it
*   into the rich, waiting earth.*

Eir is renowned for Her healing abilities. She is mentioned in the surviving Eddic lore only twice, as the "best of physicians."[4] It is said that She provides healing to all women who seek Her out,[5] making them hale and whole again. Her name, Eir (pronounced *air*, like the element), defines Her nature, translating from the Old Norse as "help" or "mercy."[6] She is also listed among the Valkyries, which connects Her to their power to awaken the dead, select the slain, and cut the threads of life. Many modern practitioners see Her specifically as a Goddess of combat medicine and surgery. Little else is known definitively about Her, but modern devotees of this Goddess know that Her healing is a gift She bestows on all levels: mental, emotional, physical, and most importantly of all, spiritual.

All healing herbs and tools are Hers, from the mortar and pestle to the Laece's (healer's) knife. She is shaman as much as healer in that She restores both body and spirit to wholeness. Anglo-Saxon lore is rich with herbal charms and remedies designed to purge illness and negativity. Perhaps the most famous of these is Wid Faerstice, a charm in which the healer commands the pain of elfshot[7] to leave the patient's body. While Eir is not mentioned specifically in this charm, it and the surviving Lacnunga manuscript[8] do provide evidence of an extremely well-developed system of healing in the pre-Christian

Heathen world. In fact, the experienced Heathen healer had a plethora of tools at his or her disposal: herbal remedies, surgical techniques, sauna, a form of acupuncture, magico-religious charms, and the power of the runes to dispel harm and bind malignant forces, including disease. The healer, like the traditional shaman, was then responsible for maintaining health (that is, wholeness) within his or her community.

Above all else, Eir is practical. There is no room for fluff or feel-good platitudes in this formidable Goddess. She is compassionate, but it is the detached, almost cold compassion of utter objectivity. There is a serenity about Her, a calm restraint that soothes, centers, and grounds. In addition to being a Goddess of Healing, She may also be considered a Goddess of psycho-spiritual and physical harmony. Many who work with Her believe that She is, first and foremost, a Goddess of natural, alternative, and noninvasive healing techniques. Often Her folk will be found in the ranks of Reiki practitioners, feng shui practitioners, acupuncturists, massage therapists, naturopaths, herbalists, reflexologists, and the like. That does not mean that more invasive (surgical) techniques don't also fall under Her domain; they do. She is a surgeon as well as an herbal and magical healer. It is simply that She, more so than physicians in our modern era, embodies the dictum "First, do no harm."

Eir is a good Goddess to call upon when facing the proverbial "dark night of the soul." She can provide a calm lifeline through the spiritual descent, and we all know how such a process can highlight our hurt, broken places. Eir provides hope coupled with efficient, practical advice—provided we are willing to work hard and diligently at the areas She reveals. Eir is all about maintaining that emotional, psychic, and spiritual balance. Eir counsels us to walk a path of discipline, mindfulness, and moderation.

Meditation and Pathworking for Eir

Begin by setting up a simple altar to Eir. The altar should be simple, even stark. Set out a mortar and pestle, a knife, a chalice of fresh water, and any other symbols that you personally associate with Eir.

First hallow the space.

Prayer
I call upon You, Eir, for help and inspiration.
I wish to be centered in You, sure in my purpose.
Assist me, Great Healer, in walking in mindfulness and kindness.
Do not let me wound by inadvertent word or deed;
Rather allow me to see clearly the right course of action.
Flow through me, bringing wholeness, health, and understanding.
Cleanse me of those things that would keep me
    from being effective or whole.
Where I am weak, I know You will be strong.
Where I am afraid, I know that I shall have Your guidance.
Hear me, mighty Eir, and know that my heart is Your vessel.
Hail Healer of the Gods.

Take the chalice of water and offer it to Eir: "I offer You this water as a symbol of Your cleansing might. I ask for insight." Take a sip of the water and place the chalice back on the altar.

Meditation

Sit before the altar with your eyes closed and begin to focus on your breath. With each exhalation, feel the stress and tension of the mundane world falling away. Exhale it all; let it flow from you with the force of a rushing tide. Consciously release every bit of tension in your body, starting at the feet and slowly but surely working your way up to the crown of your head. Continue this until you are completely relaxed.

In your mind's eye, visualize yourself at the bottom of a green, lush mountain. Herbs and flowers, trees and foliage abound, and it is a place of calm serenity. There is a small dirt path leading up the mountain. Begin to follow it. There is no need to hurry. Take your time. Healing is a journey and so is this. Pay special attention to anything you may see as you walk, be it a unique animal, a special stone, or even a particular plant. Perhaps you will meet a fellow traveler on your journey. Perhaps you will gain some insight into what needs to be done in your upcoming healing session. Perhaps you will simply have a peaceful walk up a quiet hill.

At the top of the mountain, not immediately visible from the ground below, you find a small sanctuary. Taking a moment to still yourself, you enter. Inside, it is well lit, with sunlight streaming in from high open windows, and in the center of the main room, a fountain bubbles above a small cistern. Perhaps there are other healers moving to and fro, going about their work; perhaps it is silent, and you are the only visitor. Either way, it is obviously a place of healing. There are altars and herbs, sacred statues, and desperate petitions. Within the center of this healing place is a vast pool and fountain. The water bubbles invitingly. Meditate for a moment on water and its nature. It cleanses, restores, rejuvenates. It flows, seeping into every nook and cranny, finding its way into every crack, no matter how small. It can take the shape of whatever vessel it is contained within, yet never loses its essential nature. Healing is like that. It cannot be forced, only released and gently molded.

Go to the fountain and sit or kneel before it. Spend a few moments gazing into the water and note well any images or insights gained. If anyone approaches, listen well to their counsel. Perhaps it is Eir Herself or a worthy ancestress.[9] When you feel it is right, cup your hands and scoop up a handful of the healing water. It is filled with the vital energy of Eir Herself and of Her handmaidens.[10] Wash yourself with it, pouring the water over head and heart and hands. Take a second handful and bring it to your lips, imbibing a draught from the sacred spring. Then reach into your pocket and remove an object. Even you do not know what it will be. Place it on the rim of the cistern. This is the physical manifestation of those things that would interfere with your healing, preventing you from becoming as strong and whole as possible. Reach into the bubbling water in the cistern. Reach deep down to the bottom and draw forth a second object. This is what you need for your own insight or healing. Tuck it carefully away. It may be something that will help you bring healing to another, or it may be something that will help you personally in your own spiritual journey—only you will know at the time.

Spend as long as you need sitting before the fountain or exploring the healing temple. When you are ready, offer thanks to Eir and begin your descent down the mountain. As you descend, following the well-worn dirt path that first led you to the temple, each step brings you out of your journey, closer to temporal consciousness. As you walk, begin to focus again on your breath, slowly returning to yourself with each exhalation. Take a few moments at the end of your journey to ground, focusing on sending the excess energy in your body down into the earth like the roots of a strong, supple tree. When you are ready, open your eyes.

Other good ways to honor Her include regularly giving blood, taking CPR and First Aid, donating time at a hospice, nursing home, or hospital, and donating to medical charities like Doctors Beyond Borders.

Gefion

Giving One, I ask Your blessings
on my mind and heart and life.
I would know You, Mighty Goddess,
beyond what remains of Your sacred tales.
Make me bold, as You are bold.
Make me mighty in spirit,
as You are mighty in all things.
I hail You, Gefion,
Goddess of plenty and might.

Gefion is mentioned in both Eddas and the Ynglinga Saga and is best known for the tale of how She won the island of Zealand from the Swedish king Gylfi. She appeared to him as a vagrant, and as a reward for some unspoken entertainment She had given him, he told Her that he would give Her as much land as She was able to plow around in a single day and night. What King Gylfi didn't know is that the vagrant woman was in fact a Goddess of the Aesir. She hurried off to Jotunheim, married a giant, and birthed four strong sons whom She transformed into oxen. She returned to Gylfi's realm and, using Her four sons to pull the plough, ploughed so hard and fast that the entire island of Zealand was ploughed loose from the mainland. She is remembered to this day, and there is even a fountain in Copenhagen that depicts Gefion with Her plough.

Gefion's name means "The Giving One," and many modern Heathens call upon Her for help with their finances, financial management, and investing. Given Her story, She may be hailed as a Goddess of wise acquisition, prosperity, and material wealth. She is a wise, farseeing Goddess, and Odin chides Loki in the Lokasenna for harassing Her, noting that Gefion sees the fate of all men as clearly as He Himself does.

Gná

Swift Goddess Gná, strong in purpose,
I hail You.
Divine Messenger,
with ease You traverse the Worlds.
I praise You as You guide Your steed
across Bifrost Bridge, never faltering, never hesitating,
always quick and sure.
No obstacle bars Your way.
No enemy is able to draw near.
I would be like You:
Sure of myself, sure in my purpose,
unyieldingly brave in my journey into the unknown.
Hail, Gná!

Gná is Frigga's messenger. She travels throughout the nine worlds, going about the Allmother's business. Her name comes from the Old Norse verb *gnaefa*, which means "to tower or rise high," for She rides high in the air on the back of Her steed, Hofvarpnir ("Hoof-Thrower"). Nothing else is known about Her through the lore, though it may be posited that She would be of excellent aid in overcoming obstacles and in moving forward in one's life. She may also be willing to aid in clear communication in all aspects of life. I would ask Her assistance in all problems that require a speedy resolution.

Syn

Guardian Goddess, protect me, I pray.
Let no threat breach the hall of my heart.
Protect me from the violence of others' tongues.
Protect me from the violence of their wills and words.
Let no weapon harm me. Guard the threshold of my person.
Make of me an impenetrable fortress to those who wish only ill.
I hail You, mighty Gatekeeper. I hail You, mighty Syn.

Syn is generally seen as a protective guardian Goddess, and the Eddas describe Her as the gatekeeper of Fensalir. She maintains the frith of the hall by barring the doors to those who would create disruption. Her name means "denial" or "refusal," and there is some evidence that She may have had a role on the side of the defense in legal assemblies. Simek connects Her to the Matronae, Tribal Mother Goddesses to whom votive stones were erected by the Germanic tribes.[11]

Hlín

> I call upon Your strength, Mighty Hlín.
> Defend me, I pray, for on all sides I am beset by danger.
> Still the fear that gnaws like a hungry worm at my heart;
> Shield me, Oh Goddess.
> Let nothing harm me, not fire nor water
>   nor wind nor evil intention.
> Guard me and guide me, I pray.
> Hail, Mighty Hlín.

Hlín's name means "protectress," and She is specifically charged with protecting those mortals favored by Frigga. She is a refuge of those in grave danger. In my own experiences with Her, I have found that She is reserved and formidable, almost cold in demeanor and very watchful. She is weapons-wise and a deadly warrior. Those whom She chooses to defend are unassailable by any threat.

She may also be a Goddess to call upon when in the throes of heartbreaking grief. The Völuspá notes:

> Another woe awaited Hlín,
> when forth goes Óthin to fight the wolf
> and the slayer of Beli to battle with Surt:
> then Frigg's husband will fall lifeless.[12]

Some Heathens interpret this to mean that Hlín is but a byname of Frigga, but to others, She is a companion of Frigga who will provide the fortitude to continue after the death of Frigga's husband at Ragnarok. Perhaps She was called upon by women who had lost their spouses in battle to help anneal the terrible grief and loneliness. Regardless, the Eddas list Her as a Goddess in Her own right, and She has much to teach about personal pride, integrity, and assertive self-protection.

Sjöfn and Lofn

> Gentle Goddesses, open my heart to love.
> Let me not despair, but guide me through the tangles
> of those relationships I cherish.
> Let me not cause pain to another's heart,
> but let not my own heart wither
> in the face of love's challenges.
> I hail You, for the comfort and hope You bring.
> I hail You for smoothing the way not only in love
> but in all human interactions.
> Hail Sjöfn, Hail Lofn. I thank you.

Both of these Goddesses are concerned with love. Sjöfn's name is from the Old Norse word *siafni*, which means "affection," and She helps smooth the way for productive interaction between people, not just in the realm of love, but in all dealings. She opens the heart to appreciation of those relationships that nourish us. She opens the heart to love, be it romantic love or the love of a good friend.

Lofn's name means "Comforter," and it is She that gives hope when in the midst of difficult challenges in a relationship. The Eddas note that She was so kindhearted that She would go out of Her way to procure permission from Frigga and Odin for couples to marry, even if they were previously forbidden to wed. She provides hope in the midst of relationship troubles and counsels patience and resolve. The word for "permission" *(lof)* is derived from Her name.[13]

Vor

Hail, Wise Goddess.
Nothing escapes Your sharp gaze.
You see into the deepest recesses of my heart.
You see everything, even that which I would hide in shame.
May I be bettered in Your sight.
May all the secrets of my heart be revealed to You with pride.
May I stand before You a man/woman of worth.
Hail, Vor.

Almost nothing is known about Vor, save that She was extremely perceptive. In the Prose Edda, it is noted that She is wise and careful and never misses anything. In my opinion, She may be hailed as a Goddess of self-discovery, self-exploration, and what psychologists call "shadow work." She would likewise be an excellent ally during the "dark night of the soul." She is a Goddess of all things unseen.

Var

I hail You, Var,
Guardian of all that is wise and just.
You set our souls gently yet firmly
on the path of truth and integrity.
I welcome You as a shining guide.
Let my words honor You.
Let my actions praise Your name.
May I always walk in truth, bound only by my sworn word.
I know it will be difficult.
Guide me through the fear.
May I always find shelter and guidance
beneath Your staff.
Illuminate my words, give life to the vows I make this day
that I never have cause to face You in shame.

Traditionally, Var is the Goddess who witnesses all sacred oaths, particularly marriage oaths. Her name means "vow" or "pledge," and the contracts made by oath between men and women are called *varar*. The Eddas point out that She punishes those who break their sworn word. The breaking of a sacred vow impacts the luck of all involved, including one's family and tribe. Such a thing was a grievous wrong in Germanic society. Var could then be said to maintain the strength and purity of the tribal Hamingja by punishing oath-breakers.

Meditation on Var

Hallow the space and offer up a prayer to Var. After calling to Her, sit down and engage in a brutally honest critique of the past year(s), addressing any problems and coming to workable solutions. The good should be discussed as well as the bad. What goals have you set for yourself? What promises have you made to yourself and others? Have you upheld them? Where have you fallen short? In what ways do you break your word? In what ways do you sacrifice the power of your speech by promising that which you cannot deliver? Think about this long and hard. Take as much time as necessary. Are you the kind of person you wish to be? Could you face Var at this very moment proudly, with no stain of broken oaths, broken promises, or hastily spoken words on your Hamingja?

Once you have completed your self-examination, take a glass of wine. Offer some challenging part of your life to Var for the coming year along with a promise to transform, confront, or resolve it. Offer two things: one for yourself personally and one for the good of your tribe or kin group as a whole. Heat a needle in a flame until it is red hot, and prick your finger, offering a few drops of blood to Var by dripping it into the wine and promising to adhere to the preceding oath. Thank Var for Her patience and take the wine outside, pouring it out into the earth in offering to Her. Once the rite is finished, wash and clean your hands, bandaging your finger.

(Note: Please use common sense. With any type of cut or puncture, there is a risk of infection. Never, ever, share cutting implements with anyone. This is meant to be done as a solitary meditation. Be sure to use alcohol, bacitracin, or some other antiseptic to cleanse the puncture; even small wounds can become infected. It is perfectly okay not to do this part of the meditation; a simple vow can be spoken over the wine by itself.)

Snotra

> *Gracious Goddess, clever and wise,*
> *I hail You with horn upraised.*
> *You are Goddess of right action,*
> *of courtesy and personal integrity.*
> *Yours is the steel hand in the velvet glove.*
> *You know when to conceal Your power*
> *and when it should be revealed.*
> *I praise You, Snotra, I would learn from You*
> *how best to navigate the most difficult situations.*

Snotra is another Goddess in Frigga's retinue of whom very little is known. Her name means "clever" or "wise" and is derived from the Norse word *snotr*, meaning a clever person. She is said to be a Goddess of proper behavior and courtesy. Some modern Heathens see Her as a Goddess akin to the Emily Post of the Aesir, but I personally see Her as the consummate diplomat—clever in Her speech, able to navigate the most challenging of social situations with aplomb and grace, and capable of great persuasion to Her cause, whatever it may be.

Skaði (Sceadu)

I raise this horn to the Etin bride of winter.
I praise Skaði, fierce warrior, Defender of Her father.
She is bold, fierce, and vicious in Her cunning.
She is passionate, focused, a steadfast ally.
Bride of Njorðr, Lover of Woden, fettered by none,
I will seek You, Skaði, in places of solitude.
I will seek You in the icy cold of winter.
The freezing wind is Your breath, the pristine snow Your mantle.
Formidable huntress, I will be Your willing prey.
Seek me out. I will not flee.
Come into my dark places, and we will celebrate them together.
I hail You, Skaði. I offer this to You.

I have always had a particular affinity for Skaði. She is formidable, unyielding, and fierce. Her willingness to seek vengeance with blade and shield if need be, speak of Her pride in Her heritage and Her skills as warrior, for She was willing to take on all of Asgard *by Herself*. She bows Her head to no one and can be quite vicious in protecting Her domain. She does not compromise Herself for anyone or anything, and those are virtues I quite admire. Additionally, as a woman involved in the martial arts, Skaði has been an inspiration to me—a Goddess that I have often called upon for fortitude in my training.

Skaði's name means "shadow." She is associated with the barren, winter landscape, wolves, skiing, bowhunting, and physical fitness. Modern Heathens hail Her as a huntress and Goddess of winter and as one of the Etin brides (Jotun women who married into the Aesir or Vanir and were thus elevated to Godhood). She is the cousin of the etin bride Gerða, and when Njorðr's son Frey fell ill with lovesickness after having seen Gerða from afar, it was Skaði who first noticed His malady. Many places in Scandinavia are named after Her, though there is very little about Her in lore. She is called "Shining Bride of the Gods" and Öndurdís ("Dis of the Snow Shoe"). At some point,

She and Odin were lovers, and She had at least one son by Him, from which a royal line in Norway is descended.[14] Some modern Heathens attempt to link Skaði and Ullr as a divine couple, though there is nothing to support this in lore.

Skaði is responsible for the binding of Loki after the death of Baldr. After it is discovered (by His own words, no less) that Loki was responsible for guiding Hoðr's hand, the Gods chase Him down and capture Him, though He tries to flee by changing into the shape of a salmon. He is taken to a dank cave deep in the earth and tethered to a rock with the entrails of His own son. Skaði takes a poisonous serpent and secures it above Him so that the venom will drip onto His face. Loki's wife, Sigyn, remains by His side, doing Her best to capture the venom in a bowl. It can only be assumed that Skaði's eventual enmity toward Loki hearkens back to His role in the death of Her father. She is not one to forgive such things easily.

Skaði continues to be highly honored today and provides a particularly good role model for women who, either in personal or professional life, choose not to follow society's accepted norm.

Nerthus

Holy Nerthus, Terra Mater, I hail You.
You guard Your secrets wisely and well,
and to You, we owe our sustenance.
In dawnlight and in darkness I praise You,
Mother of the damp, dark earth.
I celebrate Your bounty with words and proffered wine.
I celebrate You with action and mindful contemplation
      of the Earth and Her resources.
I remember, Goddess, Tribal Mother, that once Your sacred cart
circumnavigated the land as offerings were given to Your image.
I hold You in awe, Goddess. I hail You with deepest respect.
Hail, Mighty Nerthus.

The Goddess Nerthus is known only from Tacitus's *Germania*. She was an Earth Goddess revered by several Baltic and Germanic tribes, including the Angles who later settled England. Tacitus records a rite in which a cart bearing the veiled image of this Goddess was led by Her priest throughout the tribal lands. No one was permitted to view the holy image except for the priest:

On an island of the sea stands an inviolate grove, in which, veiled with a cloth, is a chariot that none but the priest may touch. The priest can feel the presence of the goddess in this holy of holies, and attends her with deepest reverence as her chariot is drawn along by cows. Then follow days of rejoicing and merrymaking in every place that she condescends to visit and sojourn in. No one goes to war, no one takes up arms; every iron object is locked away. Then, and then only, are peace and quiet known and welcomed until the goddess, when she has had enough of the society of men, is restored to her sacred precinct by the priest. After that, the chariot, the vestments, and (believe it if you will) the goddess herself, are cleansed in a secluded lake. This service is performed by slaves who are immediately after drowned in the lake. Thus mystery begets terror and a pious reluctance to ask what that sight can be which is only seen by men doomed to die.[15]

Tacitus compared Nerthus to the Roman Terra Mater. Examining how the Romans viewed their Earth Mother may provide useful clues to the nature of Nerthus. The Romans were well aware not only of the nourishing gifts of the Earth, but of Her terrible power as well:

earthquakes, famine, flood, storm, and destruction. She was beautiful and life-giving, terrifying and destructive all at once. There was bounty, but also immense danger contained in the holy presence of this Goddess, and so it was with Nerthus as well, as the previous passage from Tacitus attests.

Gerða (Gearde)

I hail Gerða, shining bride of Frey.
I honor Her for Her self-possession, Her independence,
Her ferocity of spirit.
She is primal power, like a river rushing beneath the ice.
She is raw force, incantations whispered in the darkness,
the embodiment of Ginnungagap's synergy.
She is silent contemplation, the holder of all things secret.
She is the loss that is not seen, the holder of life that is not born.
I hail Gerða, for all that She has taught me.
I hail Her for being the shadow that illuminates and nourishes Frey.

Very little is known about Gerða, save that She is the bride of Frey, cousin of Skaði, and that Her name means "enclosure." She is the daughter of the giants Gymir and Aurboða and listed among the Asynjur. Many scholars generally interpret the marriage of Gerða and Frey as a sacred marriage: the barren, wintry earth melting and bearing life when touched by the sun, but this is perhaps overly simplistic. Simek points out that the etymology of Her name relates not to the actual enclosed land, but to the actual act of fencing it off.[16] While She may indeed represent the barren earth seduced into new life, there is much more to Her than that. She has a certain implacable quality that is reserved, contained, and secret. It gives itself sparingly and only to those it finds worthy. Gerða is one who finds the sacred within Herself. And that, I think, is the meaning behind the translation of her name as "enclosure." She has found within herself the most sacred of temples and will not willingly open those doors to just anyone. Gerða preserves the self.

It is a very important gift she gives, that preservation of the self. We are the greatest gifts we can give our Gods, and that cannot be done unless we know truly who we are and what our foundation is. Trance work, spiritual work, pathworkings, journey work—all of this can be dangerous for the unknowing soul, which then learns only to bend to whatever wind blows the strongest. Gerða prevents that. She is staunch within herself; She guards herself and challenges the interloper. That is what I personally believe lies behind the secret of her courtship with Freyr. She does not suffer well the spiritually complaisant. She tests, as all wisdom must test. It is Gerða who treasures those thorny places within the heart. She keeps the heart from falseness. She gives only to those she has found worthy. She does not offer of Herself to please or to be liked. She watches all, observes all, and chooses very carefully where to share of Her energy. That is not something many women can say. She is content within herself.

To return again to the meaning of Her name, "enclosure" is the sacred space, the *vé* (the Norse word for "altar") upon which all offerings are made. It is a place of devotion, a place to be protected and treasured. That She is a giantess indicates that She has the potential to manifest the forces of chaos and destruction—awesome, primal power. Yet She controls them, encloses them in strictest self-mastery. She treasures Her immense passion but is not ruled by it. She puts things in their place. Hers is the inward manifestation of Skaði's outward mastery.

My own experience with Gerða has taught me that She cares about bonds, about upholding them and maintaining them. She teaches us to honor our ancestors; to listen to their voices and to find wisdom in stones, trees, and wind. There is an unspoken balance and icy clarity about Her presence. She teaches how to maintain the integrity of our bonds, to strengthen our Hamingja, and to pass on that strength. She teaches us to honor and connect past to present and to strive for future goals while nurturing our present.

I see Her very much as a solitary Goddess, for all that She is associated with Frey. They are in many ways beautifully complementary. They accept and cherish each other's differences. She is a Goddess of all loss that is not seen. I have called upon Her when counseling women who had recently miscarried. She is the shadow to Frey's light, and as He brings life, She honors life that does not come to fruition. Gerða is self-contained, and that is the lesson that She will gladly teach to those who come to Her. She teaches self-respect. Her children do not barter themselves for a moment's pleasure or comfort. They are unswerving, unyielding, and maintain the sacred enclosure of their souls. She teaches us how to bear hurt rather than yield to that which is not true. She teaches us to wait, to be content in the silence of our spirits, to seek out that silent, centered place, and from there, blossom.

Freya (Fréo)

> I will hail the Goddess of gold,
> Hostage to the Gods, delight of Her kin.
> I will praise Her with amber and wine,
> flowers and honey, for She is Goddess of beauty,
> eroticism, and desire.
> I will celebrate Her abundance, Her gifts of wealth
> and fruitful plenty.
> She brings luck, fertility, and creative fire,
>   and Her presence is found
> amid the moaning cry of lovers, hidden within
>   the rhythm of their entwined limbs.
> I will call Her luck-bringer, for Her fingers are deft
>   at untangling the snares of a gnarled wyrd,
> and sometimes the tangles are of Her making.
> I will praise Her as strong in magic, cunning,
>   skillful, and battle-wise.
> I will summon Her forth with song of steel,
> for She is fierce and shows no mercy.
> The field of combat is as sweet as the battlefield of love,
> and in both, She is the victor.
> She is sweetness and fury, molten flame, the
>   sharp edge of a killing blade.

She is danger and desire, unquenchable, unstoppable. She will
tease and entice, transforming the soul. She is pleasure
and pain so deeply bound there is no separation.
I hail Freya, Shining Goddess of the Vanir. She blinds
with Her beauty, seduces with Her fury.
I hail Her in Her fullness, in battle, witchcraft, and love.
I raise this horn in Her honor.
Hail, Freya!

Perhaps no other Goddess in Heathenry is so loved and also so often misunderstood as the Goddess Freya. She is an incredibly complex Goddess very often relegated solely to the realm of love and sex. She is most definitely a Goddess of sexual pleasure, eroticism, and desire, but She is also a Goddess of ritual sacrifice, seiðr magic, wealth, prosperity, abundance, ancestral veneration, warcraft, and power. These are not minor facets of Her nature either. So potent is Her prowess in battle that it is Freya, not Odin, who claims the first half of the slain warriors for Her hall. She is a gloriously beautiful Goddess and Her beauty is equal to Her power.

The name *Freya* means "Lady," but She has many other heiti including Syr ("Sow"),[17] Mardoll (possibly "One Who Makes the Sea Swell"), Vanadis ("Lady of the Vanir"), Heiðr ("Bright One"), Horn (possibly "Flax"), and Gefn ("Giver"). Her home is called Folkvangr ("Field of the Folk"), and within it She maintains a great hall named Sessrumnir ("Many-Roomed Hall"). She rides in a chariot drawn by some type of feline. Most Heathens assume these to be cats, but speculations range from cougars to lynx to wolverine. She is wed to Oðr, who long ago disappeared. Nothing is known about Him, save that Freya travels far and wide searching for Him, weeping tears of gold or amber. (Amber is widely associated with this Goddess.) She has a daughter, Hnoss, whose name means "treasure." It could be said that Freya gives birth to wealth.

The most famous story about Freya involves the emblem of Her power and might: the necklace Brisingamen. Though most sources call

Brisingamen a necklace, there is some textual evidence that it may in fact have been a belt or girdle. Loki, who attempted to steal this piece of jewelry bears the heiti "the Thief of Brising's belt," but elsewhere the Eddas do refer to it as a necklace. The word *brising*, or *brísingr*, means "fire," which would lead to a possible translation of its name as "fiery belt." Some scholars link it to the aurora borealis; others see it as a symbol of Freya's fertility and sexuality. In order to win Brisingamen, Freya journeyed to the dwarven realm and commissioned a piece of such beauty and power that there would be none like it in all the world. The dwarves, master craftsmen, agreed to Her request but demanded in payment that She spend one night in sexual intercourse with each of them. This Freya did, and during those four nights, Brisingamen was forged. The necklace (or belt) is a symbol of Freya's power, just as Mjolnir embodies Thor's. It represents Her power to manifest desire on levels that go far beyond the sexual. She is less a Goddess of fertility and more that of synergetic attraction, which opens the doors to blossoming abundance. She is a Goddess of sensuality and of passionate fulfillment in life, be it giving one's all in love, in battle, or in pursuit of one's chosen crafts. She teaches us to suck the proverbial marrow out of life instead of drifting through it like a shadow.

Freya is the patroness of unmarried women, who go to Her hall when they die. She is also the priestess of the Gods, charged with maintaining the rites and making proper sacrifices for the divine community. As seiðr worker, Freya is credited with bringing to the Aesir the practice of this form of magic, which involves trance work, mind control, and luck-working. She was also, by Her very presence among the Aesir, a frith-weaver, having been sent from Vanaheim to secure peace with the Aesir. Freya's husband Oðr, who apparently is a wanderer, is slowly beginning to receive cultus in the Northern Tradition, but all we really know about Him is His name, which means "Frenzy" or "Inspiration" (just like Odin's name, though breaking down His name actually gives us *the* frenzy), and that Freya mourns His absence greatly, weeping tears that turn to amber. Some people think He is Odin, but I've never found this to make sense.

Freya would surely recognize Odin as Her missing husband if the two were the same!

A note about Freya: many Pagans erroneously call Her "Queen of the Valkyries." She is not. While She does receive half the battle dead, She has nothing at all to do with the Valkyries who are in fact, handmaidens of Odin.

Meditation for Freya

Set out a pretty piece of cloth—something that appeals to your personal aesthetics. It should be at least a foot square. Think about the many ways in which we define beauty in our culture. How do you, yourself, define beauty? What do you find beautiful? What nourishes you? What attracts you? What is beautiful about you personally? Do you think you are beautiful? Why? What would you change? Why? What would you sacrifice to be beautiful? Select an item that represents your beauty and place this on the cloth. This is an offering to Freya, a gift of gratitude and love.

How are you powerful? What would you do to fully manifest your personal power? Is this power a trait you admire about yourself? Is this part of your beauty? Select an item that represents your power and put that on the cloth as a gift to Freya.

How does Freya manifest in you? How does She inspire you? Does She make you uncomfortable? What gifts of abundance has She given you? Are there any areas that you feel particularly closed off to Her? Select a gift representing Freya's presence in your life, and add that to your bundle.

Add a piece of amber to the bundle, flowers, and anything else that you either associate with Freya or would like to give to Her. Wrap the bundle up and secure it with ribbon. Take this to the nearest park, seashore, or any place in nature that is special to you. Call to Freya; speak to Her from the heart. Take as long as you wish. When you are finished, bury your offering, leave it by a tree, or cast it into the water with your thanks and a prayer of gratitude.

Sigyn

> *I will hail Sigyn, gentle Goddess,*
> *beloved wife of the Allfather's brother.*
> *She is playful and sweet, sometimes shy,*
> *yet fierce in Her own way, when She chooses to show it.*
> *This unassuming Goddess holds weighty wisdom,*
> *for those with ears to hear and eyes to see.*
> *Her name speaks of victory and daring, boldness and power,*
> *yet She is quiet and loving, simple in Her manner.*
> *I will raise a horn to Sigyn; I greet Her with pride,*
> *this Goddess who is far more than simply Loki's loyal bride.*

Sigyn is mentioned exactly three times in lore. Each time refers only to the fact that She is Loki's wife and that, when He is bound after the killing of Baldr, She faithfully remains by His side, with a bowl, capturing the poison dripping from the venomous snake hanging above Him. When She empties the bowl and the poison falls on Loki's face, His painful writhing causes earthquakes. Many modern Heathens therefore dismiss Her as everything from merely a loyal wife to the epitome of an abused wife. She is seldom given the respect due a Goddess of Her integrity and strength. There is much more to Sigyn than initially meets the eye.

Sigyn is an exceptionally gentle Goddess. The lessons that She brings have been no less transformative than Odin's, for instance, but She is gentle and sometimes even playful about the entire process. Personally, I see Her as a Goddess of love and devotion. She is also the Goddess of the inner child and will heal that child within us. In fact, my very first experience of Sigyn was that of a playful child. I don't know why She chose to take that form, but it took me completely off guard. I experienced Her as a sweet and vulnerable child, a little girl who likes Her toys, likes to laugh, and wants to be loved—and Loki loves Her dearly. I was able to relate to Her in a way that I had never experienced with a Deity before: I felt protective of Her as a mother would to a child. Over the years, I have encountered other folk who honor Sigyn and Loki regularly, and they have also reported encountering Her in this manner.[18] Many also report experiencing Loki's extreme protectiveness of His bride as well, something that allows a rare glimpse into His compassionate, loving side that is little spoken of either in lore or by modern Heathens. Sigyn has the capacity to teach those who come to Her to open and embrace the Gods with the innocence and acceptance of a child. She too strips away the facades and walls and blockages within, but She does it so gently—so very gently—that it is a sweet embrace. She is a Goddess who opens the heart.

Of course there is another aspect to Her nature: that of the grieving wife who sits by Her tortured husband, doing what She can in the dank, bleak darkness of the cave to ease His pain. Here is a Sigyn who is fierce and strong, enduring as the rock and mountain, expansive and all-encompassing—a sanctuary in the face of suffering. Her name means "Woman of Victory," and that, alone, hints at Her hidden power. There is immense wisdom, caring, and compassion in this Goddess, and that is not something to dismiss lightly.

She is Our Lady of the Staying Power, Lady of Constancy, the North Star, a Goddess of fierce protectiveness and devotion, who will not be moved from Her course. Her experience in the cave is one of the most potent mysteries in our tradition, equal to that of the Allfather hanging on Yggdrasil. Her children, Narvi and Vali, have a growing cultus among those who include the Jötnar in their devotions.

Gentle Goddess,
teach me to play.
I've seen the joy You take
in the smallest thing of beauty.
Teach me gentleness,
the sweetness of Your song.
I want to sing, as You sing,

when You know Loki is listening.
I wish to be among those nurtured
by Your tender hands,
a bright flower
pruned by Your gentle fingers.
Teach me to love,
as You love:
without condition.

Angurboða

I hail the great giantess,
Angurboða, Mother of Hela,
Mother of Fenris and the great serpent.
Great chthonic Mother, bless us with Your wisdom.
You are the dark, primal womb of all creation,
from Your bounty, the earth is filled with secrets.
You are the Silent One, Who bestowed upon Your daughter
all the magic of eternity.
In Your shadowy abode, You observed
the birth of the Aesir, and with Your magic,
You enticed Their brother Loki.
Great Mother of the beginning, bestow upon us
the silent endurance of rock and soil.
Let us always strive to see beneath the surface
of our dreams and desires for understanding.
Do not let us fall prey to pretty illusions
that sparkle and shine in easy imitation
of Your precious jewels; rather, grant us
the knowledge that wisdom need not be pretty
to be precious.
Come, Angurboða, smile upon us now.
We welcome Your blessings.

Angurboða is rarely honored as a Goddess among modern Heathens, yet She is included here because there is a small minority of modern worshippers who do choose to honor Her. Her name means "One Who Brings Grief." Nothing is known of Her in lore, save that She was the lover of Loki and that, from Their union, three children were born: Hela, Goddess of the Dead; Fenris; and the great serpent Jormungand. Those who honor Her call upon Her as a Goddess of great primal wisdom and fierce power.

Hela (Hel)

From the ice and shadow of Your obsidian abode,
You whisper to us.
You sit, carving runes of protection and defense,
knowing that, in time, all must journey to Your realm.
Your power, flowering like an ebon lotus fed by a crimson tide,
calls in dreams and sings in our blood.
Odin Himself bowed to Your wisdom,
writhing in agony on the Tree of sacrifice in exchange for Your gifts.
Your name is so often spoken in hushed, fearful
    tones; yet it is only knowledge
and comfort that You offer, a place of surcease and learning.
There is no greater joy than to be blessed by Your magic.
You sit in darkness, forging blades of power and prophecy,
offering up Your gifts to those willing to call You Mother.
Give me the strength to journey to Your dark places,
that I may learn from the hands that nestled me in
my mother's womb,
the hands that will gather my weary soul
    when my mortal time is done.
I offer myself, that I may receive Thy burning kiss
upon my humble brow.
Hela, wrap me in the grace
of Your shadow. I hail You.

Hela is the daughter of Loki and Angurboða and ruler of the realm of the dead. All those who die of natural causes, old age, and sickness go to Her realm. While some accounts present it as a rather silent, dank place, it is not in any way a place of torment as in Christian ideology. It was a resting place for the dead, represented in the literature of the time as a great hall, analogous to the hall of any other God. Traditional sources give this Goddess a rather startling appearance: half black (decayed) and half white (living). Her realm was said to have nine levels, the lowest being Niflheim (although the remaining levels do not correspond to the other eight worlds connected by Bifrost bridge), to which the worst of the dead were confined.

The dankness and darkness so often associated with Helheim need not be seen as a negative. Burial mounds were sacred places, places to make offerings to one's honored dead, places to seek out their counsel. The mounds were even seen as doorways to the dead's afterlife dwellings. Hela's presence is one of incredibly kinetically charged stillness. It is stillness filled with a solitude that has color, texture, and a voice all its own. The dead are Her children and She knows the names of all who pass into Her hall. She is an ancient Goddess of immense patience and detached demeanor (at least in my experience and that of the various Hela's folk I have communicated with), yet at the same time, there is immense compassion there. All the wisdom inherent in the ancestral connection, all the knowledge of the dead, lies in Hela's hands. She is a Goddess of deep wisdom and power.

Committing to establishing a relationship with your own dead is an excellent way to begin honoring Hela. Setting up an altar to Hela or incorporating offerings to Her on an ancestral altar is an excellent way to begin honoring Her. I often give Her coffee and coffee beans in offering, as well as a rich Chambord. The dead must be honored before power can grow. We stand on the shoulders of our foremothers and forefathers, on the foundation laid by their struggle, hopes, dreams, and sacrifices. Their blood flows in us, we are formed from their very DNA, and that is the deepest, most primordial connection we could possibly have to the realm of this Goddess.

Devotional Activity for Hela: Go to the cemetery and make offerings at a grave. Clean up the cemetery. Pour out offerings to the dead.

Laufey

> *Laufey, I wish to craft a beautiful prayer for You but words fail me in the face of the immense gift You have given me. You have returned to me my center, my roots, reconnected me to the Tree which is my strength and my foundation. I will praise You now and always.*
>
> *I sense You in the quietness of the earth, the rich synergy of the crisp forest, wood supporting the flame, and the delicious spark of synapses and nerve endings that call our senses to life. You are the richness of the forest, green tranquility, its fire as it bursts into fierce delight at the first whisperings of autumn. You are the sweet, sweet silence that restores holiness to the damaged spirit.*
>
> *You have renewed me, restored me, and returned me to the Gods I love when I was lost and hurting. I hail You, Mother of Loki. You have nurtured me like a daughter. My heart is bursting with gratitude for this unexpected gift. You have given me back reverent sight. Thank You, primal Mother. Thank You, my sanctuary. Thank You.*

Laufey, also called Nál, is the Mother of Loki. I am only aware of a handful of Heathens who actively honor Her, however I have personally derived such benefit from Her kindness that I decided to include Her here. Her name means "leafy island," and Her secondary name, Nál, translates as "needle." Nothing is known of Her in lore, save the etymology of Her name, the name of Her husband, Fárbauti ("Cruel-Striker"), and the fact that She is the mother of that most infamous of Gods, Loki.

She is sometimes seen as a Goddess of Trees, with Fárbauti embodying the burning strike of lightning. I have experienced Her as immensely centering, yet with a definite heat, rather like the molten rock in the center of the earth—hidden from view but still powerful. There is an intense synergy about Her presence: it flows and crackles like tinder submitting to the flame or the spark of electricity that causes synapses to fire and transmits sensory messages along the conduit of the nerve endings. Every time I have encountered Her, Her presence was very nurturing, like a mother bird guiding the chick in its first faltering flight. There was stillness and solitude, but through all of that a dancing rhythm—the sense of life existing in quiet harmony within the stillness. She is tranquility, and yet there is the sense of something immense, enormous, and ancient behind that benevolence.

Rán and Aegir

> I hail the Goddess of the ocean depths, Rán,
>   Mistress of wealth and hidden secrets.
> I honor You for the tumult and danger You bring.
> I honor the personal clarity You bestow, with the painful
>   precision of a harpoon sinking into the flesh.
> I honor You, for Your memory is long; You see those things we
>   mortals would forget, and You hold fast to what is Yours.
> I hail You, Rán, Goddess of the Seven Seas, and ask for Your mercy.
>
> I hail Aegir, God of the Northern Ocean.
> I hail You for Your bounty, for Your generosity, for Your wisdom.
> I celebrate the wealth and mystery of Your watery realm.
> I hail Your skill, delight of the Gods. I hail Your hospitality,
>   which is celebrated in the halls of Asgard.
> I hail You, Mighty Aegir, Bold Brewer of the Gods.

Rán is the Goddess of the sea and its depths. She hides its secrets and claims offerings from any who would make their living from Her realm. Drowning is essentially falling into Rán's hands, and those who die in such a manner, particularly by drowning at sea, do not go to Hela's realm, but remain in Rán's realm of the dead. According to Simek, She embodies the sinister side of the sea with its attendant danger.[19] Conversely, She may also encourage the ocean depths to yield up their bounty to the sailor, the fisherman, and the treasure hunter. In my own experience, I have found that She tends to evoke immense, often traumatic and painful self-discovery in those who honor Her. She dredges up all the dark parts of ourselves that we might wish long buried and forgotten. Rán forgets nothing and, when we least expect it, will remind us of that we most wish to forget. She brings an astonishing clarity of mind, but it is the clarity of one who has accepted a death of the self, a death of old habits, behaviors, and states of being that no longer serve our growth. Rán's name means "Robber," for She owns a net that captures drowning people and draws them to Her realm. She is the wife of the sea giant Aegir.

Aegir's name means "sea," and like His wife, Rán, He is a giant of the sea who often hosts the Aesir and Vanir in His hall. Given that He is so often referred to as a friend of the Gods, perhaps He may be honored as a God of celebration, hosting, and hospitality. Modern Heathens often honor Him for His brewing skills, and He has become the de facto patron of modern home brewing.[20] They also have nine daughters who receive cultus in the contemporary Northern Tradition.

Hreðe

I say hail to Hreðe, Mighty Goddess!
With explosive force, You banish winter.
With invigorating drive, You push us into
the rejuvenating arms of spring.
Cleanse me, Glorious Goddess,
of all those things that hold me back.
Unfetter my mind, heart, and will,
that I might set my feet unswervingly on the road to victory.
Hail, Hreðe, ever-victorious in every struggle!

Hreðe is mentioned only once, in Bede's *De Temporibus Ratione*. She is an Anglo-Saxon Goddess whose name translates as "The Glorious" or "The Victorious." The month of March in the old Anglo-Saxon calendar was named after Her, and She is perhaps best personified by the chill weather preceding the blossoming of Spring. There is some indication that She is a battle Goddess, given the etymology of Her name, but very little else is known.

I personally have a soft spot in my heart for this Goddess, being born at the end of March. I like to think that perhaps She can be said to embody the best characteristics of the Aries personality: forcefulness, immense creative drive, catalytic power, and a certain whimsical attractiveness.

Ostara (Eostre)

I praise Eostre, Goddess of the Dawn;
Rising mighty in the East, You bless us.
I praise Eostre, Goddess of the fertile fields.
With victory and fruitful luck, You nourish us.
I praise Eostre, Goddess of new beginnings.
With strength and resilience, You fortify us.
Shine Your light upon us, Holy Goddess.
Make our words and deeds mighty in Your eyes.
Replenish us daily with Your light.
We hail you, Gracious Goddess of the Dawn.
We hail You, Eostre, after whom spring itself is named.
Please, Make us fruitful. Hail.

Ostara, or Eostre, is mentioned only once, by Bede in *De Temporibus Ratione*, and despite the fact that one of the major Heathen holidays (the Spring Equinox) is named after Her—in addition to the Anglo-Saxon month of April—almost nothing else is known about this Goddess. It is known that the Christians gave Her name to one of their major holidays—Easter—and that much of the same symbolism currently ascribed to the secular celebration of Easter, such as rabbits and eggs, may also be given to Ostara as symbols of Her fertility and the awakening of the land.

She is a Goddess of springtime, governing all that entails: the rebirth of the land, the quickening of its natural rhythms, the lengthening of the days. She is a Goddess of new life; new beginnings; and young, newborn creatures. The impetus to reproduce may be Her gift as well. The egg is a potent symbol for Ostara (and the Spring Equinox, interestingly enough, is the only time an egg can be balanced on its end), as it contains the potential for new life, just like the land in the month that bears Her name. She brings about the warming of the earth after the ice and cold of winter. Because Her name is connected to the Old High German words for "shining" and "east" and to the Greek Eos (Goddess of dawn in their pantheon),[21] many modern Heathens see Ostara as a Goddess of the dawn, in addition to being a Goddess of springtime, prosperity, and growth.[22] Her essence is best felt in the actual moment of the equinox, when winter truly yields its hold on the land to spring. She is potential in progress.

Personal Rite to Honor Ostara

The purpose of this simple rite is to celebrate Ostara's presence and to welcome Her blessings in your life. In addition to a faining, this is a nice way to celebrate Ostara. In late March/early April (as close to the actual Spring Equinox as possible), gather a number of seeds: flowers, herbs, vegetables—whatever you personally prefer. If you live in an apartment, you will want to purchase soil and planters so that this rite may be done inside, but if you actually have land or a yard, this should be done outside. Additionally, have a selection of edible seeds in a small bowl. Set up an altar (called a *vé* in Old Norse, or *weofod* in Anglo-Saxon) either inside or outside, with the seeds, soil (if necessary), and any other images or items that you personally associate with Ostara.

Offer up a prayer to Ostara, inviting Her to witness and participate in this rite, offering its fruits to Her. The bowl of edible seeds represents potential and possibility. They are creativity that has not yet manifested, that which must be nurtured and cared for. They represent endless possibility of the spirit. Holding the bowl of seeds, spend a few moments meditating on what you wish to manifest in the coming year and speak this aloud. Ask for Ostara's blessing, and eat a few of the seeds. Ask for Her help in overcoming any obstacles and in remaining motivated. Set the rest of the edible seeds out in offering to Her, or sprinkle them outside as a gift for the birds.

Then take the seeds that you intend to plant. Prepare the soil, either putting potting soil in the containers that you will keep inside or preparing the actual ground outside to receive the seeds. With each seed (or handful of seeds, as many flower seeds are quite small), name aloud some blessing of Ostara's in your life that you are particularly grateful for. Thank Her by giving something back to the land. When you are finished, spend as long as you wish meditating upon this Goddess. Then offer your thanks and go about your day. This rite should be done in the morning.

The Valkyrja (Waelcyrgie)

While not specifically Deities, these warrior women do figure prominently in Northern cosmology, particularly in the realm of soul lore. Their name translates as "Choosers of the Slain," and They are the handmaidens of Woden. They occasionally protect His chosen heroes, keeping them from harm, but more often ride the field of battle, selecting particularly courageous fighters to join Odin's army in the halls of Valhalla. This army constantly trains in preparation for the final battle of Ragnarok. While later Germanic writings present the Valkyrja as beautiful women, civilized and wise, They were originally fierce warriors, enthralled with the fury and rage of battle. They are connected to the Nornir (Skuld occasionally being numbered among Them) in that They sever the lifethreads of those heroes They choose. Regardless of whether the Valkyrja are seen as fierce, unstoppable warriors or wise and stately protectors, They reflect and embody the powers of the God to whom They are attached, Odin. They are often referred to as Shield-Maidens and occasionally as "Óskmeyjar": Wish-women (connected to Odin as Óski, Fulfiller of Wishes). Their individual names often reflect their role as Battle Maidens: Hild ("Battle"), Thrúð ("Din of Battle"), Randgríð ("Shield Destroyer"), and Herfjötur ("Fetterer of an Army"), to name but a few.[23]

Sunna/Sigel/Sol

I hail Sunna, glorious in Her power.
It is Her life-giving warmth that nourishes and sustains us.
I give praise to this radiant Goddess. I
     celebrate Her glorious strength.
Without Her loving touch, our fields would wither.
Without Her gentle care, our world would be bleak and black.
I will praise Her gifts, more beautiful than
     amber, more precious than gold.
Hail, Sunna life-giver and protector!

Sunna, the divine personification of the sun, is rarely mentioned in the surviving lore. There is a reference to Her in the Merseburg Charm and in the Eddas. Like Mani, She was drawn across the sky in a chariot pulled by two horses and pursued by a hungry wolf. She was venerated by early Germanic peoples as a life-giver. It was Her power that helped the crops to grow, providing sustenance for a people who lived in a cold, often inhospitable land. She governed the cycle of day, and the rhythms of agricultural life largely revolved around Her rising and setting. Today we can honor Her as our Pace-setter, as most of us still rise to begin our workday by Her unchanging cycles. She may be invoked to bring rejuvenating power to us during our day, and her mere presence provides a constant reminder of the Gods' presence and power in our daily lives.

Sinthgunt

Daughter of the House of Mundilfari,
Mighty Rider across the cosmic Sky,
Wise Teacher, farseeing,
cunning and strong,
thank you for Your blessings this night.
Please show me how
You best wish to be honored.
Oh Goddess, please show me
how best to praise Your name.
Sinthgunt, I hail you,
tonight and all nights of my life.

Sinthgunt is one of Mundilfari's daughters, and sibling to Mani and Sunna. Almost nothing is known about Her, aside from being mentioned in the Merseburg Charms. What I write here is drawn from modern cultus and shared communal gnosis. Those of us who honor Her recognize Her as a Goddess of cosmic order, the movement of the stars, the flow of time, the shaping of galaxies. In this, She is very like Her father, Mundilfari, a God of Time itself. Within the House of Mundilfari, there is also the Goddess Nott, a Goddess of night, the night sky, and mystery. While not much is known via the lore about these Deities, that provides a tremendous freedom to approach Them in devotion without preconceptions.

Jorð (Eorðe/Erda)

Hal wes þu, folde, fira modor!
Beo þu growende on godes fæþme, fodre gefylled firum to nytte.
Hail be Thou, earth, mother of men,
be Thou with growing things in God's embrace,
filled with food for the good of men . . . [24]

Prayer to Jorð (Erda)

Hail to You,
Who makes the land fruitful.
May we be mindful of Your blessings.

Hail to You, Fecund Mother,
Who makes the soil rich,
may our hearts be rich as well
in love and devotion to You.

Hail to You,
from whom all good things come,
richness and bounty, abundance,
and the saturation of Your presence,
that makes our world full
of a wealth of wonder.

May we always honor You,
in our words, our deeds,
through the mindfulness
with which we walk
upon the earth that is Your body.

Hail to You, Jorð,
Hail, Gracious Mother.

Jorð is Thor's mother and Goddess of the earth. Her name is cognate to the Old English Erda but whether They may be considered the same Goddess or not is up to each individual devotee to determine for him- or herself. My general rule of thumb is to default to treating Them each individually until I have reason to do otherwise. It's just respectful. Plus, regional differences matter and can really unlock very specific mysteries of the Gods in question.

We don't know very much about Jörð, other than that she is Jotun and the Mother of Thor. Jörð is the personification of the earth itself. She is the daughter of Night, lover (possibly wife) of Odin. Throughout the lore, She is known by many different names: in Old Norse she is called Fjörgyn,[25] Hlóðynn, Fold ("Earth"), and Grund ("Ground"). In Old English she is called Folde and Fira Modor ("Mother of Mankind"). She is a Goddess of nourishing power, fearsome might, and all-encompassing strength. Because of Her benevolence, fields flourish, flowers grow, and fruits ripen. Because of Her, mankind is able to draw sustenance from the land. Her might shines forth in the earthquake, the hurricane, and the tornado. The cycle of seasons centers around Her. She is the foundation and keeper of untold wealth: land, mountains, minerals, oceans, trees, foliage, crops. An excellent means of honoring Her in our world today is to commit to mindful consumption and recycling or ongoing volunteer work at a local park.

As Goddess of Earth (Mother Earth if you will), Her sphere of influence is the land and soil, mountains, trees, blooming things, the ecosystem itself. Good ways to honor Her include donating to organizations like Big Sur Land Trust (my personal favorite) that specifically focus on preserving the land, being mindful of one's own impact on the environment, maintaining a garden, buying locally and from local farmers, and caring for the land in whatever way one is able.

Frau Hölle

> *Hail, Frau Hölle, I honor You and the secrets You hold.*
> *I ask that You teach me Your wisdom, Mother of the Hunt.*
> *I have seen You, magical, tricksterish . . . both fierce and*
> *   gleeful as You share Your knowledge. I would learn from*
> *   You. I will bring patience and industry to the task.*
> *I will not falter or back away from the unknown to which You*
> *   hold the key. I will be steadfast and bold, I promise You. I*
> *   will work with focus and care to integrate Your teaching into*
> *   my life. I welcome Your transformation. I hail You now, Frau*
> *   Hölle. Please accept this offering of wine from my hand. Hail.*

Some Heathens see Hölle as a hypostasis of Frigga—after all, Woden has His numerous disguises, so why should Frigga be any different? Others connect Her strongly with Hela, and still others see Her as a Goddess in Her own right. In Germanic folklore, She appears alternately as a motherly Goddess, rewarding industry and hard work with great blessings of abundance, or as the fierce leader of the Wild Hunt (along with Woden), Queen of Witches, and collector of souls—particularly the souls of dead children. Her realm is traditionally believed to lie beneath the earth, inside mountains, or even beneath lakes and ponds.

Nehellenia

Hail, Ancient Mother, Goddess of the primal waters,
Goddess of ships and of abundance.
You bridge the gap between the living and the dead,
You carry our offerings to the hands of our ancestors.
You carry our prayers to the ears of our honored dead.
You are Goddess of life and of death, and all passages are aided
*   by Your nourishing hands. I hail You, Ancient Mother.*

Nehellenia is a Dutch Goddess honored on numerous votary stones and altars dating from the third century CE. Many of these altars show depictions of fruit offerings, ships, and dogs, and there is some evidence that Her worship had much in common with that of the Egyptian Goddess Isis, whose worship was carried to the Northern shores by Roman invaders. According to Simek,[26] Her name may mean alternately "Goddess of Death" (from Latin *necare*, "to kill" and Germanic *helan*, "to hide"), "Goddess of seafaring," or "the helpful Goddess coming close." Given the symbols of both fertility and death so strongly associated with Her, She is honored today as a Goddess of passages.

CHAPTER 4

THE GODS

Foremost among the Aesir—indeed among all tribes of Gods—was the Allfather, Odin. We will begin with Him.

Odin (Woden)[1]

I will hail the bold God, Lord of Asgard's hosts.
I will praise the Lord of Valhalla.
I will celebrate His strength, cunning and wisdom,
This God of warriors and kings.
I will praise Him, the Allfather,
Husband of Frigga, Delight of Her arms.
I will hail the Drighten and Ring-giver,
Whose gifts inspire His chosen.
I will laud this Wooer of women,
Whisperer of charms and seduction.
I will sing of the Master of Poets,
Ensnarer of many an unwary heart.
I will raise a horn in His honor.
May victory be Yours, Valfaðr.
Hail, Woden! Hail the Wisest of Counselors![2]

Odin is a God of many names: Woden, Oðinn ("Fury" or "Frenzy"), Allfaðer ("Allfather"), Herjan ("Lord"), Wunsch ("Wish-Giver"), Yggr ("The Terrible"), Veratyr ("God of Being"), Fimbultyr ("Mighty God"), Hrjotr ("Roarer"), Svipall ("Changeable"), Gangleri ("Wanderer"), Hangagoð ("God of the Hanged"), Geirvaldr ("Spear Master"), Herteit ("Glad of War"), Glapsviðr ("Seducer"), Thekkr ("Welcoming One"), Sanngetal ("Finder of Truth"), Óski ("Fulfiller of Desire"), Sigfaðir ("Victory Father"), Grimnir ("Masked One"), Bolverk ("Bale Worker"), and Harbarðr ("Greybeard"), to name but a few.[3] The meaning of His primary name Odin, or Oðinn, is from the Old Germanic word for "berserker fury" and refers to ecstatic trance, for Odin is a God of ecstasy, of the storm, of poetry, incantation, magic, battle, death, and transformation. At the same time, He is a God of wisdom, mental acuity, knowledge-seeking, and divine order. Some modern Heathens believe that the predominance of heiti, was a product of the respect, awe, and even fear in which this God was held in pre-Christian Europe.[4] Be that as it may, the numerous praise names—more than 150 on record—certainly point to the many faces and guises this God was and is capable of taking. In fact, one of Odin's primary attributes was His tendency to disguise Himself as a common wanderer, to traverse freely through the nine worlds, gathering knowledge, furthering His plans, and interacting with mortals.

After the creation of the worlds, it was Odin who breathed life into the first man and woman. For this reason, as well as for His place in the pantheon, He is referred to as the Allfather, a paean to His life-giving power. Odin as Breath-Giver is tied indisputably with Odin as Father of Runes and Seeker of Knowledge. So many of His heiti invoke the power of the spoken word and the power of focused breath: Omi ("One Whose Voice Resounds"), Hvethrungr ("Roarer"), Vithrimnir ("Contrary Screamer"), Galdrafaðr ("Father of Galdr"), Gollnir ("Shrieker"), Eyluðr ("Ever-Booming"), and the list goes on. Odin is a God of magic and power. In magical practice, to speak is to call into being. A large part of rune magic was the chanting of special songs and the singing of runes (called *galdr*[5]) to control the unfolding of being or sometimes to call and control spirits. Therefore, to speak is to imbue with life, a power belonging first and foremost to the Gods.

So as Breath-Giver, Odin imbues creation with the animating principle. He breathes life into our most hidden, secret dreams and unhoned talents. He awakens our passions, fires of inspiration, creativity, and occasionally ferocity within us. And He has the most annoying tendency to throw open doors long thought barred and sealed within the chambers of the heart. More than breath, from the Allfather comes awareness—a frightening gift at times. We are birthed by His exhalation, and therefore, at death, we are brought back to Him and into Him by His inhalation. Our lives are the span between two breaths of a God; not only does Odin give us life, but our lives begin and end with His breath.

Adam of Bremen, in the eleventh century, declared, "Woden, id est furor" (Woden, He is fury).[6] Woden is certainly that, but even more, He is hunger. Throughout the corpus of our lore,[7] it is clear that Odin hungers for knowledge. He even subjects Himself to torture in order to acquire wisdom, knowledge, and understanding. The most notable and well-known example of this is recorded in the Havamal, where the Allfather says:

> *I know that I hung on a windy*
> *tree nine long nights,*
> *wounded with a spear, dedicated to Odin,*
> *myself to myself,*
> *on that tree of which no man knows*
> *from where its roots run.*
> *No bread did they give me nor a drink from a horn,*
> *Downwards I peered;*
> *I took up the runes, screaming I took them,*
> *Then I fell back from there.*[8]

This recounts the tale of how the runes were won. The Allfather willingly sacrificed Himself, hanging on Yggdrasil, wounded by His own weapon, for nine days and nights of agony. On the ninth night, the runes surged into His consciousness. He spied them in the abyss below and seized them up triumphantly. This one event perhaps most clearly defines Odin's essential nature: the hunger to always go further and deeper.

Certainly this is not the only example in the Eddas of Odin's quest for knowledge. We see it again in the Vafðrudnismal, where (against the advice of the Allmother Frigga), He ventures forth to challenge a wise and cunning giant to a test of riddles. Should He lose, the price would be His head. Of course Odin won, and it was the giant who forfeited his life. To gain the knowledge to use His power and wisdom wisely, Odin journeyed to the well of Mimir to barter for a draught of the magical elixir. The price for His drink was high: He was forced to tear out and sacrifice one of His eyes, which now lies hidden in Mimir's Well. Then we have His winning of the sacred mead—the mead of poetry, inspiration, and creative fire. This mead, Oðroerir, initially belonged to the Gods and was made of their spittle and the ground up parts of the giant Kvasir. It was stolen from Them and eventually ended up in the hands of the Jotun Suttung. He locked it away in a cave and set his daughter Gunnloð to guard it. Odin disguised Himself as Bolverk and won the mead through guile, shapeshifting, and eventually through His seduction of Gunnloð, exchanging three nights of passion for three sips of the mead. From this union, the God of poetry, Bragi, was born.

This episode illustrates perhaps another of His most outstanding characteristics: the Allfather loves women—all shapes, all sizes, and all ages. (This is a fact easily supportable by even the most cursory reading of the Eddas! Take, for example, the Harbarðsljoð. While Thor boasts of Jötnar He has slain, Odin, disguised as Harbard, boasts of His sexual conquests.) He cherishes women, especially those who cherish Him in return. A word should be said about Odin's boasts of sexual conquest. I do not feel that such boasts on the part of a God are ones of betrayal or machismo. Rather they are an admission of a sexuality, energy, and vital force too powerful to be contained; a symbol of life, exuberance, and strength; and above all, an expression of vitality and of seizing the moment in a life that is all the sweeter because it must seem so fragile, so threatened, to those Gods whose ears are constantly straining for the blast of Heimdall's horn. And for every person who opens to Him, who loves Him just a little, who is able to contain, for however short a time, a single drop of the enormity of His essence, more of Him is able to be in the world. We are doorways, vessels, windows for this most active of Gods.

Perhaps it is not surprising for a God so strongly associated with vital power, that we also find in Woden a God of healing, though this aspect of His nature was strongly suppressed during the Christian conversion of Scandinavia and Iceland. There are only three extant sources citing Odin as healer. The first is the Second Merseburg Charm, in which an injured horse is healed:

> *Phol and Wodan rode into the woods,*
> *There Balder's foal sprained its foot.*
> *It was charmed by Sinthgunt, her sister Sunna;*
> *It was charmed by Frija, her sister Volla;*
> *It was charmed by Wodan, as he well knew how:*
> *Bone-sprain, like blood-sprain,*
> *Like limb-sprain:*
> *Bone to bone, blood to blood;*
> *Limb to limb—like they were glued.*[9]

The second source is the "Nine Worts Galdr" from the Anglo-Saxon Lacnunga manuscript, which says:

> *. . . then Woden took up nine glory-rods, / struck the adder then*
> *so it flew apart into nine, / there apple ended it and its poison /*
> *so that it would never bend into a house. / Chervil and fennel,*

two of great might, / the wise lord shaped these plants / while he was hanging, holy in the heavens / he set them and sent them into the seven worlds / for poor and for wealthy, as a cure for all.[10]

The third source is the second rune charm from the Havamal: "I know a second which the sons of men need, those who want to live as physicians."[11]

Of course, Woden also has His darker side. He is cunning, implacable, fierce, and brilliant in battle. He leads a host of the dead in the Wild Hunt and He possesses the power to command the dead to do His bidding.[12] Many of His heiti speak of His ability in combat: Herblindi ("Host Blinder)," Hnikuðr ("Overthrower)," and Valgautr ("Slaughter God)"; others speak of His fury: Thror ("Inciter of Strife)," Woden ("Fury)," and Viðurr ("Killer)," to name but a few.[13] He is a Wanderer, wandering endlessly throughout the worlds in search of knowledge, wisdom, and some craft to hold Ragnarok at bay and perhaps increase His own knowledge hoard.

Morning Meditation Rite to Odin

Stand or sit before your personal shrine.

Light a candle or perhaps a bit of incense; this provides a focus for the subconscious mind.

Begin to focus on your breath. Spend 5–10 minutes in a simple centering breathing: inhale four even counts, hold four, exhale four, and hold four counts, while focusing on all the life energy in your body gathering at a point about two inches below the navel.

Think on Yggdrasil, the sacred Tree that supports the multiverse. Feel it strong and sturdy, with branches stretching up higher than the eye can see and roots, thick and mighty, plunging deep into the body of the earth. Feel yourself part of that Tree, connected to it in thought, drawing sustenance from it as it feeds its life-giving essence into all the worlds. Feel yourself rooted and strong as the Tree is rooted. As you exhale, feel all the energy gathered during your centering breath, plunging down and into the earth, connecting you to the body of Mother Earth, just like the roots of the Tree connect it to the source of its power. Spend five minutes consciously sending your vital force down into the earth with each exhalation, visualizing rich, sturdy roots.

Focus on your altar, and turn your attention to Woden. Breathe Him in. Consciously take in His essence as you inhale, filling yourself with the vital force of this God. Feel it filling you, with each inhalation, from toes to crown. Feel that connection with Him, open and powerful. Feel all that He is reaching down, rooting you as the roots of the Tree steady its body.

Offer up the following prayer:

*Mot þa worda min muðes ond þa geondðenca
min geðonces gelician þé, Leof min.*
[Pronunciation: Mot tha worde min muthes ond tha yeondthenke min yethonkes yelikan the, Leof min]

The translation would be, roughly, "May the words of my mouth and the contemplations of my heart be pleasing to Thee, My Beloved (Lord)." (Anglo-Saxon translation provided by Wulfgaest Thegn, Heah Blotere of the Haligwaerstow.)

Spend as much time as you would like basking in the presence of Woden, talking to Him, and meditating upon His attributes and His place in your life.

When you are finished say, "Woden, for all You are, I am grateful. Guide me this day."

Blow out the candle or extinguish the incense and go about your day.

Thor (Thunor)

I raise a horn to Thor the Mighty.
Glad I am to call Him friend.
He fiercely protects those He loves.
He watches over the weak and the innocent.
He is kind and gentle, this God, and wise—
Wise enough to save his daughter through a battle of wits.
He is loyal to His family; He does not question their affections.
He is strong but not overly prideful. What other
    God would masquerade as a woman,
to reclaim his most sacred weapon—all for the good of
    His tribe? What other God would willingly bear
    the company of Laufey's son, even though He must
    know this brings as much trouble as boon?
He is friend to all, caring and gentle. His strength nourishes,
    heals, and reclaims that which is wounded. He is
    sure and grounded, as sturdy as the roots of the sacred
    Tree. He hallows with His presence. He makes that
    which is sundered hale, healthy, and whole.
I praise You, Son of Odin, Son of Jorð. Husband
    of Sif, Father of Magni and Modi.
I hail You, strong defender of those You love,
    warder of all Your younger kin.
Hail, Thor.

Perhaps no other God is so well loved by Heathens both ancient and modern as the God Thor. He was very likely the most widely worshipped of any of the Heathen Gods throughout pre-Christian Northern Europe. He is the God of the common man, seemingly uncomplicated and down-to-earth. He is the defender of mankind, warding the world against the incursion of the forces of chaos and destruction. He hallows by His might and by His very presence, and today Heathens wear the symbol of His mighty hammer Mjolnir

("Crusher") as a sign of troth. He girds the world against its own dissolution. His is the power to restore holiness and wholeness to anything He touches. For this reason, a hammer was laid in the bride's lap at the wedding feast to ensure the fertility of the couple—a custom that continues today among modern Heathens. Thor is a God of wholeness, well-being, and protection.

Thor is kind, just, and very protective of those He cares about: His wife Sif, His daughter Thruð ("strength"), and His sons Magni and Modi ("the Strong One" and "the Angry One"). He is constantly fighting to ensure the security of His clan and extended family of the Gods so that He is primarily known for His ability at fighting Jötnar who constantly seek to undo what the Gods have wrought. In many respects, it is Thor's power that defines the inangarð. The concept of *inangarð* and *utgarð* is essential to any definition of the holy in Heathen culture. The community, clan, and tribe were viewed as the *inangarð*, a sacred enclosure protected against the forces of entropy and destruction represented by the *utgarð*. To hallow something is to bring it within the boundaries of the inangarð. Properly maintaining the integrity and wholeness of the inangarð (for instance, by proper behavior and by proper ritual performance and sacrifice) was crucial to maintaining the luck and strength of the tribe. Anything that threatened that order was dangerous and, therefore, of the utgarð. From this evolved the concept of *thew*, or tribal custom/law, which ensured that the strength of the inangarð would not be threatened by its own people. Thor constantly crossed into the untamed wilds of utgarð to slay those who threatened the peace of the Gods. In fact, He is the only God that does not use some mechanism to cross between worlds. Most use the bridge Bifrost, but Thor is too heavy so He cannot. Others utilize magical falcon cloaks or vehicles such as Freya's chariot. Thor needs none of that. His holy might is so powerful that He is able to wade through the proto-fabric of time and space on His own.

Thor will go to any lengths to protect His people, including temporarily sacrificing His masculinity! In one of the Eddic tales, Thor's hammer is stolen by a Jotun who will only return it if the Goddess

Freya promises to be his bride. Well of course Freya is not about to consent to any such bargain, so Thor (with Loki as His cunning attendant) dresses in women's clothing, disguising Himself as the Goddess, and tricks His way (with Loki's sly mind and words to help pave the way) into the Jotun's hall—ostensibly for the marriage feast. Once there, of course, the hammer is placed in His lap to hallow the "marriage," and that is the end of the Jotun and his kin.

In certain ways, though this is a controversial and by no means readily accepted theory (it is hardly agreed upon by scholars whether or not the Norse even had shamanic practitioners), Thor fulfills the function in Asgard that a traditional shaman would in a tribal community: He maintains the wholeness, health, and holiness of the community, and He protects it from otherworldly intruders and regularly travels between worlds. On at least one occasion, He cross-dresses, and He is regularly in the company of what may be seen by some as a "trickster" being (Loki). Whether one agrees with this or not, it is at least apparent that there is more to Thor than initially meets the eye.

The Strength of Thor: A Meditation

The strength of Thor is the strength that girds the world against destruction. The strength of Thor is that which contains the holy; it defines the inangarð. The strength of Thor is the supporting vessel into which the Gods may pour Their divine Maegen. Born of earth, He centers, grounds, and gives stability to that which is tenuous. He roots Midgard firmly within the multiverse; He brings to life that which lacks vigor. He centers us in the NOW. He shows us the vitality of the moment. The strength of Thor is perseverance. It is fire and thunder, lightning and quake. He is His mother's son and the pride of His father.

Fierce, He protects the lowly, the trembling, the fearful. He hallows that which connects the generations and, with His wife, blesses

Asgard, filling it with the flower of Their power. Dignity and pride, the might to defend, a forward faring spirit, cherisher of kin—these are the strength of Thor. He is shield and protector. He is companion and friend. His are the pillars that mark the frithstead. The strength of Thor does not yield in the face of loss and grief. It does not flicker away in the face of helpless vulnerability. The strength of Thor is the might of the hammer crushing the foe, but it is also the strength of compassion and care. The strength of Thor will nourish and comfort when all other comfort is lost. He strengthens the spirit and wards the soul against despair. He is the spine that supports us, often forgotten. And He never fails.

His pride is in His kin, and He battled for Thruð against the dwarf's incursion, His wit lying hidden beneath practical facade. His dignity was a small sacrifice to salvage His might when women's clothes He wore, and victorious He returned having vanquished the Jotun. He needs no vessel to cross the seas of wyrd and formless space. He stands in the liminal, making it physical and doing what must be done. He is unassuming yet mighty, a God for every man. His hammer is folk-binding—the emblem of His nature. It defines us, inspires us, and calls us to courage. It is the victory of Asgard over entropy and chaos. It rivets the fabric of being and binds us away from all harm.

Lover of Jarnsaxa, the iron-hearted; husband to Sif and defender of Her honor; Companion to Loki on many travels; bane of the Jötnar, who remain ever fearful. Warder of the Gods' halls, with many names, some very telling: Donar, Thunar, Asa-Thor, God of Thunder known to the Romans, son of Odin, beloved of the people. Called for healing, called for protection, called for insight, His wisdom held fast. Midgard's warder, God of the Country; Thrudugr, the Mighty; Thrudvald, Strong Protector; Father of Might and of Righteous Wrath; brother to Meili; Thrudvaldr Goda; Friend of Man; Giant-killer; Champion of Midgard—these names we remember.

Hail to Thor and the strength of His hammer. Hail to His insight and His willingness to aid. Ever the friend of those in need, ever the shield of those afraid.

Bragi (Brego)

Husband of Idunna, I hail You.
Your tongue is carved with runes of power,
And your mouth has become a gateway
of living inspiration. Words of beauty and fate-weaving force
pour from Your lips like pearls from an overflowing treasure hoard.
Son of Gunnloð, Son of Odin,
I praise Your poetic skill.
Hail, Bragi; I raise this horn to You.

Bragi is the progeny of Odin and the giantess Gunnloð, conceived during the three nights of sexual pleasure given by Odin to Gunnloð when He won back the sacred mead of inspiration and ecstasy. He is the husband of the Goddess Idunna and named by Odin in the Grimnismal as the "best of Poets." Poets were powerful figures within Germanic society. They were liminal figures, capable of weaving fate with their words, of passing judgments and prophesying, and of being the active voice of various supernatural beings (that is, Gods). They were visionaries capable of shaping the fabric of society and the luck of the tribe by the outpouring of their words. They ensured that the deeds of the tribe would be remembered, creating a visceral tie between the strength and might of one's ancestors and the potential deeds of living members of the community. They were a living bridge between past and present, and as such, Bragi holds a place of immense importance among the Aesir. It is fitting that He would be the progeny of Odin, Himself a God of poetry, ecstasy, and inspiration. Like the traditional role of the shaman in many cultures, among the Norse, it was the poet's duty to open doorways of consciousness through which the Gods could speak. Imbued as they were with the gift of ecstatic inspiration (and sometimes revelation), their words elevated their entire community.

Tyr (Tiw)

I will hail the grey God
Who walks in places neither light nor dark.
I will hail the One
Who holds duty to tribe and clan,
even above the binding vow of His sworn word,
in vanquishing the outlander.
I will hail Him who bears the sword as His symbol:
decisive, ruthless, just.
I will praise Him who sees what must be done
and quietly completes his duty.
He asks for neither praise nor glory,
boasts not with mighty words in the Hall.
He asks nothing but stands firm, steering His way
clearly through murky waters.
He is mighty, this God,
His glory found in His sword and the hand He sacrificed.
I will hail Him as He faces the wolf, this warrior Who betrays
for honor's sake.

Tyr is most well known for the binding of Fenris. Fenris was the son of Loki by the giantess Angurboða and had the shape of a huge, hungry wolf. At first, Fenris was welcomed (albeit with some trepidation) by the Gods, but eventually a seeress foretold that He would be the death of Odin at Ragnarok. After that, the Gods decided to bind Him so that He could wreak no harm (not wishing to kill the son of one of Their own). They took Fenris to an isolated clearing and proposed a test of His strength, promising to undo Him if any of the bonds held. They tried to bind Him with every manner of fetter, but none would hold, for the wolf was quite strong. Finally, the dwarves crafted a rope as thin and delicate as a ribbon. They called it *Gleipnir* ("Open One") and crafted it from things as impossible to conceive as the sound of a cat's footfall, the beard of a woman, the spittle of a bird, the roots of a mountain, the breath of a fish—all things that do not really exist. Fenris suspected treachery when He saw how delicate the cord was and only agreed to be bound if one of the Gods would place His right hand, His sword hand, into the wolf's jaws. Of Them all, only Tyr stepped forward to do so. When Fenris first came to the Hall of the Gods, Tyr was the one who fed and cared for Him. Once Fenris truly realized that the Gods had no intention of releasing Him, He snapped off Tyr's hand at the wrist. Tyr is known therefore for His bravery in defense of His clan.

He is generally considered to be a God of warriors, and one of the Eddic rune charms suggests carving His rune, the rune tiewaz (shaped like an upward-pointing arrow) on one's sword for protection and victory in battle. He is also a God of justice and law, right action and thew. There is ample evidence that, long before Odin became Allfather, Tyr ruled the worlds as Skyfather. His name is "cognate to Dyaus of Vedic myth and the elder Dyus Pater of Rome and Zeus of Greece, the Skyfather and progenitor of Creation."[14] By the time of the Eddas however, He had become known as Odin's son (or according to one Eddic lay, the son of a Jotun Hymir) and a patron of warriors. He is also patron of the Thing, the legal assembly in Germanic cultures through which disputes were settled by law or holmgang (ordeal by combat).

Lord Dan Halloran, a devout Tyrsman, speculates that "Tiw is less about conflict of 'war' and more about the mechanics of *recht* (right) and thus the resolution of conflict, a juridical function" and as such is concerned primarily with "clear resolution, honor and the preservation of thew."[15] One might say that Tyr is a God strongly involved in right action despite any consequences to the self, just government, legal structure and decisions, societal order, and proper maintaining of healthy customs. He is a God of valor, courage, integrity, wisdom, and of course, martial prowess—particularly that of knowing when and how to fight.

Baldur and Nanna

Brave Warrior, Shining Lord of Justice and Mercy,
we ask for Your blessings and grace.
Compassion flows from Your strong heart and noble brow.
Fearless Lord of Death and rebirth, intrepid,
*   You have braved the realm of Hel,*
So that we, children of the Gods, might have a champion
*   to greet us when we too make this perilous journey.*
Warrior-born, fill our hearts with Thy quiet courage.
Do not let us falter on our life's journey.
Teach us serenity of spirit that we might face the turmoil of our lives
joyously, embracing destiny without fear.
Open our hearts and let us not shrink in terror from our descent
into the earth, but find in Her dark depths spiritual renewal.
May we live lives of courage, passion, and valor.
Hail, Baldur!

Gentle Nanna, Baldur's devoted wife,
extend over us Your blessings and protection,
for we often struggle in our lives feeling lost and alone.
Stand with us as You stood with Baldur, even
*   joining Him in Hel's realm.*
Sustain us, nourish us, and grant us the gift of Your compassion.
Hail, Nanna, Daring and Bold, Compassionate One, Hail.

Baldur was the beloved son of Odin and Frigga, husband of the Goddess Nanna and, by some sources, father of Forseti. His death was foretold by a seeress consulted after He experienced a series of unsettling dreams. In order to protect Baldur from harm, Frigga traveled the worlds extracting an oath from every living thing that it would never harm Her son. She neglected to gain such an oath from mistletoe, however, thinking it too insignificant to do any harm. Sure that He was safe from His foretold fate, the Gods celebrated and boldly made a game of tossing weapons and darts at Baldur. Each missile bounced off harmlessly. Loki, however, made a dart out of mistletoe and gave it to Baldur's brother, the blind God Hoðr. With Loki guiding His hand, Hoðr tossed the dart, and it killed Baldur instantly. Baldur was placed on a funeral ship, and Odin whispered final words to His son, placing His holy ring Draupnir in Baldur's dead hands. Nanna died of grief upon seeing the funeral barge and was placed beside Her husband. The ship was set on fire, as was Germanic custom at the time, and so Baldur journeyed to Hel, the land of the all the dead who do not die in battle or in service to a specific God. Hoðr was slain by His half brother Váli, in vengeance for His crime.

Odin and Frigga were so distraught by His death that They sent Their other son, Hermod, to Hel, to ask Her to release Baldur and Nanna. She agreed to do this if every living thing would weep for the dead God. All did, save one: Loki took the form of an old woman and refused to weep, saying that Hel should keep what She has. (Given that Hel is Loki's daughter, it is none too surprising to find that He would not wish to rob Her of the wealth of Her realm.) Baldur and Nanna, therefore, have to remain in the land of the dead and, by doing so, survive Ragnarok.

Nanna is Baldur's wife and very little is known of Her, save that, by some accounts, Her name may translate as "the Daring One."[16] According to author Saxo Grammaticus, Nanna is married not to Baldur, but to His brother, Hoðr. Both Hoðr and Baldur survive Ragnarok.

Forseti

I hail Forseti, wise in His judgments.
I praise His farseeing wisdom.
He sets the law and orders the Thing.
He watches over His folk and protects them.
I hail this Shining God. I will praise Him often,
with raised horn and right deeds.

In the Eddas, Forseti is said to be the son of Baldur and Nanna and master of the Hall Glitnir ("Glittering") within Asgard. It is highly likely, however, that He is a much older God as He is referenced in eighth-century English sources as a Frisian God of law. When Charlemagne demanded the Frisians produce a law code, the elders of the tribe managed to delay fulfilling this request twice, but finally were punished by being sent out in a rudderless boat. They petitioned their God, and a radiant man appeared bearing a golden ax. He guided the boat ashore on an uninhabited island and threw His ax into the earth where a spring appeared. Then He began to speak, giving the Frisian elders their law code. The sacred spring was later desecrated by a Christian missionary who very nearly lost his life for the affront.

Today, Forseti is honored as overseer of the Thing assembly, as well as a God of law, judges, and just ruling. Specifically, He is one who actually creates and sets laws, giving them to His people. Personally, I see Him clothed in white linen and find edelweiss to be a welcome offering.

Heimdall (Hama)

Hail, Heimdall, Shining Watcher of Asgard.
Hail, the strength of the Aesir.
Hail to Your never-tiring vigilance;
With You on the bridge, man and Gods rest secure.
I hail Your fortitude, never resting, never sleeping.
You, too, sacrificed at the well of Mimir.
I hail Your commitment to Your duty,
Purest of the Gods, Holy watchman on the Bridge.
Your presence alone banishes fear and threat.
You maintain the integrity of the inangarð.
Your mindfulness is a gift to us all.
I hail You, Valiant One!

Heimdall is the watchman of the Gods. He stands on Bifrost bridge with a gleaming horn, which will be blown to alert the Gods when any threat approaches. He is the son of nine mothers, daughters of Aegir and Rán, and His name means "One who illuminates the world."[17] By some accounts, it was Heimdall who wandered the earth under the name Rig, siring children on each couple that offered Him hospitality, thus becoming Father of mankind. Some scholars believe Rig to have been Odin (and certainly this fits His modus operandi), but others point to the Völuspá, where mankind is referred to as "Heimdall's children."[18]

Heimdall has a number of heiti that point to His importance in Eddic cosmology. He is called Hallinskíðí ("Ram"), Gullintani ("Gold-toothed"), Vindler ("Protector Against the Wind" or possibly "Wind-Sea"), and Whitest of the Ás. He has a hall in Asgard called Himinbjorg ("Heavenly Mountain"), and it is said that He sacrificed an ear to the well of Mimir in order to gain exceptional hearing. Indeed, Heimdall is a God possessed of many exceptional abilities befitting a sentry and guardsman. His hearing is so acute that He can hear the grass growing on Midgard. He needs less sleep than a bird, and His vision is as keen as His hearing regardless of whether it be day or night. He also possesses the ability to change His shape at will. When Loki attempted to steal Freya's magical necklace (and symbol of Her power) Brisingamen, Heimdall spied Him as He fled and set off in pursuit. Eventually Heimdall caught up with Loki near the ocean, and the two Gods transformed into seals, battling for possession of the necklace in animal form. Heimdall won the battle, and the necklace was returned to Freya. Because of this, Heimdall and Loki are deadly enemies, and it is said that each will be the destruction of the other at Ragnarok.[19]

Heimdall is a God of keen, mindful vigilance, and because of that, some Heathens today honor Him as a God of spiritual growth and contemplation.[20] Because He guards the rainbow bridge, the pathways between all the worlds, it is good and proper to hail Him at the beginning of any ritual, that He may open the way for our prayers and the Gods' blessings to flow. He hallows and consecrates and helps us maintain ritual purity, mindfulness, and good, clear discernment.

Ullr (Wuldor)

Cold, You are called, and harsh.
God of barren, forgotten places—
remote, unapproachable, fierce as a wolf on the hunt.
But I have not found You thus.
I have felt Your gift of quiet strength and comfort many times.
I think that You are God of all forgotten creatures,
those neglected souls bereft of love.
You teach us to sing a song of power and beauty
in the lonely wasteland of our scarred and broken hearts.
You are Father to all those children called ugly, ignorant, or wrong.
All little creatures in need of love are welcome in Your hall.
No pain is too great for You to succor, no
    agony too great for You to bear.
Do You weep, in the solitude of Your ice-scaped dwelling,
as You seek those lost and bleeding souls, their
    number sadly beyond measure?
No one thinks to go to You for healing, yet that is the gift You bring,
God of all orphaned hearts.
All who hear the song of the ice-blessed darkness may
    count themselves blessed by its sweetness.
I hail You, Son of Sif, Mighty Ullr, Glorious God.

Ullr is another of those Gods of which very little established lore has survived. We know that He is the son of Sif, but we do not know who His father is, save that it *isn't* Thor. His name means "glory" and He lives in a realm called Ýdalir, or "Yew-Dales." He is renown as a great archer, skier, and hunter and was often invoked for aid in single combat. He was a God of the lone warrior and a common kenning for shield was "Ullr's ship." Numerous place-names, most of them with the suffixes *-vé*, *-hörgr*, or *-hof*[21] indicating that they were considered holy places, are connected to Him, indicating that He was likely very highly honored at one time. Some sources go so far as to say that Ullr ruled Asgard in Odin's absence. There is some indication that Ullr was a good God to call upon in making oaths. Today, Ullr is primarily honored as a God of hunting, and many of His heiti attest to His skill: Bogaáss ("Bow God"), Veiðáss ("Hunting God"), and Ønduráss ("Ski God").

Hoenir (Hana) and Loður

Odin's brother, holy Prophet, Shining Ás,
I raise this horn to You.
Hostage to the Vanir, Ancient Creator, Frith-weaver,
I honor Your quiet courage.
Bestower of spirit and conscious awareness,
God of mindful contemplation,
I praise You for these mighty gifts.
I have found You unassuming in Your wisdom.
I have learned to cherish simplicity from Your graceful example.
I hail You, Hoenir, with this horn and in my heart.
I hail You with reverence.

Hail, Loður, God of passion and warmth.
Because of Your gift, we are able to experience the world.
Because of Your gift, we are able to know
*   pleasure through our five senses.*
You are the beating of our hearts, the rhythm of our blood.
You have given life to our bodies as breath; sense
*   and will were given by Your brothers.*
I hail You, divine enigma, known to us only as Odin's friend.
God of beauty, You inspire growth. From You
*   we are given our evolutionary drive.*
I hail You, for Your gifts at the time the world was born.
Hail, Loður.

Hoenir is the brother of Odin, who with Him helped to create the first man and woman by bestowing the gifts of consciousness and will. Hoenir was given as hostage to the Vanir to ensure peace after the first war, and sources credit Him with maintaining that peace even after the slaying of Mimir. Hoenir is slow of speech but considered very wise, perhaps embodying the Norse ideal, exemplified in the Havamal, of wisdom going hand in hand with silence.[22] He occasionally traveled with the Gods and is generally described as tall and handsome. He apparently had a very close relationship with Mimir, who was very likely His maternal uncle. Many modern Heathens hail Him as a God of prophecy and vision. Hoenir is one of the Gods said to survive Ragnarok. He is also called Vili, meaning "will."

Even less is known about Loður. During the creation of humanity, Loður gave the gifts of the five senses and beauty of form. He gave rhythm to the beating of the heart and the pulse of the blood, the essence of life and being. His other name is Vé or "holiness." Odin, Vili, and Vé—inspired consciousness, focused intent, and holiness, respectively—represent fundamental characteristics of differentiation by which order is wrought from chaos, Being from the gaping void, and they remain essential to its continued integrity. There is skaldic evidence that Loður and Loki are the same Holy Power both in Völuspá 18 and Þrymlur I-III 21. As I noted in a recent article,[23] if Loki, as the Þrymlur implies, is in fact Loður, then that makes him one of the three creator Gods of the Northern Tradition. It gives him a primary role in the fashioning of the cosmos of nine worlds. It makes him, despite his transgressive nature, a key upholder of cosmic order, although that very order was itself created by a massively transgressive act—the slaughter of the first ancestor, Ymir, by his descendants.

Hermod

I hail You, Hermod, for Your bravery.
Hermod, I want to be like You.
I do not wish to fear the dark places within my soul
or to shy away from understanding.

You went riding into Hel
to save Your brother;
did You know then that You were saving Yourself as well?
You are God of unexpected catalysts,
of journeys and the battle we fight within.
I, too, would mount the spirit steed
that would carry me to the places
of power and change.
Will You ride with me, Hermod?
Will You protect me from myself
as I ride the path to heaven?
The loneliness held no terror for You,
Teach me, Silent One, to be staunch in my journey.
Let my heart not be turned from this path,
by the vagaries and fears of my own spirit.
Let me journey, as You did so long ago,
firm and bold, as I hold my hand unwavering
up to heaven.

Hermod is the son of Odin, brother of the God Baldur. After Baldur's death, Hermod was sent to Hela's realm to bargain for His brother's release, having borrowed Odin's eight-legged steed Sleipnir for the journey. His journey took nine long nights, during which He faced the giantess Móðguðr, Guardian of the gates of Hel. She initially challenged Him but, upon learning the reason for His journey, granted Him passage into the land of the dead. Once inside Helheim, Hermod was granted access to Baldur and Nanna, who had been given places of honor within Hel's hall. He attempted to negotiate with Hela for Baldur's return, and She agreed on the condition that every living thing weep for the fallen God. (All living things did, save one: an old woman, Þokk, who was really Loki in disguise.) Before Hermod returned to the realm of the Gods, Baldur asked Him to return Odin's armring, Draupnir, which His father had placed on the funeral ship with Him, and Nanna sends gifts back to

Frigga. Hermod is the only God known to have been granted access into the land of the dead while in living form. Even Odin never actually entered Hela's gates.

Odin has many Sons—Hoðr, Váli (not to be confused with Loki's son Vali), Vidar—all of whom are slowly gaining cultus today.

Njorðr

I hail Njorðr, God of wealth and plenty.
I celebrate the treasures He brings forth from the sea.
I praise His tranquil nature, He who was sent as peace-weaver
to the Aesir. I hail His ability to reach compromise
    in the most heated of situations.
He is wise and farseeing, gentle and open-handed.
I hail the Master of Noatun, Husband of Skaði,
Father of Frey and Freya.
Smile upon us in our endeavors, and in all things
    make our hearts fruitful, Oh Lord.
To You, God of fair trade and exploration, of
    right gain and fruitful bounty, I pray.

Njorðr is the father of Frey and Freya, and he was one of the Gods sent to the Aesir as a hostage for peace at the end of the war between the Aesir and the Vanir. As such, He is a Vanic God and, like many of the Vanir, is intimately connected to the bounty and fertility of the land. In the case of Njorðr, His realm is Noatun, the Ship-yard, and He governs wealth that is won from the sea. He is specifically considered to be a God of fair commerce and trade. Njorðr is sometimes linked with the Goddess Nerthus as brother-lover, and Their names correspond etymologically. Njorðr was often called upon to aid both sailors and fisherman for protection, as well as for luck and prosperity. Though very little is actually known about Njorðr from surviving sources, given the importance of seafaring to the Germanic culture—particularly the Vikings—His influence should not be quickly dismissed.

The most well-known story involving Njorðr is that of His marriage to the Jotun warrior Skaði. Once, Loki was captured by Thjazi, Skaði's father. Thjazi would only agree to free Loki if Loki would promise to bring him the Goddess Idunna, with Her apples of immortality and youth, in return. Having no choice, for Thjazi had Loki well and truly trapped, Loki agreed. He was freed and returned to Asgard where, at first opportunity, He lured Idunna out by tricking Her into thinking He had found an apple tree with apples just like Hers. Her curiosity was Her undoing. Once She was in Thjazi's clutches, Loki turned the tables and, upon facing the Gods' collective wrath, promised to secure Her return. He did so, but Thjazi was killed in the process. As a consequence, Skaði armed Herself and stormed Asgard demanding retribution and wergild (man-price, the legal debt paid to the kin of one slain in lieu of further blood being spilled). The Gods agreed but had to meet Skaði's conditions. She wasn't, after all, going to make it easy for Them. Odin tossed Her father's eyes into the sky where they would gleam for all eternity as stars. Additionally, She was to be allowed to choose a husband from the assembled Gods, and finally, She had to be made to laugh. As She had just lost Her father, this might have proven a difficult task had Loki not saved the day. He cavorted about and finally tied his testicles to the beard of a goat. The goat took off in fright, causing Loki to tumble in an ungainly fashion into Skaði's lap. The sight was so bizarre that She laughed out loud. Next, all the Gods assembled, and Skaði was allowed to choose Her mate. There was a catch, though: She had to choose Them by Their feet only. Skaði had Her eye set on Baldr and chose what She considered to be the most beautiful feet there, thinking that surely, as the most beautiful of Gods, Baldr would have beautiful feet. Instead of Baldr, however, She chose Njorðr, whose feet were beautiful from having been washed repeatedly in the ocean waves, for He often walked along the beaches of His seaside dwelling. Again playing the peacemaker, Njorðr married Skaði, and She became a shining Bride of the Gods. The marriage, however, was not a success. The couple tried to compromise on Their living situation, spending nine days in Noatun and nine days in Skaði's home, Thrymheim, but She could not stand the relentless squawking of the gulls, and He could not tolerate the howling of the wolves and wind. Eventually, They parted amicably.

Perhaps Njorðr could also be hailed as a God of negotiations and diplomacy. I have known many Heathens who chose to call upon Him for aid in navigating the corporate world, precisely to gain the benefit of His calm counsel and ability to find a workable compromise to any situation.

Frey (Fro Ing/Ingvi Freyr/Freá)

I hail Frey, God of the earth,
Bringer of bounty to all barren places.
I hail Your sweetness of heart, Your passion, Your strength.
I hail Your life-giving hands and Your gentleness.
God of rain, gentle breezes, and fertile fields,
I ask Your blessing on my heart, mind, and spirit.
I ask that You bring peace and abundance to my life,
and with my creativity, I will honor You.
Hail, Frey.

Frey is one of the most beloved of Heathen Gods today. His name means "lord" in Old Norse, and He is indeed Lord of fertility, sexual union, abundance, prosperity, ancestral might, and harvest. He brings blessings and fertility to crops, livestock, creative endeavors, and individuals wishing children, and luck to the community at large. Frey is a God of Kingship, and as such, His blessings make the land fruitful and prosperous. Conversely, He also plays a role in war, and the boar is His symbol, both as an emblem of fertility and also as a symbol of strength in battle. Frey owned a golden boar named Gullinbursti ("Golden Bristled"), and in sacred rituals, holy oaths were often sworn by placing one's hand on the sacrificial pig. Furthermore, a certain type of berserker drew the inspiration for battle frenzy not from the bear or wolf, as was most common, but from the boar. The image of the boar often appeared on helmets and weaponry, to imbue the strength of the sacred animal on the warrior. Frey is the only God who fights without a weapon at Ragnarok, having sacrificed His sword to win His bride Gerða.

Because He is said to have fathered a line of kings, Frey is a tribal God, and the royal line of Sweden traces its ancestry back to Him. There is some evidence that Frey's priests cross-dressed, and there are references to bells being worn by the priests and dances being performed in His honor, though this may simply be a reference to the Vanic taboo of wearing belts or knots during rites, which would result in robes flowing loosely. Some modern Heathens even believe that Morris dancing evolved from rites performed in honor of Frey. His heiti are numerous: Árguð ("Harvest God"), Bjartr ("Bright"), Bödfróðr ("Battle Wise"), Díar ("Priest"), Fégjafa ("Wealth-giver"), Máttug ("Mighty"), Nýtum ("Providing"), and Fólkvaldi goða ("Ruler of the People"), to name but a few.

Frey is also a God of sensual pleasure. The most well-known story of Frey is that of His courtship with the Jotun maiden Gerða. In Asgard, Odin had a high seat named Valaskjalf from which He could see everything that passed far and wide in any of the worlds. No one was permitted to sit in Valaskjalf but the Allfather. One day while Odin was wandering the earth on one of His many journeys, Frey snuck into Gladsheim and sat in Odin's chair. Looking out across all the worlds His attention was drawn to Jotunheim, where He saw a lovely maiden for the briefest of moments. Those few moments were enough however to kindle in Him an intense love and desire. He pined for days, unable to eat or sleep, until His stepmother Skaði sent Frey's faithful friend and servant Skirnir to find out what was wrong.

Skirnir finally coerced the source of the sickness and anguish out of his master and, at Frey's pleading, agreed to journey to Jotunheim to woo Gerða for Him (as was the custom of the Germanic tribes). In return, He asked for Frey's sword, which will fight by itself, and also His horse. Frey surrendered both horse and sword willingly, and Skirnir set off. He was granted access to Gerða's hall, but the Jotun woman was not overly keen to accept Frey's proposal and repeatedly refused. Skirnir grew frustrated and resorted to questionable methods to win her acquiescence, first threatening violence, which Gerða proudly dismissed. Eventually, Skirnir cursed her with three powerful runes, using thurisaz, the most destructive and dangerous rune in the entire futhark. The runes would have compelled an unquenchable lust, and Ann Groa Sheffield, in *Frey: God of the World*, speculates that "the magic of the runes and potions represents Frey's power to awaken sexual desire."[24] Regardless, Gerða agreed to meet Frey in a sacred grove nine nights hence and thereby accepted His suit.

It is telling that in the Lokasenna, Frey is referred to as one who has never made any girl or man's wife cry; in other words, He has never mistreated a woman. He is a God of vitality and life force so abundant that it cannot possibly be contained. Much of His iconography pictures Him with a large, erect phallus for just this reason. He brings life in all its manifold forms, and He blesses loving unions in all their many forms as well. He is a God not only of sensual pleasure, but of joy and happiness, bestowing those gifts freely upon His folk.

Loki

> I will hail the Husband of Sigyn,
> Father of Hela, Mother of Sleipnir.
> I will greet Him with warmest welcome
> to my Hall, this friend who has brought me success.
> He has nourished me, succored me,
> and brought me great comfort
> in the deepest darkness, where no other could reach.
> Shapeshifter, Skytreader, flame-haired Charmer,
> My greatest blessings have come from Your hands.
> Son of Laufey, Byleist's brother,
> to me You have always shown Yourself true.
> I praise You for all the many victories, great
>   and small, You have given me.
> I offer praises to Loki, who has been my defender.
> I offer praises to the One who is a friend to my House.

Loki is the most controversial Being in the entire Northern pantheon. To some, He is a trickster deity, capable of bringing change, evolution, and immense and surprising growth in the most unexpected of ways. To others, He is the enemy of the Aesir, the one who will lead the forces of chaos against the Gods at Ragnarok. Many Heathens refuse to honor Him at all; to others He is a beloved Friend. A growing number of Heathens are incorporating the worship of the Rokkr—Jötnar honored as Gods of primal force, shadow work, and change. *Rokkr* is from a Norse word meaning "darkness" or "twilight" and encompasses such Deities as Loki, Hela, Angurboða, and Fenris. Loki is one of the most notorious members of this divine tribe.

To begin with, Loki is blood brother of Odin. We are told in the Lokasenna that, in ages past, the two blended their blood together. This single act has puzzled scholars and caused endless consternation among modern Heathens, for this vow was an especially solemn one—a binding of souls, fate, and destiny. It was not an oath to be entered into lightly and was very nearly unbreakable. It is therefore unthinkable that Odin, a God who ordered the universe, a God charged with maintaining its integrity and balance, would bind himself to a trickster, a rule-breaker, a sly and cunning thief and finagler. Yet that is exactly what the surviving lore tells us He did. By doing so, Loki was welcomed into the company of the Gods.

Now, Loki certainly isn't a God who plays by the rules. He's not a God easily pigeonholed and He's not a God who will play within a votary's comfort zone. He strips all that away, demanding the right to act outside of any and all boundaries, like quicksilver flowing into every spiritual crevasse, every dark place where His touch is least expected. He is not a "safe" or comfortable figure and has a disconcerting tendency to alter all rules and mores to fit His own desires. Though the term is controversial when referring to Norse Deities, I would consider Loki a trickster in the same vein as Coyote or Anansi. The word *fool* is often applied to trickster figures such as Loki, though it does not carry quite the same connotation as one might think. In the medieval period, the fool was often the only member of the court who could speak painful truths to the king without facing possible execution. As such, the fool, as an archetype, is a figure unhindered by societal constraints. However, one must explore exactly what the ultimate goal of any trickster's action is.

While it is true that Loki (indeed any God that chooses for Himself the role of trickster—and it is interesting but tricksters are almost invariably male) can create a state of extreme discomfort and annoyance, I would posit that if He shows up, there is always a reason for His presence. What may on the surface appear to be totally uncontrolled chaos can then be regarded as coldly calculated strategy, with the trickster as the vehicle of truth.

Loki is the enemy of entropy, of complaisance, and He fights it with a vengeance. He is the enemy of a heart without passion, devoid of devotion. He can be wrenchingly cruel to His children, but in hindsight, it is never *cruelty*, but rather the firmness of a parent to an erring child. And therein lies the secret to His motivation: He forces us to accept the full weight of our wyrd, to open to the myriad ways in which the Gods may inspire us, and to actively claim our own potential and the responsibility that comes with it. He can be a bastard, it's true (and I say this, loving Him dearly), but He's a bastard with a purpose.

Loki forces those who work with Him to expand the boundaries of their understanding. He brings evolution and a dynamic synergy and creative power. He acts as a catalyst and facilitator of personal growth. And with that growth may come the inevitable growing pains. The trickster is not an easy one to face or to accept, and not only because boundaries are irrelevant to Him. He forces us to examine in minute detail our own shadows, egos, and facades. He is the most powerfully kinetic instrument of truth, revealing what is meaningless and unhealthy in a way that is utterly pure, odd though it may be to associate purity with Loki. The inherent difficulty in this is the element of sacrifice integral to His nature. Interestingly enough, for all that the Trickster may challenge us in facing our own masks, that very role of "trickster" is but a mask that He himself dons. What lies beneath that varies: intense grief and pain, compassion, ecstasy, and a thousand other unexpected things.

Loki is a liminal figure, always existing betwixt and between, neither fully part of the world of the Jötnar nor fully part of the world of the Gods. Belonging to neither, He is able to move between both and possesses the synergetic power of active manifestation. Because he is a being of chaos yet bound to order via his oath to Odin, he is able to manifest this quixotic and change-inducing power directly in the ordered realm of the Gods. He opens careful doorways, and through them, that power is brought under tentative control. This liminality is perhaps the most ambivalent aspect of Loki's nature, though, if we look closely enough at the surviving lore, we see that Odin possesses it too. Odin, however, always returns to the secure realm of inangarð, to the hallowed ground of the Gods. Loki is never part of that, though He may dwell there for a while. He is always an outsider, always on the fringe of the divine community.

Loki, ever existing in that liminal place where the numinous is made tangible, unites the mundane world of temporal order with the endless, fearless potential of the chaotic realms of power. He is a necessary figure, and the Gods knew this. Thor—the great defender of mankind, Who is constantly at war with the forces of chaos, Who girds the world against their intrusion—has a traveling companion on many of his quests. That companion is Loki. With his tricks and deceptions, Loki does precisely what Odin does: He brings power to the Aesir. But He doesn't do this directly. He creates discord, causes trouble, and then journeys forth (sometimes under threat) to find a solution to the trouble he has caused, and that solution almost inevitably results in greater power for the Gods. In fact, Thor received His mighty hammer Mjolnir, the symbol of his protective power, directly as a result of one of Loki's escapades.

Once upon a time, Loki, for reasons unknown, snuck into the sleeping chamber of Thor's wife, Sif, and cut off Her long, golden hair. In Norse society, a shorn head on a woman was the sign of an adulteress, so this was a grave insult. Thor was very, very angry and set off to avenge His wife. When He caught up with Loki, Loki swore that He would make everything as good as new. Thor, a bit dubious, let Him go but impressed upon Him the dire consequences if He failed to make good on His promise. So Loki journeyed to the best goldsmiths He knew of, the dwarves. He haggled, bartered, and finally induced them to make Sif a set of golden hair that would attach and grow like real hair, only a thousand times more beautiful. Given the gravity of His offense, Loki thought it best to return to Asgard with more than just new hair for Sif, so he goaded two different dwarven clans into crafting treasures for the Gods by insinuating that one could not best the other in skill. He then bet His head to the original dwarf, Brokk, that Brokk would lose the contest of skill. Loki returned to Asgard with Sif's new hair, which all the Gods agreed was even more beautiful than the original. He also brought back numerous other treasures, including Odin's spear and Thor's hammer, the latter of which, crafted by Brokk, won the bet. Just as Brokk was about to claim his reward (Loki's head), the quick-thinking trickster cried out that Brokk only had the right to His head, not any part of His neck. Of course it was impossible then to claim his reward, and the dwarf had to content himself with sewing Loki's lips together with thick sinew.

Much has been made of Loki's binding. After facilitating the death of Baldur by tricking the blind god Hoðr into throwing the fatal dart, Loki is captured and bound in a cave with the entrails of His own son. Many modern Heathens like to believe that Loki lies bound for all time, until the time of Ragnarok, when the destiny of the Gods is at hand and the forces of order and chaos explode in battle once again. But though Odin bound him, He may also have given his blood brother one final gift. Odin controls the power of speech, represented in the rune ansuz—unfettering power. Ansuz is a very unique rune. It is the attention and breath of Odin, and it washes away all that binds the spirit and the consciousness. It frees one to blend and unite with the Gods. Its Anglo-Saxon name translates as "mouth" or "God," and this is a very important clue to its true nature. To speak or to name something is to call it into being.

This is one of the reasons why I believe the dwarves bound Loki's lips: to bind what He spoke, his power of manifestation. It's also worth noting that many of Loki's more memorable escapades involve His facility for scathing speech, which He was known to use, as in the Lokasenna, to challenge everyone and everything.

Loki may lie bound on a slab in a dank, bleak cave, but nowhere is it ever recorded that his lips were sealed or his mouth gagged in this state (the lip-binding sinews of Brokk having been only temporary). He may be bound, but his voice, His power of manifestation, is not, and therefore *He* is not.

In any discussion of Loki, the problem of Ragnarok comes up. This translates as fate or destiny of the Gods and it is wise to remember that, in Norse thought, one had the power to alter one's fate. At the time of Ragnarok, Loki is said to stand against the Gods. There is a certain cyclical order in this: chaos fighting order, as in the beginning. Many modern Heathens question whether or not Loki is even a God. He is of giant stock they say, an outlander, an intruder into the dynamic balance created by the Reginn, the powers of order. He is chaos. He is the "enemy." But a little chaos is necessary for growth and evolution. Evolution is the heartchild of carefully chosen chaotic disruption, and it is worth remembering that, in the beginning of the world, Odin gave soul and spirit to mankind. In sharing His blood with Loki, perhaps he shared something more: Godhood. Order may bring stability, but it takes a touch of chaos to bring forth change, growth, and even life. The presumed binding of Loki, the binding of all potential and opportunity, is inevitably followed by the destruction of Ragnarok. Life cannot exist without a little chaos.

Loki is a very interesting Deity, regardless of whether or not one wishes to worship Him. He is a shape-changer and the only Norse God to repeatedly shift not only shape but gender as well. Not only does He change into an old woman to prevent Baldr's return from Hela's realm, but He also changes into a mare and birth's Odin's steed, Sleipnir.

When Asgard was very young and the war between the Aesir and Vanir not long past, a man arrived with his horse, Svaðilfari. He presented himself as a builder and offered to build a wall so mighty around Asgard that hostile Jötnar would never be able to breach it. As payment, he wanted the sun and moon and for Freya to be his bride. Loki urged the Gods to accept but to set a condition of their own to ensure that the giant wouldn't win the loot that he wanted. The Gods agreed and stipulated that the wall must be finished by the first day of summer, thinking that surely even for the strongest of builders, this was an impossible task.

The builder accepted the deal and set to work, and as the weeks passed, the Gods grew more and more worried. The wall was rising with astonishing speed, and the first day of summer wasn't far off at all. If something wasn't done, the Gods were going to lose their wager. Because it had been Loki's suggestion to accept the builder's offer in the first place, the Gods rounded on Him and demanded that He fix the situation because, after all, the Gods weren't about to part with the sun, the moon, and, most importantly of all, Freya.

Loki observed the builder for a while and realized that he depended on Svaðilfari to haul the large blocks of stone; it was the horse's exceptional strength and speed that were enabling the builder to complete the job so quickly. The next morning, a delicate, long-legged mare appeared not far from where the horse and his master were working. She flirted with Svaðilfari, teased him, and finally led him on a merry chase, and the two of them disappeared for three days. The builder was unable to complete the project on time and, thus, forfeited his reward. He grew so angry upon realizing this that he showed his true face—that of an angry Jotun—and he began to destroy the wall, threatening the Gods as he did so. Thor took care of the situation with his hammer, slaying the giant.

Loki was absent from the ranks of the Gods for many months, appearing some time later with an eight-legged foal. This was Sleipnir ("Sliding One"), and he is named by Odin in the Grimnismal as the "best of horses." Odin claimed him for His own, and no word was spoken of who Sleipnir's mother was, for it was, in fact, Loki who had taken the shape of the mare to lure Svaðilfari away.

Loki has six children, actually. He is mother to Sleipnir, father to Hela, Fenris, and the world-serpent Jormungand (with the giantess Angurboða), and father to Narvi and Vali, sons by His wife Sigyn. Loki's own parentage is also known: His father is a Jotun named Fárbauti ("Cruel Striker"), often thought to be the personification of lightning, and His mother is Laufey, also called Nál ("Needle," perhaps indicative of pine needles or tinder). He apparently has two brothers of which nothing more is known: Byleistr and Helblindi (which looks suspiciously like a heiti for Odin). There is much debate over the meaning of Loki's name. Some scholars speculate that it is related to words for *fire* or even *spider*, but nothing definitive has been agreed upon. Loki is seen as a God of fire, despite the fact that many of His transformations were into water creatures, such as the seal and the salmon. He has several heiti: Lopt ("the Airy One" or "the Lightning One"),[25] Sky-Traveller, Laufey's son, and Husband of Sigyn, to name but a few. Despite modern Heathen misgivings about Him, in the Prose Edda (33) He is "numbered among the Aesir."

Mimir (Meomer)

> *Wisest of Jötnar, Keeper of the well of memory,*
> *I hail You.*
> *All things hidden, all things secret, lie within Your domain.*
> *For Your wisdom, knowledge, and inspiration,*
> *I praise You.*
> *Friend of Odin, trusted Counselor,*
> *I raise this horn in Your honor.*

Mimir means "One who remembers," and He is very likely the uncle of Odin. It was Mimir and His sacred well at the spring Hvergelmir, in Jotunheim, to which Odin journeyed after His ordeal on the Tree. He asked for a draught from the well, because any who tasted of its waters would know all things. Mimir agreed, but only for a price: Odin had to pluck out His eye in exchange for His enlightenment. A single drink from Mimirsbrunnr is a gift beyond price. As noted, Odin was not the only God to drink from Mimir's Well. Heimdall also made the journey and attendant sacrifice (in His case, an ear) in exchange for exceptional hearing. One might speculate that the well contains the potential for every possible gift and wisdom, and only the willing sacrifice evokes its power, unique and individual to each God's desire. Another name for Yggdrasil is Mimameiðr: Tree of Mimir. Mimir is a God of cosmic memory,[26] wisdom, and deeply hidden power.

Andvari

Prayer to Andvari

Andvari, Lord of deep places,
grant me knowledge.
Teach me to distinguish between what I truly own and what was
*   put in my hands to flow elsewhere. Root me in that knowledge,*
and let that knowledge take root in me.

Andvari, Lord of deep consequences, grant me the gift of wisdom.
Teach me to choose my food wisely, for the earth is not
*   mine to plunder. Teach me to use energy sparingly,*
for the climate is not mine to change. Root me in that wisdom
and let that wisdom take root in me.

Andvari, Lord of deep understanding,
grant me the gift of honesty.
Teach me to own my faults and their consequences.
*   Teach me to hold my baggage if I cannot rid*
*   myself of it. Root me in that honesty,*
and let that honesty take root in me.

Andvari, Lord of deep emotions, grant me the gift of
reverence. Teach me to respect all resources, whether they
be mine or not. Teach me to respect all money, whether
I may own it or not. Root me in that reverence
and let that reverence take root in me.

Andvari, Lord of deep insight,
grant me the gift of self-esteem.
Teach me that what I am is unassailable by what others
think. Teach me that what I am is unassailable
even by my own judgment.
Root me in self-esteem
and let self-esteem take root in me.
(by Fuensanta Plaza)

Little is known of Andvari in ancient Norse texts. He is one of the Duergar, and His name means "the careful one." The Reginsmal tells how He, in the guise of a fish, was caught by Loki and had His hoard taken from Him. Andvari made no great resistance to this theft until Loki also took a gold ring, which Andvari warned was cursed; and cursed it was, bringing about the downfall of those who laid claim to it.

He has gained cultus in the modern Northern Tradition, most notably through the work of Fuensanta Plaza, a woman honored as a saint in several traditions. She recognized Him as a powerful Holy Being, a God of resources, resource management, and money. Another facet of Andvari is that of the Craftsman. When that facet of His nature and the facet of ownership collide, one gets a fleeting impression of a power and danger that feel oddly related to that of Wayland the Smith—and because Andvari is the connection of Earth and Fire, to Surt also. He, like other of the Duergar, may be called upon for help in craftwork, particularly smithing, and for help in learning to efficiently and honorably handle money. He is rather taciturn and doesn't suffer fools gladly, but His lessons are invaluable.

Saxnot/Seaxnéat

Sword Friend, strong as steel,
as loyal as a favored blade,
I hail You.
Your wisdom, from ages old,
flows in my very blood.
I will sing of You as my ancestors did.
Grant me wit and cunning wisdom,
strength of mind and heart and will,
Knife-keen focus, and a strong sword arm.
Ever will I hail You, Mighty God.
Ever to You, I pray.

Saxnot draws His name from the knife worn by Anglo-Saxon warriors, and it translates as "Sword Friend" or "Friend of the Saxons."[27] Very little is known about this God, but He was apparently once widely worshipped. Many modern Heathens consider Saxnot and Tyr to be the same God, others connect Him to Frey. By His very name, He is often seen as an early divine ancestor of the Saxon tribes. Saxnot, along with Thor and Woden, was specifically named and repudiated in a baptismal formula common to the ninth-century Saxons.

Mani (Mona)

I hail You, Mani,
You are intoxicating in Your beauty.
You seduce with the promise of magic and breathtaking stillness.
I hail Your power, subtle and secret,
the power of tides and blood and night-blooming flowers.
I hail You for the memory of Your shining
    light bathing my uplifted face.
I hail You for those moments when Your
    image, lighting the darkened sky,
stole away my breath.

I hail You, shining, exotic, and glorious. For
    Your mystery and Your allure,
I offer this horn.

Not much can be culled from the lore about Mani other than that this God is the personification of the moon. According to Simek, He steers the moon and determines its waxing and waning.[28] He is the dark, subtle reflection of the radiant power of Sunna (His sister and sun Goddess), which is not to say He has none of His own. Two humans travel with Him on His nightly rounds: a girl named Bil and a boy named Hjuki. These children are brother and sister and once had a very cruel father. Mani observed them being mistreated and came to steal them away. They now accompany and assist Him on His nightly journey. According to the shared personal gnosis of many in the community, there is some likelihood of this, for Mani truly likes humanity and likes to watch over those He cares for, even if only from afar. Mani is pursued by a ravenous wolf, Hati, who makes sure that He doesn't stray from His assigned course, but who, according to the surviving lore, at Ragnarok will capture the moon and devour Him, plunging the night into unbroken darkness.

Mani has a growing cultus in modern Heathenry and many of us find Him a mesmerizing and lovely God. There's some shared gnosis that Mani has a particular relationship with Unn, the sea Etin, one of Rán and Aegir's nine daughters. This is nowhere hinted at in lore, but it's come up many times in the devotional epiphanies of devotees to the point that many modern polytheists engaging in Mani's cult accept it as fact.

Though little is known about Him in lore, there are many ways to connect to this God. Simply going outside on a moonlit night and meditating on what qualities Mani's presence evokes are a good way to begin. In medieval herb lore, certain plants were sown and gathered at specific phases of the moon, so creating a garden of night-blooming flowers or sacred herbs is an excellent way for those with green thumbs to learn more about Mani. Women, of course, have a connection to His power through the rhythm of their menstrual cycles, which are ultimately governed by the cycles of the moon.

Weyland the Smith (Volund)

Hail to Thee, Weyland,
Crafter of Ways,
Swift nimble-fingers
Fanning the blaze.

Clever and cunning,
Scheming and wise,
Metal and Hammer
Brought forth a prize.

Ripe are your blessings
Full with great wealth
So we do greet you
Community's health.

Hail , Weyland!

Weyland (also known as Volund) is a legendary blacksmith, to whom we have references from both Norse (Þiðrekssaga and the Poetic Edda's Völundarkviða) and Anglo-Saxon (Beowulf, Deor, and Waldere) sources. In the archaeological record we see His story depicted on the Swedish Ardre image stone VIII, the Franks Casket, and a variety of stone crosses and monuments throughout England. Weyland has a reputation in folk stories that once He was paid, no matter how impossible the job asked for, He worked hard to make the impossible possible. His tools and weapons are worn by heroes in several stories, including Beowulf.

Blacksmiths represented the luck, fortune, and self-reliance of a community. The weapons the blacksmith made defended the home, supported daily aspects of everyday domesticity (cooking, sewing, dinnerware, utensils), and also helped make a very wide range of tools used to build and construct, as well as a plethora of items used in agricultural life, from working the fields to contending with the livestock. The foundational skills of a blacksmith overlap in many ways as well with jewelry-smithing, so sometimes things are created not solely for function, but also for form and decoration as well. Having a blacksmith in your community meant not only wealth, but that your community was not vulnerable to being preyed upon by others who may literally steal your fortune or figuratively in charging outrageous sums/barters for what you needed. For these reasons, blacksmiths granted a community both fortune and a certain degree of independence as well.[29]

These two chapters hardly provide an exhaustive list of Germanic Deities. There are many lesser-known Gods and Goddesses who are not included here, including Alateivia, Arvolecia, Haeva, Tamfana, the healing Goddess Sulis, Viridecdis, and Odin's sons, Váli (and His mother Rindr) and Vidar, who take vengeance on His behalf. There is the Jotun Goddess of Healing Mengloth, a colleague of Eir, and several lesser known Deities of healing: Thjodvara, Hlíf, Hlifthrasa, Bjort, Frith, Blith, Bleik, Aurboða, each with Their own specializations. There is Kari, our God of the North Wind; Surt, the Lord of Muspelheim; and Sinmara, Lady of Muspelheim; Logi, God of fire; Thor's children Thruð, Magni, and Modi; and Loki's children Narvi and Vali to name but a few. This is the beauty of polytheism, and though little is known about how They were all worshipped in elder times and in some cases we only know Their names, the door is open for modern Heathens to rediscover the power and nature of these mighty Gods and Goddesses.

CHAPTER 5

WYRD

One of the most important and complex facets of Heathen theology is the concept of *wyrd*. Awareness of wyrd and its power underlies the structure of both religious and social interactions within the Heathen community. In many ways, wyrd may be likened to fate, but is far more interactive. It encompasses the sum total of an individual's actions and choices, as well as whatever destiny may have been predetermined by the Nornir for that individual. It is the esoteric unification of all that was and all that will be, manifesting in temporal life. Wyrd is both causality and consequence, and it constantly changes and shifts. It is a web of choices: one's own choices, the choices of others, the choices of one's community, and even the choices of one's own ancestors impacting his or her current evolution and awareness.

Wyrd orders the multiverse. Even the Gods must bow to the power of Their own wyrd. In Heathen theology, the Gods are not omnipotent; They are bound, just like mankind, by the power and pattern of wyrd. Its pattern and flow is the one constant immutable law governing every aspect of existence. Humanity's relationship with wyrd is reciprocal; our lives are governed by its law, yet that law is laid in accordance with the choices and actions of our lives. We create and must abide by our own fate. The action of wyrd is analogous to a pool of water: cast a stone, ripples form. If five people each cast a stone at the exact same time, those ripples overlap. The fish swimming below create eddies that may also affect the surface of the pool. Even the wind may affect the water. The more immediate someone's involvement with the individual, the more of an effect it has on that individual's wyrd. The pool of water represents the world, and the concentric rings indicate the degree of influence of every person one meets. One's individual strand of wyrd, the part that each person has the power to affect for good or ill, is called *orlog*.

The Völuspá[1] states that the Nornir craft and decree the laws of mankind. They "set or mark fate"[2] and speak orlog. All that was, is, or shall ever be is contained within the depths of Urda's Well, which rests among the roots of the World Tree. Because our own fate is laid down in this place, it is the nexus of our connection to our ancestral path, the connection of our deeds and choices to those that came before and will come after. It is our primal memory, and memory is a very precious thing. Odin has two ravens as companions, one named Muninn, the other Huginn. He sends them out daily to observe and bring back information. Odin cherishes Muninn ("memory"), fearing its loss even over Huginn ("thought").[3] A healthy community is founded on the organic evolution of tradition that flows from that wellspring of memory. This is one of the reasons that modern Heathens are so insistent about basing the reconstruction of their religious practices and social structure on the surviving remnants of the pre-Christian world. Memory defines who and what we are, and to *remember* is to recall ourselves to ourselves. This recollection is echoed in the daily setting of law by the Nornir, and that daily repetition recalls to life our own deeds, our spiritual evolution, the growth (or not) of our character, and the enduring wisdom of our dead. Memory nourishes humankind and restores to us an awareness not only of the foundations of the world but of the proper order of things. All of that awareness and knowledge is contained in the Well.

It has the power to connect us not just to the memory of our blood kin, but to the memory of the very earth upon which we live, the memory of the Tree itself, the memory of the incarnations of our own souls, and even to the fabric of which the universe was made. Here is our essential mystery, our starting point: the Well and the Tree that is nourished by it.

The Well and the Tree form a point of intersection, the place where all choice and consequence meet. There is a reason that the Allfather had to hang on the World Tree to gain access to the runic mysteries: only beneath its boughs, in the Well of being itself, could He find the keys to wyrd and its unfolding. Actions have consequences, choices have costs. As memory and order are contained within the sphere of Urda, so the price of knowledge and decision is contained within the realm of Skuld, the Norn of the future, of that which becomes. An analysis of the name *Skuld* reveals that it denotes necessary action—even constraint and obligation. Therefore, it could be said that memory and action carry with them obligations. The individual threads of orlog, so diligently laid down beneath the Tree, are the very molecules from which our lives are formed. We even inherit part of our wyrd and its attendant obligations from our ancestors. Evolution is the sphere of Verdandi. All three names of the Nornir suggest time to be a repetitive and circular process.[4] Time flows in on itself and from itself, bound by the fabric of memory. Only our perceptions make it linear.[5] The Nornir are outside of time, not bound by the constraints of that evolution.

Urda is that which is ordered and manifest. She sets the boundaries in which our fate will form and play out. Verdandi orders our actions, weaving them into the warp and weft of those boundaries, even as we make them. Skuld binds us to the consequences of our choices, for good or ill. We choose what we give to Her, but once given, we are bound by our choice. Everything, however, begins with Urda. In Her is contained the sum total of all experience; She stands before being or presence (personified by Verdandi) just as She stands after it. It is this common origin and terminus that, more than anything else, stands in stark opposition to the extreme individualism that is so encouraged within modern Heathenry. Yes, we are responsible for our own actions, but at the same time, we are connected, through Urda's Well, to each other. At some point, all we are and do returns to the Well, where lies our ancestral memory, which forms our Hamingja, our ancestral luck.[6] In other words, part of each of our souls rests in the Well beneath the Tree.[7]

The nature of the Well hearkens back to Ginnungagap. It is apt that the substance of Being be conceived of as water. Water is changeable. It seeps into every crevice, however small. It transforms and transmutes itself from ice to liquid to steam, yet always retains its essential structure. It is necessary to life and constitutes 80 percent of our bodies. The Gylfaginning affirms the water of Urda's Well to have purifying power. Our lore tells us that the water heals the Tree. The Tree is reality itself, the direct manifestation of all that is contained within the Well. "The process of occurrence of events and the continual accumulation of more and more of them into the pattern of the past present a system of growth that is never finished."[8] This cyclical nature of the interaction of the Well and the Tree reflects the pattern that plays out in our spiritual journey as well, defining the "interrelations of all actions."[9] As the water of the Well provides nourishment and healing to the Tree—literally to the structure and support of our world—memory provides nourishment to our spirits. We are defined by what we remember, and it is the constantly shifting, interrelating layers of memory that nourish our spirits. Urda will "lead one to wisdom."[10]

We work with our wyrd by meeting it honorably and bravely. We are literally defined by the choices we make. Wyrd is the scaffolding in which we move—we inherit part of it from our ancestors, based on their actions and choices, and we will pass it on to those who come after—but we have freedom in how we meet its challenges. This provides powerful impetus to develop virtue, character, and integrity and to hone our will. We can improve our wyrd as we improve ourselves, leaving a legacy for our descendants of betterment, strength, and hope. As inescapable as wyrd might be, that we have the potential to interact with it, alter it, and transform it and ourselves is a grace and a blessing.

CHAPTER 6

THE SOUL MATRIX

Heathenry conceives the soul not as a single, undivided entity but as a composite, a microcosm of the multiverse in which we live. The soul is a matrix of interrelated and interdependent sections, each with its own realm of influence, its own power, and its own impact on one's life. To be hale and whole, the entire matrix must be kept strong and in balance. The strength and vitality of each part may be impacted by the honor of one's actions (or lack thereof), the mindfulness with which one attends to holy duties, one's devotional life, one's ancestors, and one's wyrd as well as how one meets its challenges. It is the field on which the patterns of wyrd take potent life.

Typically, the soul may be seen as having between nine and seventeen parts (some denominations combine several of the soul sections listed on the following pages). It makes sense for the soul to be comprised of multiple facets; as humankind was created by the gifts of three Gods—Odin, Hoenir, and Loður—so the structure of our souls reflects Their triune power. While it is necessary to dissect the soul matrix to gain a thorough understanding of how each part functions, it is even more important to recognize that the true power lies in the ever-evolving balance of the working whole.

The Lík/Lich:[1] The Physical Body

Perhaps surprisingly, the physical body is considered the most basic part of the soul. It is the vehicle of our incarnation, through which our wyrd plays out. It is the vehicle through which we are able to enact our will, the will of the Gods, and our highest destiny, as well as to resolve our wyrd debts. It is also the means by which we experience the world directly and by which we leave our mark. Corporeality is important, even sacred. Honoring the body is vital to maintaining a healthy soul. Maintaining mindfulness over eating; exercising and keeping fit; and pursuing martial arts, sports, dance, and yoga all help us strengthen the Lík. Additionally, when working with this soul part, it is important to carefully examine the attitudes toward our bodies, physical strength, and even sexuality and gender roles that we may have picked up from the dominant culture.

As we restore our traditions and live as polytheists, we are called to work out any issues from our birth religions and to be mindful of the impact of modernity's attitudes and values on our psyches. We must struggle to reclaim the integrated worldview of our ancestors. We can start by reorienting our attitudes toward our own corporeality. When we recognize that our bodies, our flesh, our very physicality is part of divine order, carefully crafted by our Gods—whatever the challenges that corporeality might bring—it allows us to focus on the sacred in the everyday, opening windows for our Gods and ancestors to impact us through even the most mundane of tasks. Because our corporeal forms are part of the soul, they become conduits for the experience of the sacred. Our sensorium—sight, sound, smell, taste, and touch—becomes means of engaging with the holy. Our bodies aren't something to punish or ignore, but vehicles through which we can, if we are mindful and diligent, engage with the Gods. There is no dichotomy between spiritual and physical, as might be found in other Western religions. Rather, one flows seamlessly into the other, and the holy is found as easily in one's daily work and romantic life as in the most moving of religious rites. Because the physical body is part of the soul, if one's attitudes toward the body aren't healthy, then the soul itself cannot be healthy. Looking at the soul's structure, it is clear that the body, mind, and emotions are interconnected. Working to heal and strengthen any one part will have positive effects on the whole.

Önd/Aeðem: The Divine Breath

Önd, or Aeðem, is what animates the soul. It is our connection to the Gods—the breath of Odin, breathed into us at the moment of the soul's creation. It is what gives us life and consciousness and the ability to grow and evolve. It is our connection to the Gods, our elder Kin. Each breath we take calls to mind that sacred connection. The Önd is the part of the soul that is in constant connection with the Gods and the cosmic unfolding of our spiritual evolution. It connects us to the "bigger picture" if you will. It is the animating principle, and a powerful meditation both for this soul part and for Odin is to consciously think of each intake of breath as being given from Him and each exhalation of breath as something we give back to Him. We exist within the span of a God's breath, and that is a powerful thing.

Hamingja: Luck

The Hamingja is one's personal luck. It may be nourished or diminished by our actions and choices. It is a living, ever-changing thing that we are constantly creating. Our Hamingja determines the quality of our lives, the effort we will have to expend to reach our goals, and our chances of success. A certain degree of luck is inherited from our ancestors and the result of their choices, actions, victories, and struggles. It flows from the mother to the child and, like our very DNA, connects us to those who have gone before and those that will follow us. We are charged with living rightly so that our own Hamingja will leave no debt for our children to work out. There are many ways of strengthening and increasing one's personal luck. The strength or weakness of our Hamingja can affect us in many intangible ways—not only with lack of personal success, but also with physical illness, depression, and emotional crisis. Living honorably, keeping one's sworn word, paying mindful attention to one's personal obligations, giving back to one's community, honoring one's ancestors, and striving to better oneself are all good places to begin. It goes hand in hand with one's Maegen, or vital force. Hamingja tends to be particularly strongly passed on through the women in one's line, and women can take a powerful role in tending this soul part, for themselves and their entire households.

Maegen: Vital Force

Maegen is the vital force that flows through every living thing. It is intimately connected with one's luck and, like the Hamingja, may be directly impacted by the way in which we live our lives. Dishonorable choices, the breaking of one's word, doing harm to kin and community, or living in a way that brings harm to oneself all indirectly weaken one's vital force. Whereas luck is affected directly by our actions, those same actions cannot affect the vital energy itself. What those actions affect is our ability to be a strong container for that force and to tap into that vital power. Maegen is comparable to what Chinese tradition calls qi or chi, and it allows us to act in the world. It gives us the power to alter our wyrd and strengthen or weaken our luck and power. It may be seen as fertility of the spirit, increased or diminished by the quality of our deeds. Maegen is like a reservoir of power that keeps us hale and whole. Strengthening the will, the Hamingja, and the Lík all contribute to maintaining a strong Maegen. Maegen is our ability to access our luck and all the blessings the Gods have given. Developing discernment and being able to recognize the Gods' blessings in our lives both flow from and contribute to our Maegen.

Vili/The Willa: The Will

By will we assert our desires. It is a direct expression of our personal power, inspiring our talents, creative drive, intellect, and passion, the means by which we reach our goals and impact the world around us. Like the other parts of the soul matrix, the will must be balanced between desire and intelligence, duty and wyrd, the good of the individual and the good of the tribe/community. Our challenge is to align our personal will with that of the Gods. We want to be working in alignment with divine order, not against it. Given the depredations of modernity, the poor examples for spiritual living that we've been given, the way devotion and piety are often pathologized in our culture, this can be quite a challenge. It often involves a drastic reordering of priorities to learn to live in ways more conducive to devotion and that develop character and virtue. Like everything else, this is a choice, one we're called to make every single day, choosing to believe in our Gods, to venerate Them and our ancestors, and to live in a way that celebrates that devotion.

Hugr/Hyge: The Intellect

The Hugr is our intellect, our capacity for rational thought. This part of the soul matrix gives us our ability to make sense of our experiences. It enables us to learn, grow, and process our interactions with each other and with the world at large. This capacity for rational decision-making enables us to live rightly and choose to impact our communities in a positive way. Our consciousness is, just like the animating breath, a gift from the Gods, in this case Hoenir. Our capacity for thought allows us to decide cleanly to turn our lives to our Gods, to make choices about how we will live in the world and what kind of person we shall become, what kind of world to create. There is tremendous beauty and profundity in the way we were designed, in the power of our minds to reach out to the Gods and experience in some infinitesimal way all that They are. We connect with the mysteries of creation every time we make a decision that aligns us with our Gods and against entropy, despair, and the empty promises of modernity, monotheism, and Marxism. In some respect, we are called to be cocreators with our Gods—not that we have a hand in creating the worlds, but we can again and again align ourselves with the primordial acts of creation by aligning our minds and hearts and wills with our Gods. We participate by consciously choosing to order our values as polytheists, no small thing.

Mynd/Minni: Memory

It might seem strange to find memory included in the soul matrix, but this aspect of the soul was so precious to the Germanic tribes (a primarily oral culture) that the God Odin worried more about the loss of memory than about the loss of His ability to think cogently. Memory connects us to our tribe, our self-definition, our ancestors, and our own evolution. It is our foundation, nourishing our growth and strength like a tree's roots. It enables us each to celebrate our uniqueness and our identity and to learn from past experiences. It may be that there is an integral connection between the function of memory and our ability to care for and love another.[2] Intellect and memory are personified by Odin's two ravens, Huginn and Muninn. Memory also allows us to connect rightly to our ancestors, to recognize our own place in the chain, and to cultivate that mindfulness in our children. To determine who we are, we need to know where we've been; and it's not just memory of who we are now, but the entire journey of our soul, its *longue durée* that our Gods nurture and cherish.

Oðr/Wod: Passion, Ecstasy, and Inspiration

Just as intellect is part of the soul, so is our ability to feel passion. This isn't necessarily sexual passion, but a drive and determination that shows in devotion, inspiration, and excellence. It is our ability to give ourselves fully to an endeavor without hesitation or compromise. The Wod is responsible not only for the creative inspiration of the poet and artist but also for the raging destructive power of the berserker. Inspiration was often believed to go hand in hand with madness and frenzy, which gives some indication of what occurs when this part of the soul is nourished by itself, without being properly integrated into the functioning whole. Facing one's inner demons, dealing with any unresolved issues, facing our fears, shadow work— all of these things help to encourage balanced expression of one's personal Wod.

Fylgja/Fæcce: Guardian Spirit

The Fylgja is one's guardian spirit and may often appear in animal form or as the opposite gender. The Fylgja assists in helping us to reach our full potential, aiding us in fulfilling our wyrd and governing the distribution of Maegen and the flow of Hamingja. Working directly with the Fylgja can lead to amazing insights and inspiration. Often one's Fylgja may appear or communicate through dreams but can also be directly contacted through meditation. In many respects, it's analogous to the personal agathos daimôn of Greek polytheism, the animus/anima of Roman polytheism, the Ori in Lukumi, and the guardian angel of Catholicism. We have help in this life if we just ask for and recognize it. That's a beautiful thing. I find it helpful to occasionally make offerings to one's Fylgja, to recognize its help, and to do cleansings with the intention of making certain those lines of connection and communication stay clear and strong.

Orlog/Orlæg: Personal Wyrd

Wyrd, as we have already discussed, is the web of all being, constantly woven and rewoven. Orlog is one's individual strand, connecting us to that greater web, and it is this strand that we have the ability to directly affect, the field upon which our decisions take shape, affecting our Hamingja, Maegen, and the other parts of the soul matrix.

Kin-fylgja

Kin-fylgja is your connection to your ancestors, your ability to access their wisdom and protection as well as that of the Dísir (powerful female ancestors) or tribal Mothers (Matronae) of your ancestral lines.

Hamr/Hama: Etheric Soul Skin

In *Runelore* Edred Thorsson speculates that the Hamr is the power of imagination that can, at times, take active shape and form in our world.[3] It is more commonly thought of as a type of soul skin containing the various parts of the soul matrix and which we might shape and direct. Norse literature is replete with stories of sorcerers going into trances and sending forth their Hamr to work their will. Odin Himself is said to possess this ability. The Hamr gives us the ability to journey forth and act in other worlds, realms, and states of being. The Hamr is strongly connected to the Lík, and it's important to develop healthy practices (getting enough sleep, eating well, moderate exercise, dealing healthily with stress) with respect to the physical body, in order for the Hamr to be as strong as it possibly can be.

Mod: Self-Consciousness, Emotions, Heart

The Mod, cognate with our word "mood," is essentially the self in the here and now, containing all that we are—our awareness, consciousness, and temporal being. The Mod is "a reflection of the integrated self"[4] and of a properly integrated soul matrix. It's also the seat of our emotions, and is well-nourished insofar as we have full access to our emotions, understanding and acknowledging their motivations. Our Mod is the fabric and color of our emotions and our response to our world. One way to develop the Mod is to foster habits of integrity and honesty with respect to one's emotions. It's important to get therapy if there is hurt in one's past and to do whatever one can to heal any emotional traumas. As with all parts of the soul, the work we do here is ongoing and, in fact, the task of our entire lives.

Litr

Litr means "color" or "hue" and is the gift given by Loður at the moment of humanity's creation. It's our physical health, but more importantly our vitality, the raw animating principle of life.

Vé/Wih

Vé means "holiness" and, in terms of our souls, refers to the amount of spiritual power that we contain as children of our Gods. It can be cultivated by devotion, clean service to the Gods, and piety in moving through our world. It may also refer to one's psychic or spiritual abilities, the former of which may be inherited, the latter, as already noted, developed by consistent discipline.

Gyðja/Goði

Meaning "priest" in Old Norse (Gyðja is the grammatically feminine form, Goði, the masculine), it refers to that part of our soul, throughout our incarnations and lives, that is always directly connected to the Gods, ensuring that if we try, if we cultivate our characters and a strong devotional practice, we can find our way onto the paths the Gods would have us walk. This part of the soul grants a deep, spiritual, inborn knowledge and inspiration of what the Gods want for us. It tends to be uniquely connected to our Fylgja, through which we may have more direct communication.

Wyrd/Urda

Whereas orlog is our individual thread, wyrd is the tapestry, the web in which we move, the scaffolding into which we were born, our connection to the world, the Gods, our ancestors, all other lives that we may ever touch. Wyrd is the interconnectedness of everything, the causality, consequence, and inherited debt joining all things. In terms of the soul matrix, wyrd is immediately and directly that part of the web that is ours to navigate; our orlog, the path we carve by that conscious navigation.

It is obvious from the nature of the soul matrix that Germanic theology did not (and does not) contain a split between this world and the spiritual world. The two were intimately connected, equal partners. One could not truly succeed in the spiritual by neglecting the physical or in the physical by neglecting the spiritual. Living well meant living in a way that benefited not only oneself but one's community as well; it meant living with honor. One of the beautiful things about the Northern Tradition soul matrix is that we have the ability to strengthen our souls. We can focus on one particular part and consciously work to better it. We can create and recreate ourselves in ways that are fruitful and pleasing to our Gods, and that is a glorious thing.

The Germanic Concept of the Afterlife

Heathen cosmology has no concept of heaven and hell comparable to what is found in the Abrahamic religions. There were several destinations a soul might take after physical death. Just as Heathen cosmology affirms multiple worlds, so the afterlife consists of several realms. Death is not thought to be the end of existence, nor is it a static, unchanging state. The soul of the newly deceased has options.

In simplest form, it may be said that life continues after death in the realm of the ancestors, much as it does in temporal life. Ancient Heathens would erect elaborate burial mounds over the graves of their ancestors, and offerings would be left there to honor the dead. Those seeking wisdom would spend the night at the burial mound (*howe*), and often their perseverance was rewarded and their ancestors came forth to speak directly to them. The howe was considered a doorway to the realm of the ancestors, and the dead were by no means locked away from the world of the living. Female ancestors (called *Dísir*, or singular, *Dís*) were especially influential in the life of the living family, and stories abound about powerful Dísir warning their descendants of danger and sharing wisdom and advice, often in dreams.

Those who die of natural causes—sickness or old age—go to Hela's realm. This is in no way a place of torment, but rather a great ancestral hall where the dead reside. Some modern Heathens believe that particularly vile people will end up in Nastrond, a dank pit in the lowest, darkest region of Hel. With the exception of Nastrond, Hel is not an unpleasant place. Those killed in battle, by bladed weapon, or in special service to the God Odin were said to dwell in Odin's hall, Valhalla, a hall of warriors, where the chosen few continued training so that they would be ready to fight the final battle of Ragnarok. Odin was often said to meddle in the affairs of mortals to hone his chosen warriors, eventually setting in motion events that would lead to their death at the height of their strength and power. (It's important to realize that His ultimate goal is ensuring the continued survival of both humanity and the Gods.) Half of the fallen warriors go to Freya's hall, as She has first pick of the slain. Death in battle was considered preferable to death of old age or disease, and the Germanic peoples were fierce fighters because of this. The host of Odin's hall were called the *Einherjar*, and many modern Heathens conduct special fainings in their honor on Veterans Day and Memorial Day. Military service is still considered a great honor among modern Heathens, and those who serve either in the military or as police or firefighters have places of honor within the community.

Today we live in a world far different from that of our ancestors, and it is no longer likely that we will die in actual combat. Therefore, we must look at the attitude and mindset of the warrior to see what we can glean. Living honorably; holding to one's word; committing to a set of values; doing what is right, even in the face of fierce opposition; being willing to defend oneself and one's loved ones; standing up for what is right; rejecting complaisance, cowardice, and moral relativism; and constantly striving for excellence in every area of life—all of these things are ways in which we can live a warrior's life today. Doing what is right, even when it is most difficult; speaking out and speaking up when necessary; being forthright in one's dealings; and avoiding those actions, however small, that diminish us as people are all actions of a warrior and all ways that we can connect with our honored dead.

Those who died by drowning belong to the Sea Goddess Rán and are believed to be drawn down into Her realm by Her fishing net. Those who die devoted to a specific God or Goddess may go to that Deity's hall after death. A spirit may also choose to remain and watch over his or her family, lending strength, wisdom, and protection. The important point to remember is that the dead have options. Many Heathens also believe in reincarnation: that the souls of the dead are born again and again into the temporal world. Unlike some forms of reincarnation belief, Heathens do not believe that the soul may take animal or plant form. Most believe that the dead will reincarnate within their family line.

Honoring the Ancestors

You have been paid for. Each of you, Black, White, Brown, Yellow, Red—whatever pigment you use to describe yourselves—has been paid for. But for the sacrifices made by some of your ancestors, you would not be here; they have paid for you. So, when you enter a challenging situation, bring them on the stage with you; let their distant voices add timbre and strength to your words. For it is your job to pay for those who are yet to come.

—*Maya Angelou,* Rainbow in the Cloud:
The Wisdom and Spirit of Maya Angelou

Nothing is more important, more crucial, than honoring one's ancestors consistently, rightly, and well. If one does nothing else in life devotionally, this would be enough. Every pre-Christian polytheist would have engaged in ancestor veneration of some culturally and religiously defined sort as a matter of course. It wasn't something reserved for spirit workers or priests or any other specialist. It was what one did as a mature, responsible adult. Stepping into the full obligation of honoring the ancestors was one of the defining facets of adulthood. It defined and determined family, what made you a part of your family. For if you know who you are and where you come from, if you are truly rooted in your ancestral lineage and power, if you know that every time you bow your head or speak your prayers your entire ancestral line does so with you, you cannot be spiritually corrupted. Many of us today feel very isolated, but if you're honoring your dead, you have a whole community, no matter where you are. You have people in your court, people who love you, care about you, who want you to succeed, and they'll support you as you support them.

Ancestor work is the single biggest commonality across indigenous cultures. We as polytheists are working to restore our indigenous religions: all the religions our ancestors practiced, replete with their Gods and spirits, before monotheism swept across the world. This is sacred work but I don't believe it can be done cleanly, wisely, or well, without the help of the ancestors. It's going to take both sides, living and dead, to right the imbalances in our world and to restore our broken, sundered, desecrated traditions. There's nothing more important that one can do than consistently honor one's dead.

I'm betting that some of you already honor your ancestors at least a little. I believe it's deeply ingrained, that we're hardwired to make these connections. We visit graves, name children after our dead, tell their stories. We may not do it in a sacred context—we've lost that— but vestiges exist. If some of you were fortunate enough to grow up not in monotheisms but in your indigenous traditions, most likely there are sacred practices relative to the ancestors there. But regardless of where your ancestors came from, your people had cohesive, sacred, ancestral traditions too. We can reclaim those. We must. It's one of the most crucial parts of polytheistic restoration, but it's also one of the most spiritually and even physically nourishing things you can do for yourselves, your loved ones, and all those who will come after you. Ancestor work makes one's life better.

Before we go further, let's take a moment to clarify what is meant by the term *ancestor*. It's really something of a catchall term. There are many types of honored dead that can be classed as ancestors:

- Ancestors by blood

- Ancestors by adoption

- Deceased friends

- Deceased teachers, mentors, etc.

- Heroes or saints that one might honor

- Those of your work lineage (A doctor can honor any and all physicians who preceded him as part of his or her lineage ancestors.)

- Spirits of dead children in your line, aborted, or miscarried children

- Groups you may feel called to honor (the military dead, for instance)

- Your partner's/partners' dead

- Personal or cultural heroes

- Elemental powers

- Deceased pets

There's no right or wrong place to start. Some of you may be wondering if you need any special psychic abilities or talents to do this work, and the answer is absolutely not. This is something everyone can do. Mediums may have a leg up on clear communication, but they're specialists. You don't have to be a specialist to honor your dead. We all have dead. It's the one unifying, universal thing. It is right and proper that we honor them. Once we take those first stumbling steps, they'll meet us halfway, finding ways to communicate. It might not be with words, but they'll find a way and you will too. I've seen it happen again and again. So don't doubt your ability. You'll each find your own unique way of engaging.

As you get started, there are only a few taboos that I'd like you to remember, and I think they're pretty easy: Most importantly, don't ever put a picture of a living person on your ancestor altar. It's considered disrespectful and "courting death." It literally marks the person as dead. Engage as consistently as possible. Be respectful. Those are the only "rules" to worry about. Your ancestors may eventually give you more involved guidelines as you deepen your connection to them, but that's something you'll work out with them as your practices evolve. There is no one right way to do ancestor work. It is flexible because the ancestors aren't archetypes or metaphors: they're individuals, people with all the quirks that individuals have. Like any other relationship, the ones with your ancestors will take time and care to develop. Above all else, it helps to keep in mind that essentially, we are our entire ancestor lines walking.

In many traditional cultures, including the pre-Christian Norse and Germanic cultures, it was generally believed that when the living properly and respectfully fulfilled their obligations to the dead, luck, wealth, blessings, and abundance would fall upon the family, and they would have powerful allies in the unseen world. Where those attendant obligations were neglected, the entire living family would suffer. One of the most painful aspects attendant to the spread of Christianity across the world has been the severing of those ancestral ties, the neglect, and at times, the open vilification of such practices. We stand on the shoulders of our dead; their struggles, hopes, sacrifices, and even their errors have contributed to the quality of our own lives and who we are today. We are here because of them. Good or bad, they are ours and through ancestor work, we can even bring healing to our lines. We need not know their names to honor them. The dead, no matter how far back in one's ancestral line, know their children. They generally maintain an interest in their family line. Even those who chose not to have children still take their place in the web of ancestors as guides, teachers, and examples. One does not have to be a blood relative to be honored as an ancestor. There are connections of spirit that are equally powerful to—in some ways more powerful than—those of blood.

None of us come into this world alone; we come with a line of ancestors, foremothers and forefathers stretching back untold generations. If we can do nothing else to reclaim our sacred traditions, to build again strong, autonomous communities, we can honor our progenitors. A life spent with mindful awareness of that holy connection is a life well lived. Speak their names. Tell their stories. Research their cultures. Learn their languages. Delve into your own genealogy. Visit graves. Set up an altar to your dead. Bring them gifts. Bring them your attention as an ongoing devotional act. For those who are adopted, you have two sets of ancestors to celebrate—those of your blood family and those of your adopted family. It isn't necessary to know their names. Simply make the call and they will know you. For those who come from abusive families, reach further back or call upon spiritual ancestors—those people and perhaps heroes who inspired and taught you on your journey. There is no shame and much power in such an act. Opening the door to one's honored dead opens the door to a reservoir of support, knowledge, and personal might unimaginable to those who live with their eyes on the living world alone. It restores the sacred to the death process. It restores the sacred to our communities. It nourishes our spirits. Even more than honoring the Gods Themselves, venerating one's ancestors is fundamental to Heathen practice.

Ritual for Honoring the Ancestors

For those who have never worked with their dead on an ongoing basis, for whom the concept of ancestral veneration is a new one, setting up an ancestral shrine provides an excellent time to begin the process of reconnecting to one's lineage and forebears. It doesn't matter where you are from, what your ethnic background might be, we all have ancestors and it's right and proper for all of us to honor them. This is not an excuse for any type of racism. *Everyone* has ancestors, and they and their cultures should be celebrated. Period. Different indigenous cultures have their own methods of honoring them, but I will share the one that has worked for me and is fairly common within Heathenry: that of the ancestral shrine and feast.

Begin by setting up a shrine. It doesn't have to be elaborate, but it should be separate from your devotional altar. A windowsill or bookshelf will do. I know a woman who has four cats. She simply cannot keep a regular altar, so she has constructed a reliquary box. Her altar is contained within a large carved box. When she wishes to honor her ancestors, she opens the box, sets out her offerings, and talks to her grandmother. She doesn't leave the offerings out, but commits them to the earth after she is finished. Adapt the practice of altar meditations in whatever way best suits your lifestyle. Form is less important than the act of mindful contemplation. Choose where and how you will construct your altar. Many traditions, such as Lukumi, often use white altar cloths and white flowers, with nine glasses of water on their altars. I too have found this helpful. Water is the most basic offering possible and a good place to start. It also represents nourishing your dead. Creating an ancestral altar is an act of hospitality. You are inviting your ancestors not only into your house, but into your life. By setting out water, you provide them with symbolic refreshment, as you would any guest.

Once you have decided where you want your shrine to go, begin by consecrating the space in whatever way is common in your spiritual tradition. Offer incense and a prayer to the Goddess of the Underworld (Hela), asking that She help facilitate communication in your new endeavor. The prayer, like the action of crafting a shrine, should come from the heart. Once you feel Her presence strongly, begin constructing your altar, verbally speaking aloud the reason you are including each object.

Anything can go on an ancestral altar that reminds you of that sacred connection: pictures of the dead, if you have them; items from the culture in which your ancestors lived (for instance, I use an altar cloth that was handwoven in Lithuania to represent the generations of Lithuanian ancestors on my father's side, about whom, sadly, I know next to nothing); a genealogical chart; flowers; incense; elemental symbols, if you like; objects belonging to your dead—these are just suggestions. Each shrine will be as individual as the person constructing it. Spiritual ancestors and heroes should absolutely be included here.

Once your shrine is constructed, spend as much time as you like meditating in front of it. When you feel ready, call to your ancestors. If you know their names, call them by name, welcome them into your life, and explain what you are doing and why. I realize that many of our ancestors will be Christian or Jewish or Islamic. That's okay. It's the honoring that is important, not what religious tradition they followed. I've almost never had issues arise because our religion is different from that of a particular ancestor. Sometimes, we may have to teach them how to engage—this relationship after all, like any relationship, has two sides. Just as we're learning how to engage with them effectively, they are often learning the same thing with us. This is not about which God or Goddess we worship, but about reconnecting with one's family and the source of one's strength.[5] Ask them to be a part of your life again, and tell them that you will be honoring them regularly. If a dead relative was abusive to you, he or she need not be honored. I have seen people make peace with abusive family members after they were dead, but that does not happen in every case. It is important to honor those relatives you want in your life. While you may or may not choose to pray for the others, they need not be honored on a regular basis if doing so causes pain. If you don't know any names to call, that's fine. Simply call to the ancestors of your maternal line, the ancestors of your paternal line. It may be that you will learn their names in time.

When you have talked to them for a time, offer them food and drink: rice, bread, beer, wine, coffee, sweets, and even full dinners are appropriate. I usually set out a glass of wine or cup of coffee and a bit of bread or coffee cake for weekly offerings. On birth and death anniversaries, special holidays, or if I have received their aid in a very special way, I will offer more elaborate fare. Juice and water may be offered in lieu of wine and beer. I usually leave the food sitting out, but after a few hours it may be discarded. Tobacco, flowers, and incense are also appropriate offerings; in fact, you may offer anything that you personally feel called to give. This is not going to waste. The dead will take its vital essence. After a few hours (I usually leave offerings overnight), dispose of them the same way you would the remains of a dinner party with honored guests. Nor do you have to buy offerings outside your means. Share your life with them and if you have little, a glass of water, a bit of your food, your prayers and love are enough. Talk to your ancestors, tell them about yourself, your dreams, you goals. Tell them that you would like them to be a part of your life now. Understand that if you have not done this before, it may take time to develop a connection—just like with any other relationship. Invite them to communicate with you, and indicate your commitment to getting to know them. It's a process, one without end.

Once you feel that you have said all you wish to say, make your offerings. Thank them for their presence and for being there in your life. Thank the Goddess that you initially called for aid, and then end the ritual. Honoring the dead in such a fashion is not a onetime occurrence. It is a process of developing a very conscious awareness of our connection to the ancestors. This is something that you should commit to doing on a regular basis: weekly or at least monthly, if you really want to reap the benefits that having a strong relationship with the dead can bring. If you are able to do it, light a candle and put it on the shrine, allowing it to burn out. (It's okay to blow the candles out when you have to leave the house. Recently I've begun using battery-powered candles. Those work really well too.) Pay attention to your dreams for the first few nights after your offerings. I have found that the dead often choose to communicate in dreams.

In addition to honoring the dead, we also honor the spirits of the land around us. The Norse word for these beings is *Vaettir* (singular *Vaet*),[6] and they are responsible for maintaining harmony in the natural world. This term may also be used to refer to the various nonhuman beings that may inhabit a house or dwelling. There are some who are beneficial to humankind and others who just want to be left alone. Every stone, tree, and blade of grass has Vaettir attached to it. Any damage done to the natural world directly affects and often harms the indigenous Vaettir. As our relationship with them is, in many respects, symbiotic, they may be honored the same way as the ancestors, with a bit of beer or milk and honey, bread, and butter set out prior to any rite. Taking care to recycle and even committing an hour or so a week to picking up garbage at a local park or beach is also a nice way of honoring Vaettir.

Humanity exists in a balance between the world of the dead and the natural world, a balance of respect and mindfulness that each living person is charged to maintain. Consciously honoring one's ancestors, honoring the Vaettir, and living rightly, courageously, and with devotion are all means of doing just that.

Ritual of Ancestor Elevation

Over the past couple of years, I've gained insight into the process of ancestor elevation. I used to do it because it needed to be done, but I would do it rather by rote. There's a Baltic proverb that says *the work will teach you how to do it,* and I think that definitely happened with me. After over two decades of doing ancestor elevations I finally feel like I have some sense of what it takes to do one well.

First is the ritual itself. Ancestor elevation comes to us originally through nineteenth-century spiritualism and was adapted almost immediately by the African Traditional Religions (ATR), but can be done by anyone. The ritual is meant to be flexible and fluid, adapted to the needs of one's specific ancestors. That is how it was designed. Ancient polytheisms had their rites and rituals for tending and healing the troubled or hurting dead, but since we no longer have access to those rites, this will do. It's a powerful ritual when done well.

The Ritual

Ancestor elevation is done to help the soul of a dead family member who was troubled in life, perhaps having done harmful things to themselves or others, never able to live a happy life due to their own inner demons. By doing this ritual, we aid their souls in finding peace. It is an act of mercy and can also bring emotional freedom to the living, especially if their own lives were negatively affected by that individual when they were alive. It is ironically a lot easier to do this work for someone after they are dead. Unlike simply wiping them from one's life, this practice actually helps the problem at its root.

An elevation can be done for a beloved ancestor just because you love that ancestor and want the best for him or her. While they are usually done in the case of troubled, aggressive, unhappy, unhealthy ancestors or conditions, they don't need to be reserved only for those cases. The only prerequisite to doing an elevation is that you must already have a primary ancestral altar and an engaged ancestral practice.

Begin by laying an altar on the floor. This is done in part because the ancestors are our roots and in part because during the course of this nine-day ritual, we will be raising the altar and thus symbolically lifting our ancestor up. Be sure to place the altar somewhere where it can remain out for nine consecutive days. If you have pets, that's okay. It's not going to harm anything to have them drinking out of offering glasses.

The altar should be white: white cloth, flowers, candles. In doing an elevation for a particular ancestor, we are engaging in ancestral healing, clearing blockage, pain, or hurt from that particular line. White, representing cleanliness, is a good color to use for this.

Set up a picture of the dead person you wish to elevate centrally on the altar. (If you don't have a photo, write their name on a piece of white paper in your best handwriting.)

Put out flowers. Prepare a candle, a glass of clean, fresh water, incense, and whatever other offerings you wish to make.

When you are ready to begin your ritual, set a candle at each of the four corners of the altar and light them, offering a prayer that fire will cleanse and consecrate this space, making it sacred, making it a place where clear communication may occur between you, the ancestors, and the Holy Powers. Call upon any God or Goddess whose help you might wish in this endeavor. Ancestral work is a very personal thing. It not only involves us and our spiritual connections but specific ancestors and their spiritual connections. Regardless of the fact that we are Heathen, Norse Pagan, or Northern Tradition, etc., we may find ourselves called to put representations of Deities our ancestors honored on the altar or to call upon Them. If you have a grandmother, for example, who had a close connection to the Virgin Mary and, in the course of an elevation, you get a sense that you should put an image of the Virgin on the altar, I'd suggest doing it because, really, who is better positioned to help elevate that grand-mother than the God or Goddess she prayed to her entire life? It's not about our comfort levels or our devotional relationships, it's about connecting with our dead and doing what is best for them. If they had certain devotional commitments, they may want those included, for their own comfort and peace of mind. They drew nourishment from their traditions. It's fine to acknowledge that.

Sit on the floor in front of the shrine and call to the ancestor you are elevating. Light incense and the main ancestral candle. Begin by offering the following two prayers on behalf of this ancestor (feel free to use others if you wish):

First Prayer

Hail to the Gods and Goddesses.
Your grace illumines all things.
Your gifts shine forth,
Making fruitful nine mighty worlds.
Blessed are those that serve You.
Blessed are those that seek You out.

Holy Powers, Makers of all things,
Bless and protect us in Your mercy.
Lead us along the twisting pathways of our wyrd
And when it is time, guide us safely along the Hel-road.

Second Prayer

This prayer was originally written by Fuensanta Plaza for the Gods she loved above all others, Loki and Sigyn, but you can readily adapt it to your own devotional connections.

My Lord and My Lady, my Beloved Ones,
May those You call always hear Your voice.
May I always love You beyond trust and mistrust.
May my surrender be complete and voluntary.
Give me this day the grace of Your presence.
When I fail You of Your kindness,
Permit me to make amends.
Use me and teach me according to Your will,
And deliver me from all complacency.

Third Prayer

Call directly to the ancestor you are elevating and say:

Oh clement and merciful Gods,
Magnificent Holy Powers hear my prayer.
I offer these prayers for the soul of X,
And for all good spirits who wish our prayers and recognition.
Please let X know that someone here on Midgard
Is stepping forth to speak for him/her.

Merciful Holy Powers,
And all other good spirits and ancestors
Who might intercede for the relief of this soul:
Grant him/her hope.
Grant him/her the awareness
That he/she is illuminated by the divine light,
That he/she is younger kin to the Gods,
Beloved of the Holy Powers.
Let him/her see those tangles in the wyrd,
Those hurts and imperfections
Which keep him/her away from peaceful tenure in the realms of Hel,
From rebirth, from renewal.
Open his/her heart to understanding,
Grieving, repentance, and restoration.
Let him/her understand that by his/her own efforts
He/she can make the time of his/her testing easier.
Wyrd unfolds always, and living or dead,
The power to weave it well is in our hands.
May the Holy Powers and other helpful ancestors
Give him/her the strength to persevere in all good resolution,
To meet the tests of his/her wyrd rightly and well.
May these benevolent and loving words
Mitigate and soothe his/her pain.
May they give him/her a demonstration
That someone in Midgard acknowledges, remembers,
And takes part in his/her sorrows.
May X know that we wish him/her happiness.

At this point, offer the glass of water to X. Put X's picture and the glass of water on a book (cover it with a pretty cloth so it's aesthetically pleasing). Remain meditating and praying for as long as you wish. When you are ready to end the ritual, you may leave the candle to burn for a bit or blow it out. Thank the elemental power of fire for holding and consecrating the space as you blow out the four corner candles. Thank the Gods and ancestors and then your ritual is over.

Repeat this for nine consecutive nights. Each night, clean, fresh water should be offered and the water and picture lifted by the addition of a new book. After the ninth day, the picture and offering glass of water can be placed on top of the main ancestral altar.

A few caveats: If the candle or the glass breaks, you should do three things:

1. Start the entire elevation over.
2. Call upon your Dísir, and other strong and protective ancestors to guide and watch over the ritual.
3. Put pieces of camphor in the water. In traditional folk magic and in spiritualism, from which the concept of elevations originally evolved, camphor is protective, keeping destructive spirits away. If you want to use a more traditional northern herb, sprinkle dried agrimony or mugwort in the water.

If the shrine is very active, change the camphor, agrimony, or mugwort every day and do not use the candle. Usually your strongest ancestors will come forward to help with the elevation.

I have found that the dead like to be remembered with food and drink offerings but also with music. It would not be inappropriate to offer music during this ritual. At the end of the nine-day ritual, when the elevation is complete, it is always good to make an offering to all your ancestors, and to make an offering to the Gods upon whom you called for help.

You may do elevations for the same ancestor multiple times. It does not hurt. In fact, with particularly damaged or angry ancestors, or tangled wyrd, you may have to. It's not a bad gift to give a beloved and healthy ancestor, too.

Note: When doing elevations, it's important to keep notes on your dreams for the next few days. It's also really important to do nightly cleansings—a cleansing bath, for example—every night of the elevation.

You can't do this type of work alone. When we decide to do an elevation, we act as the living keystones here in the corporeal world. We are letting our ancestor-in-need know that someone living remembers them, cares about them, and is deeply concerned for their welfare. We should not be the only ones doing the elevation, though. It is crucially important that we bring our other ancestors and perhaps even our Gods into this practice. Ask your ancestors to participate in the elevation right along with you. Just as it is right and proper for us to elevate our dead, so too is it proper for our ancestors to participate. This is a family ritual. In fact, other ancestors will suggest that a certain Deity be called upon. Once, when I was praying about halfway through a nine-day elevation for my great-grandmother, I got the strong sense that I should petition Asklepios too, which I did, even though He's not a Norse Deity. When I started, one of my dead had asked that I pray to Mary. If you can, take their suggestions. It can transform an elevation.

Elevations can be exhausting and grueling on a spiritual level especially if one's ancestor is carrying deep wounds or has committed terrible deeds. In some cases, we're directly confronting and challenging an intergenerational cycle of abuse. There can be intense resistance on the part of the ancestor, and a lot of emotions like fear, anger, despair, outright terror, shame, and grief can bombard the person doing the elevation. This is normal, but it really can have significant repercussions on the ancestor worker. It's a heavy weight to bear, and sometimes, as the ancestor is fighting for their healing, or in their damaged state, fighting against the healing, the person working the elevation faces moments where they are shouldering the weight of that damage. This is why it's important to always begin this process clean and to take special care with purification during the nine days of the rite. Depending on the reasons for elevating one's ancestor, a great deal of miasma and pollution may be released during the ritual and that will need to be dealt with or we'll end up mired in it.

When I begin each night's prayer cycle, I usually start by taking a cleansing bath, and then I use a scent diffuser in which I use Van-Van oil, Blessing oil, or something similar to help prepare the space. I asperge with khernips myself, my shrine, and the space where I'm doing the elevation. (Khernips is not Norse, but rather Hellenic holy water, made by dousing a burning bay leaf in clean, fresh water.) Then I go through a cycle of two ancestor songs, one for fire before I kindle any candles, and one for my ancestors in general. I refresh all the offerings on my main ancestor shrine (usually just water at this point) and make offerings to whatever Deities I'm going to be petitioning too. Then I prepare the elevation shrine, refresh the offerings there, talk to that ancestor a little bit, invite my other ancestors (and Gods) to participate, and begin the nightly prayer cycle for the elevation. Afterward, I cleanse myself again and throughout those nine days, being more mindful of cleansing practices than perhaps I normally would. During an elevation it's important to neglect nothing. There are times, I will admit, when we can let protocols slide a tiny bit. This is not one of those times.

It's also really, really important not to start one's ancestor practice with an elevation. Before even thinking of performing an elevation ritual, take the time to develop a working, devotional relationship with your dead. Set up an ancestor shrine, make regular offerings, pray to them and for them. Don't just plop down one day and decide to do an elevation. This ritual is part of a healthy, ongoing ancestor practice, not the beginning of one. It's one possible part of getting right with one's ancestors, but not the appropriate place to start.

Step by faltering step, our ancestors, in the best of times, pushed us forward. There were those so damaged or broken that they failed even in this, yes, but overall, they did the best they could. We carry our dead. We should do it proudly and we should do it well. To that end, every day, ask yourself: What have I done for my ancestors today? Have I made them proud? There are far worse rubrics by which to live one's life.

Miasma and Pollution

In ancient Greek religion, *miasma* was the word given to spiritual pollution. Heathens don't give much thought to the idea of miasma. I didn't either for a very long time until my father died and I was helping to prepare the body for cremation. Contact with dead bodies is a primary cause of miasma, and I realized in the heartbeat of that moment that I was in a state of spiritual pollution. There was no other word for it. I could feel it clinging to me, and only ritual purification set me right again. It wasn't bad, but it was there and it rendered me ritually unclean.

Now, I almost hesitate to use the word *pollution* to describe miasma, because of its negative connotations. Miasma is a natural thing, neither good nor bad, but a natural consequence of certain actions or contact with certain things. Sometimes this is inevitable, and then you perform the appropriate ritual cleansing. No big deal— except it is. Ritual purity was practically an obsession to ancient Greeks, and maybe it should be for us as well.[7] There is more opportunity in our contemporary world to enter into a state of miasma than in the world our ancestors faced. After all, so much of what is common in our world stands diametrically opposed to the values and virtues the Gods would have us cultivate.

Not all miasma is the same either. There is the miasma that comes when one accidentally blunders into an unclean situation or from doing a necessary or kind act but that led to contact with something unclean. There is also miasma that comes of consciously choosing to expose oneself to something disrespectful to one's Gods. And there is the miasma of certain horrible crimes.[8] How one deals with a state of spiritual contamination depends largely on what caused it.

There is positive contamination too. Anyone who has had direct experience with the holy may be in a state of what I term positive miasma. It's not bad. In fact, it's very, very good. But it leaves a mark, an energetic signature by which others may be contaminated who have not prepared themselves properly for such contact. Shamans have this signature, as does anyone who has just been possessed by a Deity. Anyone who has just had a powerful encounter with the sacred carries it. The sacred is a type of positive contamination. This is why in *Till We Have Faces*, one of C. S. Lewis's characters speaks about "the smell of the holy." It does have a smell, a feel, a sense, a taste even, I suppose. This type of miasma, I would go so far as to say, should be reverenced. It should be respected and attended to appropriately. I would, however, counsel that the person in this state of holy miasma understand that transitioning back into mundane headspace might be difficult, painful, or even cause a moment or two of emotional and cognitive disconnect. I would counsel such a person to be gentle with him- or herself and take the time necessary to process and experience the aftereffects of such contact. I would also counsel them not to rush back into mundane situations.

Miasma can come about because of the conscious (and poor) choice on the part of the individual, through a lack of mindfulness, or accidentally, through not having all the necessary facts beforehand. I'll give you two examples from my own experience.

A couple of years ago there was a public Winter Solstice ritual held in my town, and I was invited. There was, of course, a bonfire. The woman serving as ritual facilitator was incredibly unskilled. She had no concept of the sacred whatsoever. The man building, lighting, and tending the fire did to some degree, but not enough to challenge what occurred. The ritual was already suspect from the beginning because there was a sense from these two facilitators that it was a performance piece. While there is an element of performance inherent in a good ritual, the purpose of this is to enhance the cultivation and experience of the ritual state, not as an end in itself. So, as the fire was blazing, after invoking the elemental powers (poorly), the man said that now it was time to give offerings to fire. Fire blazed up at that. The woman interrupted and said, "No, we'll do it later." (This is already a violation of ritual protocols. Banter and incompetence have no place in ritual.) She went on to deny fire the promised offerings. At that point, being initiated to fire as I am, I was in a state of massive miasma. All of my taboos as a fire worker had been violated, ritual protocol had been violated, and a family of spirits with whom I am very close had been shown massive disrespect. I pushed my way to the fire, made offerings despite what the two of them had said—Gods and spirits trump humans any day of the year in my book—and left. When I got home, I made massive offerings to the spirits of fire, with my apologies, and underwent a full ritual cleansing. Then I wrote an article about it to educate other people on how to behave both in ritual and around fire. Because I recognized the ritual violation and knew that miasma would attend it, I was able to deal with it appropriately right away, instead of waiting until it ran its course (never a good thing), bringing with it misfortune, possible illness, and the anger of a family of good and gracious allies.

The second example is far more mundane. I went to the movies. As a child, I'd loved the original *Clash of the Titans* (I went through a period when I was seven or so when I was obsessed with Greek cosmology), so when the remake came out, I eventually got around to watching it. I was appalled. It was nothing like the original and was, in fact, one of the most vile and singularly disrespectful presentations of myth I have ever seen before or since. I was sickened. I also came away from the movie feeling polluted, tainted, and utterly ritually and spiritually unclean to the core of my being. I wrote about this at the time, and I was heartened to find other polytheists had experienced the same thing. Perhaps this wouldn't have affected someone else as deeply, but for me, it was several days of meditation, prayer, and deep cleansing before I felt like anything approaching normal again and even longer before I felt ready to approach the Gods properly in ritual space. I had exposed myself *willingly* to that which impugned the Gods, which rendered my head- and heartspace not conducive to piety.[9]

This second incident really brought home to me something about the nature of miasma. We should consider where we go, with whom we spend our time, to what influences we expose ourselves. They matter, be they however small and mundane. There is a concept in Buddhism called "right mindfulness," which means (as I understand it) directing your thoughts and attention to spiritually wholesome endeavors, focusing on those things which will enhance one's spirituality. By doing so, one enhances one's life. That starts with the small things, like what movies one chooses to watch, and should expand until it encompasses the greater things, like how one treats the homeless man hungry on the street and how one reacts when legislators threaten to begin fracking in one's neighborhood. We court miasma by the harm we choose to let pass unattended, unchallenged.

Some people have specific taboos that render certain types of miasma more damaging or have duties that put them more often in a position courting miasma. The advice I offer there is to develop a ritual of cleansing and purification before and after engaging in such acts. For instance, according to ancient Greek religion, performing a sacrifice was curative of a state of miasma in the one requesting the sacrifice, but also rendered the priest performing the ritual in a state of miasma. But this was, I would warrant, easily cleansed away, as anyone trained in such rituals would have doubtless learned in the course of training.

Understanding miasma, what it is, and how negatively it can impact someone, is an essential component to ritual studies, one that I feel has been sadly neglected within contemporary polytheisms until now. We need more mindfulness in our communities, both within our rituals and without. It's not like the Gods are going to smack one down for being in a miasmic state, but it corrodes and compromises one's relationship with Them. Often the consequences aren't immediately noticed, in fact they may not be felt at all, until suddenly the spiritual relationships that were once so vital, present, and true are blurry, distant, and hard to reach. A miasmic state impairs luck and health. It twists all that is spiritual into something mundane and gross. Indeed, part of the reason that people may not recognize when they are in this state, or approaching it, is that our society is so out of balance, riddled with spiritual pollution on every level. In a society where people are blowing up mountaintops from sheer greed, where our food is poisoned, where children are picking through garbage, and the Kardashians are considered role models, it's difficult for people to recognize spiritual disease. When once piety and purification were the norm, now people look askance, even in our own communities, when one seeks to take proper precautions around one's spiritual health by insisting on healthy boundaries.

To deal with miasma, I recommend regular cleansings. *Spiritual Protection* by Sophie Reicher provides cleansing protocols and meditation exercises to develop discernment. Incorporate things like regularly asperging with blessed water before rituals, weekly cleansing salt baths—in addition, of course, to one's regular hygiene!—and regular prayer practice. I'll also light candles and bear them around my space before and after rituals, asking fire to cleanse and purify. Be mindful that we must prepare ourselves for engagement with the sacred, and what we watch and hear and engage in can impact our spirits and either strengthen or diminish our commitment to piety. Understand that when we transition into ritual headspace to engage with our Gods and ancestors and back into ordinary headspace, something important is occurring. Learning to attend to miasma and purification at the beginning of one's practice will pay dividends later in our devotional lives.

CHAPTER 7

HEATHEN ETHICS AND VALUES

B eing Heathen is more than just honoring the Norse Gods and Goddesses. To truly be Heathen means living one's life in a particular way, adhering to a specific set of values, and following a particular code of ethics. Where that code of ethics is lacking, so is true Heathenry. The values of the Germanic tribe or warband—honor, loyalty, forthrightness, and courage— are greatly prized; cowardice and unconditional pacifism are condemned. It is this sensibility that creates the greatest gulf between Heathenry and Neo-Paganism. Within Heathenry, warriorship is not a mental or theoretical pursuit. Many Heathens own weapons and know how to use them, choose to serve in the military, excel at hunting and the study of the martial arts, and find numerous other ways to develop in themselves a warrior's sensibilities. Willingness and readiness to defend oneself and one's family are of paramount importance to the average Heathen. While not every Heathen would define him- or herself as a warrior, the virtues of honor, integrity, and bold action are valued by all.

This code of ethics is drawn from the tribal structure. It can be very difficult for a newcomer to the religion, at first, for this very reason. Developing an understanding of Heathen ethics, learning to embody them, and turning one's back on the values instilled in a non-Heathen childhood are an ongoing challenge. One way to do this is to consciously seek out opportunities to hone these newfound values and to engage in pursuits that enhance such Heathen consciousness. Developing and striving to live by this code of ethics are some things that Heathens do to better serve their communities and their ancestors and to better honor the Gods. Simply choosing to address conflict directly, intelligently, and honestly rather than fleeing or avoiding is a good step in the right direction. It goes without saying that this does not mean meeting every conflict with violence. There are times when that is indeed the appropriate response, but that is hardly the case in the majority of situations. Most Heathens are peaceful, family-oriented folk. Violence would be considered appropriate only in the case of injury or threat to oneself or one's family.

The Nine Noble Virtues (NNV), though never directly found in any piece of Heathen lore, are culled from the Havamal[1] and reflect, in brief, the important values of Heathenry. The Nine Noble Virtues are not static ideals, but rather constantly evolving goals toward which we must always strive.

They are as follows:

1. Courage
2. Discipline
3. Fidelity
4. Honor
5. Hospitality
6. Industriousness
7. Perseverance
8. Self-Reliance
9. Truth

Now let's break these down for further study.

Courage: Courage is the brother to fear. There is no courage that doesn't rise from terror. It is knowing when to speak and when to remain silent and having the will to act, despite difficulty or overwhelming fear. It means facing darkness, and it is the first step in learning to live by one's convictions.

Discipline: What a bad word this has become in modern society! It is key to deepening one's commitment and relationship to the Gods. It is the first and most important building block in the foundation of an honorable life. It goes hand in hand with the virtue of perseverance and, as a whetstone hones a finely crafted blade, so discipline hones the spirit, stripping away all that is not spiritually healthy. Discipline is a gift we give to ourselves, allowing us to succeed in every aspect of life.

Fidelity: Developing one's relationship with the Gods is akin to falling in love—a passionate, all-consuming love. Fidelity is the long-term commitment, not only to the Gods but to the Kindred and tribe that walk the path with you and to the ethics which, as a Heathen, you have chosen to live by. It is a strength that gives one the ability to forbear and means not turning back when the path becomes difficult. Another word might be *loyalty.*

Honor: This is the most difficult of all the virtues to describe. It defines the condition of one's spirit and, in many ways, is the accumulation of all the other virtues lived out. In a specifically religious context, it is a matter of not compromising in one's relationship *or* service to Deity, no matter how difficult or trying that may, at times, become. It is consciously and willingly tearing away the comfort zone that we place between ourselves and the Gods and standing vulnerable yet strong in purpose.

It means doing what is right, even when it is difficult or might bring uncomfortable consequences. Honor is living one's duty.

Hospitality: This is a virtue that impacts many diverse elements of our lives. It is not only being courteous, but acknowledging Kindred as kin. It means approaching others in the spirit of "right good will," which means that you accept that those who approach you within the community are doing so honorably and without any hidden agenda or malicious intent. It gives the benefit of the doubt that all are adhering to the same ethics and values, that we are all acting with each other's good in mind. The virtue of hospitality also involves acting honorably and with generosity. Hospitality entails one's responsibility to the world around you, including being aware of where you can make a difference. It means being willing to reach out to help the least of one's Kindred.

Industriousness: This virtue is about constantly striving to develop one's gifts and talents and sharing those gifts with one's Kindred, as well as using them to make an impact on the non-Kindred world at large. It entails accepting the responsibility to do your life's work as the Gods define it. It is also the responsibility to be productive with your knowledge. It's taking pride in doing the smallest task well, for every act should be a prayer and a celebration of everything that makes one Heathen.

Perseverance: Has to do with developing one's will and fortitude, and goes hand in hand with discipline. It means grasping each difficulty, each failure, each fear, and each pain as a gift, blessing, challenge, and opportunity to grow stronger, wiser, and closer to the Gods. It means not giving up, keeping to your goals, and holding the Gods, one's kin, and thew always in mind and central to your life.

Self-Reliance: Ridding oneself of any unconscious motivations, tearing down blockages of ego, and moving past the codependency and self-pity that we, as a society, have been taught lead to self-reliance. It means not only taking responsibility for one's actions and their consequences, but also claiming one's active place as part of the Kindred. It means not going to the Gods only for what we must work to get.

Truth: More than simply speaking or doing no falsehood, it means having the courage to walk honorably, despite the difficulties or discomforts. It means facing the challenges that will inevitably emerge as we cast off unneeded facades in the course of our spiritual journey and growing awareness of what it means to live in thew.

A good way to develop an understanding of these virtues is to take some time to define them for yourself—to elaborate on what they mean to you personally and how you manifest them in your daily life. Where do you fall short? Where and how can you improve? What special talents and gifts do you bring to your Gods and your community?

There is a saying within Heathenry: "We are our deeds."[2] This defines Heathen ethics better than anything else. The quality of one's deeds and the spirit in which they are performed either strengthens or weakens oneself and one's community. Heathen values are not based on a concept of sin and redemption, but of right action and divine order. There is that which enhances one's wyrd, one's tribe, and one's own life and luck to the benefit of all—and that which does not. There are consequences either way.

Over the past couple of years, there has been some pushback against the NNV. It sometimes seems as though having any ethical guidelines at all offends some people. There's little attempt by naysayers to replace the NNV with a different set of values, but rather a desire to negate any values that might constrain or properly shape character. We live in a strange world and must reorient ourselves mentally as polytheists. Our ancestors understood the importance of building a strong, incorruptible character. Values and virtues were things worth having and cultivating. Each person is a link in a larger chain, one that forms family, community, and tradition. Doing that well starts with cultivating good character and firm values, and sadly very little in our modern world encourages that.

Examples of these virtues can easily be found in the Havamal and the Sagas. They are fitting for a society in which existence was a constant struggle. If you think that isn't applicable today, try living below the poverty line. None of these virtues are objectionable to a reasonable person. Do you really want to be a person without honor? Without courage? Who is incapable of hospitality or personal discipline? Who lacks fidelity in relationships, or who is incapable of telling the truth or holding to his or her word? The NNV may be simplistic, but they are meant as touchstones. Note that they do not tell you how to be courageous or how to be truthful. One is encouraged to be introspective in discovering this for oneself. I rather like that. It's not the end of the conversation, but the beginning. What is truth? What does it mean to me as a devotee of Deity X? How can I cultivate that in my life? These are important questions to ponder for anyone trying to live rightly and well, particularly within a faith tradition.

Of course, given how pervasive the NNV are within Heathen traditions, it is inevitable that someone holding objectionable views will subscribe to them. So do many people holding views that are diametrically opposed. One of the reasons these accusations occur is that the list of the NNV were created by (depending on your source) the Asatru Folk Assembly (AFA) or Odinic Rite, which are known to be adamantly folkish. Folkish Heathenry is not synonymous with racism, but as with every other religious position in the history of the world, has sometimes been misused. But we should never relinquish what is good and true within our traditions to those who would misrepresent those traditions. We are called to hold the line against racism and hatred, but also against diminishing our traditions out of fear, ignorance, or for any other reason. I've also often seen the NNV condemned as ableist. Those disabled in some way (and I write this as a disabled woman) can fulfill every one of these virtues; otherwise what the detractors of the NNV are actually saying is that disabled people are disabled not only in body but in mind, heart, and character. That's pretty foul. It's infantilizing and really quite disrespectful to the struggle of differently abled people in our communities.

We should be encouraged to define the NNV for ourselves in our own lives, with respect to our own relationships with the Holy Powers. Or we should be encouraged to come up with our own system of values sustainable within and coherent with our traditions. Either way, character matters, and it's often difficult for people coming from monotheisms where they're told what to believe and how to act, to encounter a system of ethics encouraging self-reflection and independence. I'd love to see discussions of other philosophies and different ethical guidelines. The NNV are guidelines and principles. Let's have conversations on what it means to have courage in the modern world, what it means in each person's individual circumstances, what it means to show hospitality, especially when one is impoverished or living with scarcity. How does the hospitality shown to one's Gods differ from what one shows to one's friends or to strangers? We need to be having these conversations, and this is a challenge to you, my readers, to do just that.

In addition to the Nine Noble Virtues, there are also the "Twelve Aetheling Thews,"[3] some of which are contained within the Nine Noble Virtues, while others expand upon and complement them. Because this particular code of ethics evolved within the Anglo-Saxon Heathen community, the name for each virtue is in Old English. The Twelve Aetheling Thews are:

Besignes—Industriousness

Efnes—Equality and equal justice for everyone, regardless of gender, race, social standing, etc.

Ellen—Courage

Geférscipe—This is perhaps the essence of tribalism: putting the good and needs of the community above one's self and utilizing one's own unique talents to enhance the luck of the tribe as a whole.

Giefu—Generosity

Giestlíðness—Hospitality

Metgung—Moderation and self-control. Though it's never stated explicitly, moderation is stressed throughout the Havamal as the primary attribute of an honorable person.

Selfdóm—Nurturing one's individual talents, being true to oneself

Sóð—Truth and honesty

Stedefaestnes—Steadfastness

Tréowð—Loyalty, troth

Wísdóm—Wisdom

Also underlying the ethics and values of Heathen society is the concept of *frith*. Many folk define frith as "peace," but that is not quite accurate. A far better translation of the term would be "right order."[4] Adherence to frith ensured a cohesive, harmonious, well-functioning community by keeping discord at a minimum and providing means by which grievances could be addressed. Frith is the foundation of thew. A *frithstead* is a place wherein no violence or ill action may be committed, for to do so not only damages one's luck, but may lead to various community penalties, from being forced to pay a *shild*, or debt of honor, to being cast out from the community. The fact that many Goddesses, especially Frigga, were referred to as "Frith-weavers" underscores its importance in Heathen culture. Sometimes violence was necessary to maintain or restore frith, as the conflict between the Aesir and Vanir show. Frith was never peace at any cost, especially not the cost of the community's luck and integrity.

In addition to the virtues mentioned, many other qualities are valued within Heathen society, including wisdom, eloquence, compassion, and freedom of conscience. All of these attributes are considered necessary building blocks of civilized Heathen culture. Ultimately, however, each person is responsible for his or her orlog, responsible for ensuring that he or she is remembered with honor.

The Question of Evil

We don't talk much about evil as polytheists. Our traditions aren't focused around it; we don't have a figure like the Christian Satan, and for the most part, our traditions aren't really fixated on any definitive eschatology. Instead we tend to be much more focused on celebrating the divine order and all the blessings our Gods bestow. That does not mean, however, that evil doesn't exist. Christians weren't the first to wrestle with this. Polytheist philosophers engaged with the question of evil, and perhaps from time immemorial men and women have been asking why bad things happen.[5]

First, there's the question of what evil actually is, which has been as vexing through the centuries as why it happens or whether it exists at all. Before we attempt to answer that, it's important to articulate some of the underpinnings of our cosmology. The baseline understanding in Heathenry is that our Gods are inherently good. That doesn't mean that Their nature is good according to human understanding, which is necessarily limited, but that Their nature is inherently good on a cosmic, eternal, superhuman level. They are the good from which all other good things flow. They are good in a way that supports and sustains everything in our world and the fabric of Being itself. Whatever evil there is in the world, it does not come from our Gods.

Misfortune can't necessarily be equated with evil. Life is subject to multiple, sometimes conflicting variables we can't control. Sometimes what seems like misfortune now turns out to be a blessing later. More importantly, we each have our individual wyrd and our ancestral wyrd. Wyrd is the sum total of every decision we have made or chose not to make, everything we've done or not done. Ordered by the Nornir, it intersects with the wyrd of those with whom we engage and is likewise impacted by the deeds of our ancestors. Sometimes misfortune results from ancestral debt that has traveled down to us,[6] or from our own poor choices, or sometimes just painful necessity. Dealing with it can strengthen our character. None of that is "evil." Wyrd is part of the natural—and divine—order. Evil is not part of that order. If the Gods are good, then evil cannot come from Them. It must, of necessity, be something external to that divinely ordained architecture. So if that is the case, what is it and where does it come from?

I was taught that whatever evil exists external to us, it has only those openings that we choose to give to it. This is why it is so important to cultivate virtue, to train ourselves to make the morally correct choices, as much as we can determine what those might be, as a habit, and to do so even when it is difficult (perhaps most especially when it's difficult). Virtue is something that we are absolutely capable of cultivating. Of all the ways in which we have free will, the choice to cultivate good character is the most powerful. That cultivation allows us to strengthen our soul matrix, just like working out at a gym strengthens our physical muscles. And just like eating well, getting enough sleep, and exercise bolster our resistance to illness, so too developing virtue bolsters our soul's resistance to evil.

It is not the Gods' job to instill in us a sense of morality or virtue. That is the job of philosophy, of our families, upbringing, and education—in short, in a properly ordered community, of our culture.[7] The Roman author A. Gellius wrote: *Dii immortales virtutem adprobare, non adhibere debent* ("The immortal Gods ought to support, not supply virtue," Gellius, *Noctes Atticae*, 1.6.8). We have our cosmologies, our sacred stories, the discipline of devotional work, the powerful tool of prayer, and our relationships with the Gods, the land, and ancestors, which, if properly ordered, impact everything else in our world. We shouldn't need our Gods to list for us everything it is right or wrong to do. Developing virtue comes down to behaving as the kind of people we would like best to be. That is on us. That is our work to do. The Gods will guide and support us in that endeavor, but we have to do that work, learning from our mistakes as we go. Living in a world the ethics and morality of which are not only quite different from what our traditions might teach, but in many cases destructive and diametrically opposed to traditional wisdom and devotion, we need to start the cultivation of virtue not by looking to our society's elders and teachers, but by first addressing our own brainwashing.

But there is something else I believe we must take into account when speaking of evil, what I call the Nameless, that malignant sentience which stands against the order the Gods have decreed. This is not directly a Heathen concept, but it is I think what truly lies at the core of the mythos of Ragnarok.[8] Other traditions, like ancient Egyptian/modern Kemetic or certain Native American religions, have a much better developed idea of the Nameless, but literacy came to the Northlands only with Christianity and it is difficult to untangle our surviving eschatological structures from the medieval Christian scribes who recorded them and their worldview. The Nameless is the evil external to cosmic Good. It is not the Jötnar. I want to say that again: it is *not* the Jötnar, who are themselves part of cosmic order. This is the malignancy that will jump at any chance to seep into our minds, twisting our perceptions, whispering in the darkness, cultivating despair, indolence, apathy, and hate. Without the work of having developed character and virtue, we are sitting ducks for it. This is why I believe that the maxim at the Oracle of Delphi is vitally crucial to us all: Know Thyself. We must know the pattern of our thoughts and emotions, our motivations, and above all else the lay of our inner landscape, the good, the bad, and the ugly, so that when genuine evil comes to whisper in our minds, to plunge us into darkness, to twist our perception and nurture ugliness in our souls, to cut us off from our Gods and the abundance of good They bring, we will recognize it as not being of us. If we can recognize it, we can resist it and cleanse ourselves of its miasma before we are changed by it for the worse.

We have free will. Even those of us bound in service to our Gods have free will to do the things that cultivate devotion and virtue or not, to serve graciously and willingly or not. Because of this we have the freedom to choose to let evil in, to nourish it, or not. Because the Gods have made us free, They aren't going to step in and stop us when we're opening the door to evil, whether from weakness or poor character, need, want, or a thousand other things. It is for us to choose. This is why regular devotional practice is so vital. It creates an environment in our hearts, minds, and spirits that is not conducive to evil. It affords us a greater chance of recognizing that which would pull us out of true with our Holy Powers and helps us foster the moral habits that develop a character capable of resisting the malignant. It is the same with honoring our ancestors. They are our first line of defense.

We might not recognize it at first. It might be that insidious whisper in the night that tells us what we're doing is for naught, whispering that there are no Gods to hear us, so why bother? I have looked into the eyes of people—thankfully not many—who were riddled, willingly, with its influence, and it was horrible to see. I've heard from many people who have in some way encountered what they conceived of as evil, something that tainted them, terrified them, and in some cases harmed them spiritually. What do you do when confronted with something like that?

I can only tell you what I was taught by a woman far more devout than I. When you are faced with evil, when you are standing in the presence of something foul and unholy, do not flinch or flee. Stand up. Look it right in the eye. Yield no space, and call upon your Gods. Surround yourself with that which is holy, articulate your acceptance and support of the divine order. Stand confidently in it. Root yourself in your devotion to the Gods and ancestors. Call upon Them and do not be afraid. Evil may be very good at tricking us into creating openings for it, but if we remember our relationships with the Gods, if we remember that we do not ever stand alone, that we always stand with thousands of ancestors ranked at our backs ready to protect us, then we have nothing to fear. Fear is the weapon it utilizes the most, but in the end, we must recognize that our Gods are stronger. And we must be aware that when we start feeling aversion to holy things, to our Gods, and to our dead, that this is a sign of infection.

We have a tendency as moderns to compartmentalize our devotional world into what we do before our shrines, out of sight. I've often encountered the attitude that one's practices are just a small part of one's life. (This is true not just of polytheisms but pretty much across the board in the modern world with all religions to some degree or another.) Unconsciously we treat our spiritual lives as a hobby, opening us up to the despair that is so much a part of the modern world. Doing devotion well, tending those relationships, means making one's internal landscape a place where gods and spirits might dwell. This in turn means being careful about what we expose ourselves to and choosing carefully those things we put into our heads. And this means learning to desire the right things, things that augment our devotional consciousness, that make us more receptive to the Gods and spirits rather than those things that entrain us away from Them. Living devoutly means allowing devotion to transform us from the inside out. Nothing in our contemporary world teaches us how to cultivate devotion.[9] In fact, what we too often see is the commodification of spirituality, rendered down to its most shallow components, together with suspicion of religion and disrespect for devotion. Therefore it's up to us to do this for ourselves.

CHAPTER 8

THE BASIC BLÓT

All denominations of Heathenry share in common the blót. Taken from an Old Norse word for "sacrifice," the term *blót* (pronounced to rhyme with *boat*) is used by modern Heathens to indicate a generic Heathen ritual. Indeed, it forms the foundation for all of Heathen worship, and many important tenets of practice and faith can be found in this relatively simple rite. The word *blót* has sometimes been thought to mean "to strengthen" (the Gods).[1] Given the reciprocal obligations of gift-giving among the Norse, it would follow that strengthening the Gods strengthened one's personal health, wealth, luck, and well-being, as well as that of one's kin. One of the most thorough descriptions of a blót can be found in Snorri Sturluson's Heimskringla:

It was an old custom, that when there was to be sacrifice all the bondes should come to the spot where the temple stood and bring with them all that they required while the festival of the sacrifice lasted. To this festival all the men brought ale with them; and all kinds of cattle, as well as horses, were slaughtered, and all the blood that came from them was called hlaut, and the vessels in which it was collected were called hlaut-vessels. Hlaut-staves were made, like sprinkling brushes, with which the whole of the altars and the temple walls, both outside and inside, were sprinkled over, and also the people were sprinkled with the blood; but the flesh was boiled into savoury meat for those present. The fire was in the middle of the floor of the temple, and over it hung the kettles, and the full goblets were handed across the fire; and he who made the feast, and was a chief, blessed the full goblets, and all the meat of the sacrifice. And first Odin's goblet was emptied for victory and power to his king; thereafter, Niord's and Freyja's goblets for peace and a good season. Then it was the custom of many to empty the brage-goblet;[2] and then the guests emptied a goblet to the memory of departed friends, called the remembrance goblet.[3]

. . . .

The standard ritual format within modern Heathenry is largely drawn from descriptions such as this. The motivation behind the blót comes from the Havamal and its exhortations toward gift-giving and sharing of wealth among the tribe. As we are given many good things by the Gods, so the blót provides an opportunity for us to show our gratitude and to give something back. The purpose of the blót is twofold: an opportunity for communion with the Gods and also a "folk-binding" ritual, bringing folk together in celebration and friendship, increasing their feeling of kinship, and strengthening the bonds of hospitality.

At its core, the blót is about sacrifice. The concept of sacrifice is one of the integral tenets of Heathenry. It is enshrined in our lore where we are called to remember Odin hanging on the Tree, in nine nights of agony, in exchange for the runes. It is essential to frith where the exchange of gifts, food, drink, and hospitality creates a bond of reciprocity between giver and receiver. This, perhaps more than any other practice, ethic, or virtue, sets Heathenry apart from Neo-Paganism: we commune with our Gods in part through an established system of gift-giving. The Havamal exhorts us to go often to our friends' homes and to exchange gifts. By doing so, a bond of affection and obligation is established. The blót provides the opportunity for just such an exchange with the Gods. Far from being self-serving bribery, it is a well-established ancient tradition wherein two parties enter into a web of duty, obligation, and—yes—affection, thereby also entering into a pact of frith (right order, harmony, peace). The blót invites the Gods to participate in the household and community, to come and be welcomed as honored guests with all that this entails to the Heathen mind.

Through the Sagas we do have surviving accounts of how a blót was performed. Let's examine the various parts of this ritual.

Folk gather.

Congregants come together at a designated time and place to honor the Gods. They may bring wine, food, and other offerings. If there is to be a feast, the preparations would take place at this time or slightly before.

The space is hallowed.

Once everyone is gathered and it is time for the rite to begin, the officiant hallows the space. Depending on one's denomination, this may be done by a sacred chant calling upon the protective power of the God Thor to banish all evil. Or it may be done by a mini-rite called a "Hammer Hallowing," which invokes the power of Thor's hammer to protect the sacred area. For one new to the religion or one performing a blót by him- or herself, carrying a candle around the ritual space and sincerely asking Thor to hallow and bless the space are perfectly acceptable and efficient.

The offerings (usually wine and food) are blessed. Folk may be sprinkled with wine in lieu of the sacrificial blood mentioned in the Sagas.

The officiant blesses the offerings and the feast. An evergreen sprig is dipped in the offering wine, and the congregants are sprinkled with the wine. Some may choose to omit this part of the rite if there is no attendant feast.

The Gods are called in invocation and prayer.

The officiant hails the Gods and Goddesses. There is no limit to how many Deities may be called, but usually blóts are either Deity-specific (such as a Woden blót, Frigga blót, etc.) or for some special occasion (baby blessing, holy day, etc.). One would not hail every single God and Goddess in the span of one blót.

A horn, symbolizing the Well of memory and fate, is passed around the gathered folk. People may offer prayers to the Gods, hail their ancestors, or boast of their own deeds.

Sometimes the horn will just be passed person to person; sometimes a woman of high regard and status within the group will carry the horn from person to person. The first time the horn is carried around, each person raises the horn and offers a prayer to a God or Goddess. The second time, each person may hail an ancestor. The third time, one may boast of deeds that have been accomplished. This threefold action is later expanded into the most sacred of all Heathen rituals: symbel.

If the rite includes a feast, it takes place at this point. Some of the food and drink is set aside for Vaettir (land spirits), ancestors, and Gods.

The officiant offers alcohol and part of the feast to the Gods, Vaettir and ancestors, placing it before the altar or pouring it out in a special bowl used only for ritual (a blessing bowl). The remainder of the feast is then shared among the participants. If there is no feast, wine is offered to the Gods, ancestors, and Vaettir with accompanying thanks.

Thanks are offered to the Gods, and the rite is adjourned.

The officiant gives thanks to the Gods and ancestors, and the remains of the wine, mead, or beer is poured out in offering. A prayer may be said in closing. I personally like to sing the Valkyrie's prayer from the Sigdrifumal in the Poetic Edda:

> *Hail to the Day, and Day's sons.*
> *Hail to Night and Her daughters.*
> *With loving eyes, look upon us here*
> *And bring victory.*
> *Hail to the Gods,*
> *Hail to the Goddesses,*
> *Hail to the mighty, fecund earth.*
> *Eloquence, wisdom, and native wit*
> *Bestow on Your children here.*
> *And healing hands while we live.*[4]

At this point, the rite is closed, and folk may mingle as they wish.

In the past, before Christianity spread across Europe, the average blót would generally have involved some sort of animal sacrifice. It was a communal feast. In some denominations of Heathenry, the word *blót* refers *only* to rites in which animal sacrifice takes place. In such rites, the animal, usually a swine or goat, sometimes poultry, is honored and treated with great solemnity. The space is hallowed with a sacred song, the Gods are invoked, the horn is passed among all participants, and then the animal is sacrificed cleanly and quickly, in as painless a manner as possible and with a blade. If the animal suffers in any way, it is a hideously bad omen. The blood of the animal is captured in the blót bowl and sprinkled on the attending participants, in an act of blessing. The ritual is then concluded. At this point, the animal is cleaned, cooked, and later served as part of a sacred feast. Every part of the animal must be eaten or consigned to a sacred fire as an offering to the Gods. Nothing is wasted. Such sacrifice is done only at very special occasions, such as Yule or Midsummer, and affects the luck of the entire tribe. Generic rituals, done to honor the Gods but without blood sacrifice, are called *fainings*.

It goes without saying that only someone trained and qualified as a blótere or sacrificial priest is qualified to actually do the sacrifice. This takes specific ritual training as well as practical training in the mechanics of clean butchering. If you want to give this to your Gods, contact a goði or gyðia trained in the practice and have them facilitate your blót. This is the holiest sacrament we have.

The concept of sharing food as a means of communing with the Gods may be found in nearly every religion. It is a very potent act. By entering into sacred space and sharing these things symbolically with our Gods, we are opening ourselves to being nourished by the Gods just as much as we are celebrating the blessings the Gods have given. When a blót involves the sacrifice of an animal and communal feast, it is commonly called *husel*, a word that early English Christians adopted for their own rite of communion.

Numerous things, including animals, might be sacrificed in the course of husels of old, and this holds true today. Certain animals tended to be associated with certain Deities (for example, boars for Frey, horses for Odin, and goats for Thor), and making such a sacrifice, which in most cases culminated in a feast, was yet another way of bringing the community together and of celebrating kinship and frith. Animal sacrifice is only practiced by a small minority of modern Heathens. It's far more common to simply cook up a roast purchased at the local supermarket. Of course other items might be offered as well. It is important to understand that, at its root, the word *sacrifice* means "to make sacred." It is not a matter of sacrificing for the sake of sacrifice alone, but of sacrificing in order to draw closer to the Gods—very much like giving a gift to a loved one.

By extending that metaphorical hand in welcome to the Gods, by gift-giving and throwing open the doors of our homes, hearts, and consciousness, we sanctify, we make sacred not only the dwelling in which we celebrate, but ourselves and that which is being offered as well. Therefore, the offering need not be an animal. Modern Heathens may offer anything from flowers to beer to food to volunteer work. It is the willingness to enter into a relationship with the Gods that is important.

Eric Wodening, in his article "Knowest How to Blót," points out that the Old English word *bletsian* ("to bless") may be related etymologically to the Norse word *blót*. Both have connotations of "to bless with blood." In the description of a blót quoted previously, the gathered folk are sprinkled with sacrificial blood. This hallowing with blood is highly potent symbolically. Our connection to our folk, our kin, and our ancestors is one forged not only in spirit, but in blood. The Hamingja (one's personal, ancestral luck) is passed on through the blood. And we are said to be blood kin to the Gods, descended from and tutored by Them. The Eddic poem "Rigsthula" tells the story of how the God Heimdall wandered disguised among humanity, fathering children on every woman who showed him hospitality. Some scholars believe that this may have actually been Odin, not Heimdall, for it is well attested in the lore that Odin likes the ladies; however, modern Heathens generally agree that humanity is the kin of Heimdall. This ritualized sprinkling with blood can be seen as a vivid reminder of that sacred connection.

The hallowing is an awakening of memory and spiritual duty. The same could be said for lifting the horn, for though not every blót will include an animal sacrifice and feast, every blót should include that mindful awareness that each of us stands as an ongoing link in a chain of ancestors stretching back to the beginning, and are the ancestors upon whose shoulders those who follow us will stand. It is that mindfulness—that connection with the Gods and our honored dead—that creates the blót. All else, however potent a symbol, is merely a reminder of that essential fact.

A Note on Animal Sacrifice

It's easy to forget how disconnected our society is from its food cycles, from offertory traditions, from life and death, and from the ways of our ancestors. People don't die at home anymore. They get shipped off to hospitals and hospice to make that passage, which denies us contact with them in their last days and with the process surrounding their dying. Unlike our ancestors, we buy our food pasteurized, sanitized, sterilized, and sealed in plastic. There are kids today that don't know hamburgers come from cows. Disconnection seems too mild a word.

Sacrifice is *essential* to polytheistic religions. But how many of us have grown up slaughtering our own food? That separation from the origins of what nourishes us leaves no place for the act of slaughtering an animal either practically or sacrally. Even for those devoted to restoring our traditions, this particular tradition can make some of us cringe. But across the board, to one degree or another, this was the accepted view of our ancestors and of religious traditions that sustained their people for generations upon generations: Without butchery, the slaughter of animals, there is no piety. There is no religion. There is no being in right relationship with one's Gods. Railing against the necessity of such sacrifice is just one more way that we assume we know better than our ancestors. It's one more way that we assume the death of our traditions was some sort of moral "progress." It's what my colleague Raven Kaldera, in our book *Northern Tradition for the Solitary Practitioner*, called "Urdummheit," the idea that our ancestors were stupid.

I have found over the past couple of years that in some sections of modern polytheism even the idea of giving any offerings is problematic. After all, it does highlight that we and our feelings are not the central point of the religious equation, doesn't it? If I could see our contemporary polytheisms nurture any attitude in their followers, it would be that we cannot give too much to our Gods. But our culture says "Don't waste that" when one is about to lay out an offering of food or drink, as if giving tangibly to one's Gods and ancestors is a waste. We as a culture think ourselves better than our pious ancestors, an arrogance unthinkable to the ancient mind.

Sacrifice is the most solemn and sacred of all rituals. It renews, restores, and nourishes in a way that no other offering can. Granted, not every Deity requires blood sacrifice, but many, many do. The role of the sacrificial priest is an awesome responsibility. One must learn the mechanics of slaughter adeptly, so that the animal in no way suffers. One must develop (or have an assistant with this skill) the ability to communicate with and soothe the animal. It is important that the animal suffer neither pain nor terror. They are fulfilling a tremendously sacred role, the apex of what their own wyrd may be, and participating in this cycle in a way denied us as people. It is an act worthy of recognition, respect, and care. This type of priest must learn all the necessary prayers and purificatory rites required before, during, and after, both for oneself and for the animal. It is necessary to develop a very strong connection with one's ancestors and one's lineage because the power released during a sacrifice is enormous and the broken threads of our traditions, imperfectly restored, may not be able to sustain the force of that which once would have nourished a living community. Not everyone is meant to be a sacrificial priest. Even though I've done this work for years, I still divine before each and every ritual involving blood sacrifice to make certain that I am cleared to serve in this capacity. Our ancestors had the option in many cases of going to a temple, purchasing an animal, and having the sacrifice done for them. One should not attempt a sacrifice without proper training and, for the first few rituals, oversight. There's no room for error here.

I will always divine before planning such a sacrifice, even if I am sure one is desired. Maybe it isn't. Maybe I'm wrong. I let the Gods and ancestors speak for themselves. I will divine, and if there is any further question, I will see another diviner for absolute impartiality. I will also divine just before the sacrifice is to be performed and immediately after to make sure that it was accepted. Well in advance, I will seek the Gods' counsel on whether the offering is meant to be cooked up to feed and nourish a community, or to be given in total immolation to the Gods. Is it meant to be buried or disposed of in a particular place? What do the Gods wish? This is one of the purposes of divination, to give the Gods a chance to convey Their wishes. Even if I am certain that I have heard and understood a Deity directly, I will still confirm with divination. I do this not to question the Deity, but in deference to my flawed human understanding. I do not want *my* errors of comprehension or interpretation to mar the process.

I give thanks for those clergy, of all our various traditions, who have dedicated themselves to the task of learning and restoring these rituals and protocols. I give thanks to the Gods and ancestors for those who teach and those who do, for those who take up the knife so that our Gods may have the offerings best suited to Their glory. I give thanks for our sacrificial priests (and yes, I am one, but I give thanks to those who taught me, to those from whom I continue to learn, and to the Gods for Their continued patience). I give thanks to the farmers who provide the feast for the Powers. I give thanks to the fire that carries the fullness of the sacrifice away via immolation, and I give thanks to those who dress and prepare the sacrifices for feasting, when that is appropriate. I give thanks to the knife and the ones who craft it. I give thanks for the animals, and I give thanks for the land that catches the blood as it is spilled. These things are sacred. The hands of the sacrificial priest are sacred and the process and cycle itself. For these things, I am grateful. I know how they nourish wyrd. I know what it means to restore these rites after two thousand years of our ritual places lying fallow.

Personal Faining

This is a basic outline of how I do personal faining; it's important to remember that any sacred ritual needs to leave room for fluidity of experience. Before the rite begins, I set up an altar. Like many Heathen clergy, I maintain an altar all the time, but before any rite, I may change its design and make it more Deity-specific.

Before every ritual or blót, the ritual room is purified both by being physically cleaned and smudged with *recels* (incense). Because the Goddess Frigga is specifically associated with a strong, hallowed home, I have created an incense that is dedicated to Her and Her 12 handmaidens—all powerful Goddesses in Their own right.

Purification and Protection Incense

Start with 7 tablespoons of white sandalwood.

For Frigga, the Allmother,
  add: 1 tablespoon of rosemary.

For Fulla, Her sister and most cherished companion,
  add: 1 tablespoon of mistletoe.

For Saga, Goddess of lore, history, and sacred stories,
  add: 1 tablespoon of hyssop.

For Eir, the Divine Physician,
  add: 1 tablespoon of mullein.

For Var, who hears all sacred vows,
  add: 1 tablespoon of mint.

For Hlín, who defends and protects,
  add: 1 tablespoon of ash.

For Vor, who knows all secrets,
  add: 1 tablespoon of mugwort.

For Sjöfn, who inclines the heart to love,
   add: 1 tablespoon of linden.

For Lofn, who helps loved ones come together against all opposition,
   add: 1 tablespoon of vetivert.

For Gefion, Goddess of abundance,
   add: 1 tablespoon of juniper.

For Gná, Frigga's speedy messenger,
   add: 1 tablespoon of comfrey.

For Syn, who wards and shields,
   add: 1 tablespoon of alkanet.

For Snotra, Goddess of graciousness and frith,
   add: 1 tablespoon of elder.

Blend all of the herbs together thoroughly and store the mixture in an airtight jar. This is an excellent cleansing and purification incense. I personally like to cleanse my ritual room before and after any rite, particularly if guests attended. It's good metaphysical hygiene. This incense is burned over small charcoal pieces that can be purchased at any metaphysical or occult supply store.

If there is to be a feast, I make all the necessary preparations a couple of hours before the rite. Several bottles of mead or wine are uncorked and set before the altar.

1. Hallowing

I use Thorsson's Hammer Hallowing[5] in Old Norse or the Ealdriht Weonde[6] song in Old English. I love the resonance of the languages. One might also simply light two candles on the altar and ask Thor to bless and ward the room.

II. Prayer to the Ancestors and Offering to the Vaettir

I hail my honored dead, mothers and fathers generations back.

I hail your triumphs and honor your sorrows.

I remember you and will speak your names with welcome in my home. For I am here, strong and whole and proud because of your struggles and sacrifices. I carry your blood in my veins and your courage in my heart. [Name specific ancestors], I remember you and hail you here tonight. [Pour out wine or mead in offering.] I offer this to you in remembrance.

[Pour out more wine.] I offer this to the Vaettir and ask that you lend your blessings to this rite that we are about to perform. Hail and welcome.

III. Prayer to Odin

Allfather, I ask for Your blessings.

Breathe into me, Oh God of gainful counsel.

Nourish me, Wish-Giver, that I might know You more fully and well.

Remove any blockages that might keep me from being truly open to Your presence.

I hail You, God of wisdom, cunning, and inspiration.

Wondrous Healer, Nourisher, Welcome One,

Be welcome in my life, my home, my heart. Master of the Tree, I sacrifice to You

My fears, my doubt, my hesitation.

Breathe into me.

Open me, Wisest Lord.

I will seek You with the fervor with which You sought the runes.

Be my mead, be my joy, be the prize at the end of my seeking.

Hail, Allfather, Woden, Wondrous Lord.[7]

At this point, aquavit, which I personally associate with Odin, is tasted and poured out in the blessing bowl for Him.

IV. Faining

The horn is filled with mead or wine and passed around to each person in the group several times. The first time, Odin is honored. After that, other Gods, Goddesses, and finally individual ancestors may be hailed. Sometimes folks may choose to tell stories about specific ancestors or relate experiences with the Gods that moved them deeply. If one does not own a drinking horn, a chalice may be used instead.

V. Feasting

The food is brought out, blessed in the name of Frigga and Odin, and shared among the participants, after first offering sizable portions to Odin, the Vaettir, and ancestors.

VI. Thanksgiving

Odin may be thanked extempore, the Vaettir and ancestors are thanked, and any remaining alcohol is given to them. The altar candles are blown out, the rite ended, and participants dispersed. The contents of the blessing bowl should be poured out in the garden or, for city dwellers, outside. (It can be poured down the sink in a pinch, but personally, I feel this lacks finesse.)

After everyone is gone, the ritual room should again be purified in some way.

This basic format for the faining process can be expanded upon as one gains more confidence and ritual technique. Of course, variations may be encountered from Kindred to Kindred, and one can be incredibly creative in how one structures one's rituals to the Gods. The important thing is to enter into the rite with mindfulness, respect, devotion, and a conscious desire to honor the Gods. As a rite, blót or faining may stand alone or as part of a larger celebration. It is the foundation of Heathen worship.

CHAPTER 9

SYMBEL

One of the holiest and most significant of Heathen rites is called *symbel* (which can also be spelled *sumbel*). Symbel is essentially a rite of libation. Alcohol (or a suitable non-alcoholic substance, if desired) is passed around and consumed by the attendees while honoring the Gods and calling to mind the luck and deeds of the gathered folk. Symbel serves many purposes: it is a folk-binding ritual; it reinforces the duties and worth of every attendee; and it celebrates Heathen values and heroic culture. This rite can be seen as the quintessence of tribal unity. Its importance in Heathen liturgy and communion cannot be overestimated. So integral was symbel to Germanic culture, that accounts were even incorporated into Christian texts such as the Heliand, or Saxon Gospel. Here, we find the Last Supper referred to as "the last meadhall feast with the warrior-companions," and the atmosphere of the wedding of Canaan is described in terms that directly hearken back to the atmosphere of the meadhall: "The conviviality of the earls in the drinking hall was a beautiful sight, and the men on the benches had received a very high level of bliss . . . "[1]

Obviously the rite of symbel continued to hold power even over the Christian mind well after conversion. Much as certain Gods and Goddesses later became revered as Christian saints,[2] this ritual was a unifying thread between Heathen society and that which followed it.

There are four primary parts to a good symbel, each of which will be discussed:

Hallowing

The Fulls

Beots and gielps

Gift-giving

Symbel is a ritual of mindfulness in both speech and action. Each sacred action serves to strengthen the unity and interconnected luck between all participants. It is important to remember that, to the Heathen mind, luck is part of the soul, a living thing that may be nourished and strengthened by mindful care or damaged by careless speech, ill-conceived actions, and cowardly nonaction. In symbel, Heathens are called to remember those past deeds which strengthened their luck and brought might to the group, and they are called to rise above those deeds that may have been less shining. It is an opportunity to commit oneself to personal betterment. Symbel is, above all else, a ritual of fate-weaving. It is a celebration of frith, community, and commitment to future evolution. Though it bears some cursory resemblance to blót and faining in its initial structure, it is far more complex and tightly ordered.

Examples of symbel permeate the surviving lore, giving modern practitioners a fairly clear idea of how the rite was practiced in pre-Christian Northern Europe. We find examples not only within the Anglo-Saxon, but in Scandinavian and Norse texts as well. The most well-known and clear-cut example of symbel in the lore occurs in *Beowulf.*

Then a bench was cleared, room made in the hall for
    the gathered warriors, standing in a troop;
the courageous men took their seats,
proud in their strength; a thane did his office, carried in his hands
    the gold ale-flagons, poured bright mead. At times the scop sang,
bright-voiced in Heorot; there was joy of warriors . . .

Here we see that symbol was held inside, in the feasting hall, after the primary feast, and that the ritual incorporated both praise songs and sacred speech. The nobility of the rite is emphasized, as well as its importance to the gathered warriors. Later on, we are given even greater insight into the nature of this ritual:

The noble lady gave the first cup,
filled to the brim, to the king of the Danes, bade him rejoice
    in this mead-serving, beloved by his people, he took it
    happily, victory-famed king, the hall-cup and feast.
The lady of the Helmings walked through the hall, offered the
    jeweled cup to veterans and youths, until the time came that
    courteous queen, splendid in rings, excellent in virtues,
came to Beowulf, brought him the mead. She
    greeted him well, gave thanks to God,
wise in her words, that her wish came to pass, that
    she might expect help against crimes
from any man. He accepted the cup,
battle-fierce warrior, from Wealhtheow's hand, then
    made a speech, eager for combat . . .[3]

This excerpt illustrates several important parts of a traditional symbol—most notably, the important role women play in structuring the ritual and maintaining a sense of the sacred.[4] We also see that symbol included mighty boasts. In fact, though there may be minor variations from Kindred to Kindred, the basic outline of a symbel may be broken down into the following parts:

Hallowing

In many cases, the rite begins with a ritual blessing, either the Hammer Hallowing or the Weonde. In other cases, this is omitted in favor of a simple declaration that symbel has now begun. The defining aspect of symbel is that it is a ritual of mindful, sacred speech. What is said becomes active fate. What is spoken directly impacts the luck of the individual, as well as of the tribe as a whole. Verbally intoning that symbel has begun can be as effective as any type of hallowing. Generally, folk are seated according to their position or rank within the Kindred or tribe before this hallowing takes place. At this time, the host or hostess may also give a brief introductory speech, stating the purpose of the gathering, praising the group's accomplishments, expressing joy at being united with everyone again, or otherwise speaking in a manner that eloquently sets the mood and tone of the ritual to come.

The *valkyrie* (Old Norse) or *ealu bora* (Old English) pours the beverage of choice into the ritual horn. She first offers the horn to the host or hostess and later carries it around to the assembled guests, hailing them with wise words and offering them a draught.

In many respects, the ealu bora is the most important person in the entire symbel. In traditional Heathenry, this role is *always* fulfilled by a woman. At first, this may seem like a gender bias that casts the woman in a subservient role, but nothing could be further from the truth. Germanic culture has always regarded women as being innately holy. Women were believed to have a special connection to the numinous, and many were said to possess the gift of prophecy. Tacitus records with some surprise the high regard in which the Germanic tribes held their women, particularly esteemed seeresses such as the renowned Veleda, who foretold the defeat of the Roman legions.[5]

Women were connected to fate and the structuring of wyrd in a way that no man could hope to be. In traditional Germanic culture, one of the primary feminine arts was that of spinning and weaving, which was absolutely necessary to the smooth running of a household. There were no stores from which to buy one's clothing. Everything was made by hand at home, usually under the auspices of the lady of the house, if not by her own hand. The ancient Heathens early on recognized a symbolic parallel between the mortal arts of spinning and weaving and the actions of the Nornir who spun and wove layers of fate, and it is as Their representative that a woman presides over symbel. As the Nornir weave strands of fate, so women weave frith during symbel, ensuring that the oaths and boasts are layered properly into the tribal orlog. The ealu bora, deciding the order in which the horn is passed from person to person, also reinforces social structure and tribal hierarchy. It is the wisdom and power of the woman that makes the symbel a holy rite.

In symbel we see a balance of *worth* and *frith*—of might and right order. In many orthodox denominations of Heathenry, men are said to predominantly manifest worth, and women, frith. This does not mean that a man cannot be a peace-weaver or a woman manifest sacred might. We are discussing general sacred roles patterned largely after the Allfather and Allmother, both of course mighty in Their own right. Because one of the main actions during symbel is the taking of oaths and the boasting of honorable deeds over the horn (all acts of worth), it is all the more necessary to have the rite ordered by one embodying frith and that unique connection to Hamingja and fate. That being said, the horn-bearer should be inconspicuous. She should not make herself the focus of the ritual. The horn and what it symbolizes—the communion of the Gods, ancestors, and people within a tradition—is what is important. There may be occasions where no women are present, though this is rare. If symbel cannot be postponed until a woman is able to attend, the horn should be passed by a man who has a strong connection to one of the Goddesses. Certain denominations will find this unacceptable and would simply not hold symbel. Other, more liberal denominations do not adhere much to the tradition of having only women pass the horn.

A word should be said about the prevalence of alcohol in Heathen rituals. The passing of a horn is highly symbolic. The horn represents the Well of Wyrd, Urðabrunnr, into which all fate and memory eventually flow. The waters of this Well nourish the World Tree, and both the Well and the Tree are tended by Urð, the Norn of all that has been and all that will become. During symbel, in sacred thought, the Well and the horn become one, and the ealu bora becomes the embodiment of Urð. This is why words spoken over the horn during this rite create strands of fate that are then ordered into the collective wyrd. The use of alcohol, generally mead, is representative of Oðroerir, the mead of poetry, eloquence, and ecstatic inspiration. Verbal eloquence and poetic skill were highly prized among the Germanic and Scandinavian peoples. Poets were regarded with an almost sacred reverence. Additionally, the liquid in the horn symbolizes the healing power of the waters of Urðabrunnr. Of course, nonalcoholic beverages may also be used, and many Kindreds, particularly those in which there are folk in recovery, choose to have two horns carried by the valkyrie: one with mead or wine and another with juice. If it is the best that can be offered, there is nothing inherently wrong with filling a horn with plain drinking water.

The Fulls

Before bearing the horn to anyone else, the valkyrie passes it first to the *symbelgerefa*, the host or hostess, saluting him or her with carefully thought-out words. The symbelgerefa, upon accepting the horn, makes a series of three prayers, or *fulls*, and thereby sets the tone for the entire symbel.

The first full consists of prayers or hails to the Gods. Here, the symbelgerefa usually honors the group's (be it Kindred, Mot, or Maethel) three most popular Gods or Goddesses. For instance, my Kindred is given to Woden primarily. Let's say that the Maethel that we are part of is under Ingvi Frey's protection, and as a Kindred, we have dedicated the year's work to Eir. Therefore, at a Kindred symbel,

I would most likely hail first Woden, then Frey, and then Eir, offering a toast to each. At a Tribal symbel, Frey would be hailed first.

Next, the symbelgerefa hails and toasts the luck, or Maegen of the gathered group. He or she may call to mention specific deeds and even speak briefly about the history of the group and everything that has passed since the last symbel. This is not meant to be a tediously long toast, but a concise and vivid reconstruction of those actions that have had the most potent influence on the group as a whole, a time to call the collective Maegen into the spotlight, putting it on the table, so to speak, in full metaphorical view of the gathered folk, Gods, and Nornir.

The third full is commonly called the *bragafull* and usually consists of boasts for the group's upcoming goals and plans of action. The symbelgerefa openly discusses his or her plans for the group's upcoming season. Goals are set into motion, verbally and esoterically laid into the warp and weft of the group wyrd. This is a very important part of the ritual, for what is spoken over the horn becomes woven inexorably into being and fate and carries with it a definite obligation. Failure to fulfill oaths and boasts thus made can lead to a weakening of might and luck for everyone concerned. It is, in many ways, equivalent to spiritual *devolution*.

After the symbelgerefa has made the requisite fulls, the ealu bora carries the horn around to each person gathered, usually in order of rank. Less hierarchical Kindreds may simply pass the horn as in blót: clockwise around the gathered folk, but always to and from the hand of the valkyrie. The first round is given completely to the ancestors and is called the *Minni-horn*, or horn of memory. In later rounds, as the horn is being passed, each person may hail friends, ancestors, and kinsman.

Unlike a faining, which is specifically oriented toward Gods, symbel is folk-oriented. It brings everything full circle. Whereas a blót or faining has as its primary purpose honoring the Gods, in symbel, the ultimate goal is binding the folk together, increasing their collective luck, and weaving new collective wyrd. While the Gods and Goddesses may certainly be hailed in the various rounds, it is just as common to hail friends, family, and the honored dead.

Beots and Gielps

The horn is usually passed several times around the gathered folk. The first time, as mentioned previously, kinsman and friends are hailed. During the later rounds, one may continue to do this, or conversely, one may choose to make a beot or gielp.

A *beot* is an oath, or sacred promise, made in the presence of Gods and kin. It is often a vow to perform some deed or undertake some specific work that will bring honor to oneself and one's Kindred. For example, at the Kindred symbel on Yule of 2003, I made a beot to complete a book of devotionals to Woden within the year. It was to be a gift to Him, and this vow was completed in July 2004.[6] As Pollington points out, calling a beot and gielp a *vow* or *boast* does not truly capture the power of uttering these ritual words.[7] They were incantations, a conscious, active structuring of one's personal fate. In fact, they may be seen as a way of challenging fate and improving one's lot. One's Maegen or Hamingja may be strengthened by fulfilling difficult oaths. Pollington goes on to point out that the word *beot* is "derived from *bi-hat* 'calling' (*hatan* 'to call, to name')" and it is connected to the "Germanic notion of single-combat and dueling."[8]

A *gielp* is a boast of past deeds. It is of utmost importance never to exaggerate or speak falsely when making either a gielp or a beot. This is not a time for overly prideful bragging, but a time to honestly and sincerely recount those ways in which one contributed to the good of the whole. The Havamal states that:

> *Cattle die, kinsmen die, the self must also die, but glory never dies,*
> *for the man who is able to achieve it.*
> *Cattle die, kinsmen die, The self must also die;*
> *I know one thing which never dies: The*
> *reputation of each dead man.*[9]

This excerpt brilliantly illustrates the warrior ethos of the Arch-Heathens, one that is being resurrected today. One's *gefrain* (good name or reputation), one's deeds, and the work of one's hands are of utmost importance to the modern Heathen mind. They are the measure of a man or woman, which is allowed to shine forth in symbel.

Every gielp or beot is woven directly into the fabric of wyrd. They are powerful and binding both in the eyes of the Gods and in the flow of wyrd. A broken oath or a misspoken gielp can have negative repercussions for all involved—even those who only witnessed the ill-chosen words. Ensuring that no ill consequences befall the group from poorly spoken words and acting to counterbalance the force of the speaker's will is the role of the *Thyle*. The Thyle maintains the order and integrity of all words spoken within symbel and may challenge anyone's gielps or beots without breaking the frith. In fact, in symbel, the Thyle is instrumental in maintaining frith, which, after all, is not just harmony and peace, but right order as well. The role of the Thyle is usually maintained by the man or woman most knowledgeable in lore, tribal customs, Kindred history, and ritual structure. It is the *obligation* of the Thyle to challenge any toast, oath, or boast not based in honesty and integrity. The Thyle is the one person in all of symbel who ensures that nothing untoward is laid into the communal wyrd. He or she guards and maintains the luck-weaving, thereby removing this burden from the symbelgerefa and ealu bora for the duration of the ritual.

Gift-giving

During the third round of passing the horn, the symbelgerefa and/or the lord/lady of the Maethel or hall may choose to bestow gifts on their gathered folk. In Anglo-Saxon and Scandinavian society, the lord was a ring-giver, the lady, a loaf-giver. They bestowed gifts and nourishment on their folk in exchange for loyalty, friendship, and service. These gifts were marks of trust and the reciprocal relationship maintained by everyone within the social hierarchy. Though in some modern symbels everyone exchanges gifts, historically and in more traditional denominations of Heathenry, it is only those in the leadership position who bestow gifts on the gathered folk. Each gift carries with it reciprocal obligations of loyalty and friendship and is a token of esteem and honor[10] and is imbued with the luck of the group. Gifts are given to each person in order of their rank and social station.

After the third round, the horn may be passed as many more times as desired. Songs may be sung, stories told, and poems recited in place of toasts or beots or gielps. Though a solemn ritual, symbel should not be devoid of joy and laughter. It is a celebration of everything that makes a Kindred or Maethel a community. At the end of symbel, the remaining alcohol should be poured into a *blótorc*, or blessing bowl. The symbelgerefa formally announces that symbel has come to an end and may choose to offer thanks to the three Gods hailed at the beginning of symbel. After this, folk are free to disperse. Someone, either a priest or the ealu bora, takes the blessing bowl and pours its contents into the earth, in offering to the Gods, ancestors, and Vaettir.

This is the full, most formal type of symbel. Variations on this rite abound, some more formal, some less. What doesn't change is the importance and solemnity of the words spoken over the horn, promises made, community honored, Gods hailed, and threads of wyrd woven deeply in Urda's Well. One doesn't have to follow this format. Devotion comes in many forms and ritual is a creative act. This style is, however, what one will most often find in Heathen liturgy.

CHAPTER 10

PERSONAL DEVOTIONS

S piritual opening is difficult, a process that demands all the vigilance of a master warrior and the patience of a master gardener. And most frightening of all, it is a process that we ourselves seldom control or even comprehend. Opening to the ineffable presence of the Divine can be terrifying. It strips us away from all that is safe, comfortable, and known. It challenges us to be better than we are, better than anything in our spiritually bereft world tells us to be. An open connection to the Gods is a prize worth struggling for, but hard-won. In a world filled with moral relativism, situational ethics, and endless distractions, it is also a gift easily lost. Our sacred stories point the way for us, mapping out a road both exhilarating and frightening in its immensity. The Gods, by Their own struggles, show us where and how to go, as in the story of Odin journeying to Yggdrasil and sacrificing Himself by spear and rope, for nine nights of agony, until wisdom is revealed to Him.

Our forebears lived in a world that made room for mystical experience, a world where the Gods and Goddesses were easily and openly honored. We do not. Often, we must struggle on alone, without the presence of a spiritual community or supportive folk. What is to keep us from despair? How do we fight to bring the holy into our lives? They key may lie in an examination of the word *holy*. It comes from the Anglo-Saxon *halig*, meaning "to make whole or healthy" (ultimately the word derives from the Proto-Indo-European root *kailo*, from which *hale*, *whole*, *health*, and *hail* are drawn). True health is not dependent on the body and mind alone; there must be emotional and spiritual health, as well. Spiritual wholeness is maintained by devotional practices that nurture our connection with the Divine. Our awakening spirits can be likened to seeds buried deep in rich, dark earth. They must be cared for and nourished with water, sunlight, and proper care in order to grow and thrive, as we must learn to sustain ourselves through disciplined practice.

Our piety, our regard for the Gods and the respect with which we treat Them, should permeate every aspect of our lives and define our ethics and goals. It is the rule against which everything else must be measured, if we are to truly nourish holiness and devotional consciousness in ourselves. This means not doing that which will diminish us as spiritual beings, not sating every pleasure or desire, but instead looking at the larger picture, the larger tapestry of one's life, soul, and purpose. It means doing what is right, even if it means standing up and confronting a wrong. There is an old saying: God is in the details. It's from such seemingly small, insignificant things that our spiritual integrity can be forged or broken. Such discipline, such care, is largely alien to us in our dominant culture. Indeed, we are often taught exactly the opposite. It is all the more necessary then that we take pains to cultivate such mindfulness within ourselves, drawing our inspiration from wherever we can and seeking out like-minded individuals. There is no greater work that we shall ever do. This cannot be emphasized enough; the occasional ritual or reading of lore is simply not enough. Spiritual health, that which enables us to maintain a strong connection to the Gods, must be an ongoing practice.

There is a medieval proverb that goes *"Lex orandi, lex credendi"*: the rule of prayer precedes the rule of belief. Prayer is fundamental, the first and most important building block in the road to spiritual health. It precedes everything else. It's also an act of immense courage. Prayer has the potential to change everything. It opens us to the experience of the Gods like nothing else can. It nurtures our relationship with Them as courtship nurtures the relationship between lovers. It cannot be overestimated. There is a reciprocity about this seemingly simple act. Prayer is an acknowledgment of one's willingness to accept responsibility for acting as cocreators with the Gods in our lives. This is a surrender; it brings us to the point of release, but only of those blockages and doubts that keep us from truly being all that we can be. We surrender those things that keep us from standing in the source of our personal power, that keep us from being spiritually healthy or whole, and we surrender those things that keep us from truly loving and knowing the Gods.

With prayer goes meditation. As prayer allows us to speak to the Gods from the heart, so meditation puts us in the proper frame of mind to truly listen to Their response. There are many types of meditation, but the first and, in my opinion, one of the most powerful meditations that one can begin with is *shrine work*. As human beings, we crave the sacred. We crave a palpable connection with the Divine. Nowhere is this more obvious than in the nearly universal practice of creating shrines. You see them in one form or another in every culture. And in times of great tragedy or stress, they often spring up automatically. Shrines create a nexus of spiritual focus, a reservoir of power to guide the dead to their ancestral halls. Shrine work is instinctual. It is healing. We create them in our homes without even realizing it, gathering those symbols that recall to us the sacredness of life. They are a source of connection, reconnection, and comfort.

Setting up a personal shrine is simplicity itself. In fact, as one's spiritual practice grows, any flat space becomes fair game. Shrines have this amazing tendency to grow! The entire process of creating a shrine makes a statement that you are consciously inviting a God or spirit into your life, that you are opening a door and extending an invitation. Place on a shrine those things symbolic of important places in your spiritual landscape, those things that call to mind the bounty and blessings of the Gods. Pray before it regularly, light candles, and meditate, for a shrine should be a living thing reflecting the spiritual evolution of its creator. There is nothing worse than seeing a shrine lying stagnant and in disarray. Set aside time each day to talk with the Gods, even if it is only for ten minutes. This is the way to begin working those spiritual muscles. Ritual work is important as well, but not everyone has the means to immediately begin there. It can be too intimidating. Many people, instead of seeing ritual as a process through which the experience of the Divine is internalized, get caught up with preconceptions of static ceremony and dull repetition; or they worry about not "doing things right." Ritual is what the devotee makes of it, and learning to pray well and center one's life around the Gods is an excellent place to begin. All else will, in time, flow naturally from that beginning.

One often-neglected aspect of spiritual growth and development is volunteer work. We are all interconnected. We have a responsibility to work, in whatever capacity we can, for the well-being of our neighbors. By giving of our time and effort, we are given the powerful opportunity to become vessels of divine energy and compassion, and we ourselves are strengthened spiritually. It also helps maintain a certain perspective when in the more painful throes of the spiritual descent. Giving back, contributing, and making one's community stronger are a vital and necessary part of one's spiritual development. It takes us out of ourselves, removes us, ever so slightly, from our culture-induced narcissism. It can be, in many cases, the best therapy in the world.

Part of the process of spiritual emergence involves clearing out emotional and psychic dreck, cleansing one's space and one's self. Most ancient religions had some laws of ritual purity for those who maintained their temples and shrines, and I'm sure we've all heard the old saying "Cleanliness is next to Godliness." Well, there's some truth to that. It's more than physical cleansing, though. It is often necessary to cleanse oneself etherically as well. But the effect of such techniques as fumigation, cleansing baths, floor washes, and the like—magical or psychological—does aid in putting one in the proper frame of mind for spiritual work. They help us center ourselves and purge extraneous and unwanted energies and influences from our unconscious mind.

The easiest thing to do is to take a cleansing bath. I have often found it helpful to do special baths along with prayers for a certain number of nights. For instance, nine is Odin's sacred number. If I feel the need to clean away blockages in my relationship with Him or simply want to open more fully to His energy, I will mix up an Odin bath using herbs associated in Nordic and Anglo-Saxon lore with Him and then take a cleansing bath for nine consecutive nights, often utilizing the same prayer each night as I bathe. It is powerfully effective. Cleansing baths are quite common in the Hoodoo tradition of the American South and in the Afro-Caribbean traditions, where practitioners have raised it to a high ritual art. There's no reason, however, that we can't also benefit from such a tradition. There is evidence that cleansing baths were part of European folk practices as well.[1] For those uncomfortable with practices not specifically noted in the lore, smoking oneself with burning recels, such as mugwort, may be used in place of the cleansing bath. Or even better, use a sauna. The Anglo-Saxon medical texts make reference to this practice, and these texts draw from the healing knowledge of pre-Christian Heathen culture.

When I feel the need for a major cleansing, I usually turn to the Goddess Frigga. She is extremely no-nonsense. Those who honor Frigga as their patroness often joke about the initial requirement She demands: housecleaning. I think the reason behind this is more esoteric than one might initially think. Frigga is, in many respects, a power broker. Cleaning removes clutter and blockages, allowing a free flow of vital energy necessary for health, abundance, and luck to blossom. Just as we cleanse ourselves, our homes should be given the same care. Regular floor washes, smudging, and even keeping glasses of water with a bit of ammonia in each room, changing them weekly, all encourage positive energy in the home. Fortunately, both floor washes and sacred baths are very simple to make. Here's a basic example:

Frigga Cleansing Bath

In a large soup pot mix together the following:

1 cup each of: rosemary, basil, cinnamon (sticks are fine), lavender, chamomile, rue, sage, and fresh-squeezed lime juice.[2]

Add 2–3 gallons of spring water and bring to a boil. Remove from heat. Let sit until cool, then cover and refrigerate.

For seven consecutive days, take a soothing bath, adding a cup of sea salt to the water. *After* you bathe, pour 2 cups of the herbal mixture (strained into a container) over your body. This is the traditional way to take a cleansing bath. First you take a regular bath, *then* you pour the cleansing mixture over your head and body. As you do so, ask Frigga to cleanse you of any blockages or negativity that may be holding you back spiritually. To make a floor wash, simply add one cup of ammonia to the blend and add it to your bucket of mop water. This need only be done once, not seven consecutive days.

Practices such as this, though simple, involve all our senses. I am an extremely kinetic person, so I prefer those techniques that incorporate not only sight (a beautiful altar) or sound (singing a prayer), but also smell, feeling, and at times, movement. I strongly believe that devotional work should speak not only to the mind but that it should be a full-body experience. So incorporate regular cleansing into your spiritual routine, even if only a weekly housecleaning and smudging with sage or asperging with an infusion of basil or marjoram around the perimeter of each room (both are said to bring happiness and peace). This is good preventive medicine. It's like taking a daily vitamin. It keeps sluggish and unhealthy energies away. The same can be said of using a Tibetan bowl to smudge a room or playing sacred music before meditation or ritual to "set the mood." The process of spiritual emergence is an ongoing fight against entropy.

These are tools at our disposal to give us the upper hand against that insidious foe.

Warding and maintaining one's spiritual boundaries makes oneself a sacred enclosure welcoming to the Gods, but also shields oneself from spiritual harm. There are numerous books on the market with daunting titles, such as *Spiritual Protection* by Sophie Reicher, *Psychic Self-Defense* by Dion Fortune, and *Practical Guide to Psychic Self-Defense and Well-Being* by Melita Denning. What these works really teach are the techniques whereby we retain our spiritual and psychic integrity and develop good discernment. These practices are a necessity not only for spiritual health but for mental and emotional health, as well. Grounding, centering, and basic wardings of both self and home are fundamental. In many ways, all of these practices come down to choosing to center one's life around the Gods and filtering all other experiences and choices through that lens of spiritual devotion. That's the key to spiritual emergence: consciously centering one's life around the Gods. Everything else is decoration. The devotee who keeps that goal foremost in his or her mind will find the spiritual process easier in the long run. We are spiritual beings. It's a difficult thing to remember in a world that emphasizes anything but. We are challenged to holiness, challenged not only to make ourselves holy and to recognize our spiritual callings, but to carry that awareness into our daily lives, to everyone we touch. It is a difficult task. Moreover, it is one that we must do over and over again, in a never-ending process. We are growing toward the Gods.

It's easy to love the Gods when things are going well in our lives. It's not so easy when every day is a struggle. It's not so easy when mired in depression or pain or when one's life is shattering. It's when we need the Gods the most that it's the hardest to reach out to Them. It's so hard then not to become like churlish children, blaming Them, spewing vitriol at Them, pushing Them away in a myriad of ways. I think They understand when we do this—and no matter how devoted we are, I think we all do this sooner or later. I don't think They blame us for our humanity, but I have, in my own moments where I clutched at whatever shards of grace were allowed me, had glimpses of how deeply They ache for us when we suffer. Loving the Gods makes things better, but it doesn't remove challenges and obstacles and the pain of living. We are human. There is fragility and magnificence, cruelty and kindness in our state of being. It's up to us what we choose to nourish. One of the most courageous and healthy things we can do is choose, consciously, to nourish devotion in the midst of crises.

The Gods will wait for us. They are there even when we deny or try to push Them away. One of the most important things we can do for ourselves spiritually is to not allow jealousy or bitterness or pain to twist our devotional relationships with Them out of true. This is why it's so important to develop good devotional habits when things are going well, consistencies that we hold to as a matter of course, a baseline that can sustain us when our world falls apart. How we choose to respond can bring us so much deeper into devotion and faith, can provide us with the most potent of all lifelines.

So don't be afraid to try. Don't be afraid to reach out to Them. Yes, you will make mistakes, but through those mistakes you'll learn and you will grow in faith and piety. The Gods are, by and large, patient with our fumbling. I also urge newcomers not to worry if belief comes and goes. Belief is a funny thing, and while it's important to cultivate, it's equally important not to fetishize it. I know the Gods exist like I know gravity exists. I don't have to think about it all the time. If for a span of days I don't feel Them palpably in my world, so what? I don't consciously feel the presence of gravity either, thinking every time I drop something: Behold its power. The most devout person I ever knew, a woman I considered a living saint, told me once that there were times she didn't believe; but she continued, "*Whether Loki exists at those times or doesn't exist, I love Him anyway.*" That was all that mattered. It was that commitment, dedication, and love that guided her devotional life, not abstract musings on belief.

It is normal, given that we are fighting for restoration, picking up and reweaving sundered threads rather than inheriting the full tapestry of tradition passed down in an unbroken ancestral inheritance, that sometimes we will be self-conscious about our internal processes around belief. I am not saying that nonbelief is right; however, part of building a devotional relationship is learning how to *cultivate* belief. It's difficult not to fetishize belief when we are working at a nexus of communities wherein we must fight for space for our Gods to exist, but I'll share with you what I was once taught about it, by the saint I mention above: Belief is a choice. You make it over and over every day, throughout the day. You make it every time you choose to engage in devotional work, every time you choose to do something that deepens your relationship with the Gods, that prioritizes Them in your world, and like working a muscle, the more you do that, the easier it becomes. Belief moves from the realm of the abstract into a bone- and soul-deep certainty that sustains.

Any particular right belief is also less important than understanding that the existence of the Gods has consequences in our lives. Because we are seeking to cultivate devotional relationships with Them, to prioritize Them in our lives, our behavior with respect to things sacred, and everything else, will be impacted. If we contemplate our belief only at those times when it is palpable, then we must realize that what we are dealing with is an emotion and emotions are questionable guides to any truth. Just because we do not *feel* belief at a given point in time does not mean that our belief isn't there. What it means is that feelings are, at best, only vague indicators of *what is*. Feelings can be affected by anything from lack of sleep to indigestion! We're all going to have times where we're just not where we want to be in terms of *feeling* belief. That's when you make the choice to carry on with devotion anyway, to act in right relationship with the Gods anyway, because emotions are variable but the Gods are not. One can be respectful regardless of the state of one's belief. One can treat Them well, as proper guests, honorably even if one is struggling spiritually. One can likewise struggle toward organic belief, and doing so is one of the things that helps to build a strong spiritual life. No Deity expects perfection of practice, not now, not ever. Our struggles and sometimes even our failures add color and texture to the fabric of our spiritual lives. Working toward belief can bring us closer to our Gods than simply moving through devotion by rote. It's not enough to just believe in the Gods, and in the end, it's not enough to just venerate Them.

It's easy to think that devotion is all about feeling the presence of the Gods. Maybe one is particularly gifted and can hear or even see Them. I won't deny that the capacity to experience the Gods in this way is a tremendous grace, but those things are unimportant in the end and focusing on them too much can be a powerful distraction to actual devotion, especially when they are sought or embraced without even a hint of discernment. If our devotion is predicated on seeing, hearing, or feeling the Gods, what happens when we can't do that? What happens when we're in a dark place, a dark night of the soul, or going through some type of emotional upset that has impacted our receptivity? What happens when feeling or seeing or hearing is not forthcoming? Does our devotion go away? Moreover, demanding that we have that feedback every single time we make an offering or prayer is putting the Gods on our timetable, holding Them hostage, subordinating Them to our whims and our needs. It is a violation of the hierarchy of being of which the Gods are part. They are Gods after all, not our invisible friends, for all that They may care for us, nurture us, and engage in a friendly, loving manner with us at times. It prioritizes our desires over what is good and right and proper: maintaining right relationship with the Powers. It reduces the Gods to playthings and elevates us in Their place.

This is where getting ourselves out of the way comes in. I strongly believe that we are deeply loved by our Gods, and that They want the best for us that is possible. I also think that our own world is poisoned and out of balance, and our wants and desires, our egos and hungers have been shaped by that lack of balance. We've been taught to value things that are detrimental to our spiritual life. We've been raised to prioritize things that are not in alignment with the goals the Gods have for us and that are certainly not in alignment with any developed and authentic spiritual expression. When the time comes to raise ourselves up, to curb the corruption or atrophy of our very souls, when the time comes to change, to move beyond the immediate reinforcement of seeing or feeling, we balk. Sometimes we run like hell. Sometimes we throw tantrums and immerse ourselves even more in things that are spiritually detrimental.

Take popular culture, for instance. I think that absorbing pop culture uncritically can have devastating consequences on our spiritual senses. The problem isn't, believe it or not, pop culture itself. Pop culture has existed as long as we have possessed the ability to craft and convey stories. In the ancient world, Homer might have been considered "pop culture." Certainly, later philosophers challenged the Homeric corpus (at least the *Iliad* and *Odyssey*) on the grounds that in it the Gods and heroes were presented impiously. The problem is less the stories we tell than the context in which they're told. The cultures of the ancient world were steeped in polytheism. Not having yet had the dubious benefit of modernity and the Enlightenment, devotion and piety were not yet positioned culturally as primitive, foolish, or potential mental illness. The culture itself was steeped in religion so as to allow for the intergenerational transmission of piety, and these things countered any potential harm from the pop culture of the time. Even those who may have had a paucity of actual faith were encouraged by the philosophers, by their culture, by their traditions to attend to the proper rituals and otherwise behave themselves. We don't have that. Instead we have a culture that encourages us to prioritize the shallowest aspects of our lives, to treat the Gods as errant children, that encourages us to behave, in effect, with gross (though usually ignorant) impiety. This complicates the process of opening ourselves up to the Gods. It complicates our growing in faith and spiritual awareness and into fully developed human beings in right relationship with our Gods and dead.

Does all of this mean we should never expose ourselves to popular culture? Maybe. But maybe it means that we approach the popular culture that we imbibe critically, with eyes open, aware that it carries with it seeds that could blossom into gross impiety and ugliness in our souls. It's an opportunity to have conversations, to challenge ourselves and the culture in which we were raised, to reconsider and to do better. Sometimes I will leave a movie or turn off a particular television show, even if I'm enjoying it on some level, because I don't want to give that pollution space in my head, taking up real estate that would otherwise become fertile ground for devotion. I want the seeds planted through my conscious devotion to grow in rich, clean soil. Then there are times where I'll watch anyway, but make offerings and cleanse afterward, and maybe discuss with whomever else was present why it was problematic, even though it might have been enjoyable as hell. It depends. I think we're called to do this not just with pop culture but with our cultural assumptions, our values, the foundations of our morality, our goals, priorities, and everything in our world. We are called to consider everything. Devotion requires conscious choice across the fabric of our lives. It is a challenge to allow ourselves to be reshaped from the inside out by our piety, rather than to reshape our piety to suit our undeveloped souls. We may not know all the time what our Gods want, but we can do those things that make us receptive to finding out. We can immerse ourselves in those practices that help us develop deeper piety, deeper devotion. We can accept that this process of doing devotion well is going to have its ups and downs, its fallow periods and its periods of deep insight and communion, and that it will, if done right, change everything about how we view our world, how we position ourselves in it, and ultimately how we will set ourselves to changing it.

Lectio Divina—Heathen Style

It could be said that Heathens tend toward being fixated on lore. With a demographic drawn largely from Protestant Christianity and working in an over-culture that is doggedly Protestant Christian in its attitudes, it is perhaps not surprising that there is deep suspicion and even hostility among Heathens toward anything not immediately and apparently mediated by the written word. There is also a noticeable insecurity and ambivalence in the Heathen community toward mysticism—i.e., direct experience, often dismissed in Heathen circles as UPG, the dreaded "unverified personal gnosis." I've touched on this in earlier chapters, but I'm going to revisit this issue here, because it has direct impact on how devotion is often approached, or not, within our traditions.

Before going further, let me clarify what lore is in Heathenry. When one of us speaks of lore, we're referring to written texts including the Prose and Poetic Eddas, the Icelandic Sagas, Anglo-Saxon texts, and contemporary historical, archaeological, and linguistic research, as well as any other relevant scholarly work. None of these texts may be considered "revealed" texts, nor were they ever intended to serve the purpose of scripture in the way we are accustomed to think of that term. But this is the context in which most Heathens frame their religion, and in many cases, it's also the context by which their experiences are consciously limited. I find that unfortunate. It is not, however, unexpected.

One of the dominant features of Protestant Christianity is a focus on scripture. This was, historically, one of its chief criticisms of Catholicism: that the latter's praxis and liturgy veered too far away from scripture. But even before the Protestant Reformation, Christianity was always a "religion of the book." For religions of the book, there is holy writ, and it has tremendous authority in guiding practice and faith. Since Vatican II, unfortunately, Catholicism has also been—in the spirit of "modernism" and "ecumenism"—doing its best to cull its more mystical elements, including devotion to Mary, on the grounds that they are not textually authentic. I find it depressing and sad that a rich, complex, mystical theology would be exchanged for a pseudo-rational, unemotional, scripture-based approach. But that's just me. Were this restricted to the Christians, it wouldn't be something I felt the need to address, but it's been a struggle to avoid having this same reductionist approach dominate Heathenry.

We are raised surrounded by the cultural and social trappings of Protestant Christianity. That is the dominant voice of American culture, even among those not nominally Christian. One of the unspoken aspects of this is that we assume religious experience to have a textual base. We look for scripture to tell us what to do, what to believe, and whether or not we're doing our religion right. This is one of the reasons why it's so important to examine our religious expectations, to drag all our unspoken, ingrained assumptions about how a tradition works and how we ought to engage out into the light. There will be parts that are useful and parts that are not, but it's important to see it all clearly.[3]

Our Heathen ancestors knew the wisdom of piety and reverence, when to go on their knees in the dirt before their Gods out of awe, when to sacrifice without complaining about giving too much, and that the Gods were Powers capable of impacting our world and us. In a way, we're having to do now exactly what the very early Christians had to do in order to grow their faith. It's an ironic role reversal: early Christians developed their monastic traditions and powerful traditions of interiority and prayer because they had to worship in secret or at best in small groups away from the public eye. It wasn't until later, once they'd gained political power, that they were able to create public spheres of worship (and oppression). First, there were small groups and individual prayer. This made the hunger for texts, I would think, all the more powerful. If I can't be celebrating my God with a group of my coreligionists, then allow me to summon that community, and the presence of my God, to my memory by reading stories and accounts that we all share in common. Let the absence be filled by memory evoked by engagement with the text. Let me engage with my community, spread out and hidden but united in that very absence, as it were. Now, Christians are everywhere and it is the polytheists who meet in small groups, often quite spread out, and perhaps we also find ourselves deferring to written texts for prayer and meditation more than our polytheist ancestors may have done, ancestors for whom the core beliefs of religion were contained and transmitted via intergenerational household and social practice. They could see their religion and veneration for the Gods reinforced all around them. We who don't have that depend much more on written media.

But Christians didn't just read and take pride in their ability to memorize and regurgitate. They engaged in a certain amount of exegesis. Each reading opened the door to meditation and prayer, and that in turn opened the door to the potential at least—with the grace of their God—for direct experience. Each text led one on a meditative journey with the goal of drawing closer to one's God. This was brought home to me when, in a graduate class in medieval studies, I had to read an article, "Praying with Anselm at Admont: A Meditation on Practice" by Rachel Fulton (*Speculum* 81.3 [2006], pp. 700–33) about how small prayer books were used for personal devotion in the eleventh and twelfth centuries. I won't quote the description of the process one would go through when using a Christian breviary for private use, but I am going to recontextualize that process for a Heathen audience. So drawing upon and expanding the description offered in Fulton's article, here is how I as a Heathen would practice sacred reading—*lectio divina*—as a way of engaging with our lore.

First, as Fulton notes, to own a book was to participate in privilege. Now, I realize that may not be quite the same for us today, but there are parts of the world where reading and writing are still a privilege. There's magic there, too. Think about the first of our ancestors who realized the potential in making marks on the surface of a rock or a bit of bark or clay. Think about the work that went into the book you hold or read, first formed in the mind of its creator, brought into being, translated to text, and pushed through the publishing process, disseminated online or to bookstores and finally ending up in your hands. This process was much more laborious in the medieval period, but each book is still a miracle, still an act of creation and craft. There is something very special in text that ties us to each and every reader who may likewise be influenced and inspired. This is all the more true of religious texts where the readers share a common cosmology and devotional practice.

Many medieval prayer books, like prayer books today, were drawn from scriptural readings, as well as set prayers. So, using that as my paradigm, I'll choose a section from the Poetic Edda focusing on one of Odin's mysteries, the Runatal section of the Havamal. (The process below might be used to equal effect with a prayer, too.) Here's the text, for those who might be unfamiliar with it:

> Veit ec at ec hecc vindga meiði a
> netr allar nío,
> geiri vndaþr oc gefinn Oðni,
> sialfr sialfom mer,
> a þeim meiþi, er mangi veit, hvers hann af rótom renn.
> Við hleifi mic seldo ne við hornigi,
> nysta ec niþr,
> nam ec vp rvnar,
> opandi nam,
> fell ec aptr þaðan.

> I know that I hung on a windy tree
> nine long nights,
> wounded with a spear, dedicated to Odin,
> myself to myself,
> on that tree of which no man knows
> from where its roots run.
> No bread did they give me nor a drink from a horn,
> downwards I peered;
> I took up the runes, screaming I took them,
> then I fell back from there.[4]

First, I might read it quietly aloud in Norse and English. There is a rhythm to the Norse verse that the English translation lacks, however well done. Certain of the Norse phrases I might have (in fact personally do have) committed to memory. These I might linger over, letting the tones of the words resonate through my body.

Odin is, after all, a God of empowered speech, of galdr, of poetry, of incantation. I would strive in my private prayer to make of these phrases, whichever I choose, an incantation that reverberates through the memory hall of my heart, that strikes at the core of my soul, kindling devotion, opening me up, bolstering a desire to connect, to reach outward to Him.

Perhaps I have recently read academic commentary on this section that brought some insight applicable to my spiritual life. I might mull that over for a time. My mind might segue to an image of a tree that calls to mind Yggdrasil. Perhaps I'll parse that word out: "Steed of the Terrible One." What does that mean about this Tree? What does it mean about its agency and awareness? When I think of Odin hanging, there are a thousand images that come to my mind. Perhaps I have included one, a prayer card, or even a photocopy of the image, in my Edda where I can look at it as I read and pray. Or perhaps I have an image on my altar or shrine, and I am praying and reading with this in my sight.

In my case, part of my devotion to Odin involved a hook suspension in *imitatio* of this exact experience. (I do not recommend this to everyone. This was predicated on twenty years of devotion to Odin and very specific work as a *vitki* and shaman that I was engaged in for Him.) It is Odin's greatest mystery and the point of most powerful (for me at any rate) connection to Him. When I read about the windy tree, I think of the November night that I underwent this ordeal. I think about how cold and damp it was, what effect that had on my skin and my muscles, how I watched the sun set with growing dread. I wonder what it was like for Odin approaching the Tree, what preparations He might have made, and what it must be like to be a God and still be afraid.

I have a chant that I use for Him that recounts His time on the Tree and perhaps that will come to mind, and if I am alone, I might even offer it to Him aloud. We don't yet have the tradition of devotional images to which medieval Christians could turn in illuminating their psalters and prayer books, but we do have some.

Many, particularly older images show Him in armor on the Tree, or at least with a helmet. I wonder why, when it was the moment of His greatest power but also His greatest self-chosen vulnerability? I think about all the images I've seen of Him on the Tree—does He have both eyes, or has the artist portrayed Him as He is after having made His offering to the Well? What does my own experience tell me about the nature of mythic time? What about the fact that Mimir is His maternal uncle? That was a powerful role in many cultures, including the early Germanic. What do I know of Mimir? What do I know of the wells that sit at the base of the Tree? Are they all one well, or many? Why are they located with the Tree? What came first: offering to the Well or offering to the Tree? When I read the line about Him being wounded by His own spear, I think about sitting beneath my tree, the hooks going into my flesh: how that felt, what it did to me, where it allowed me to go. I remember the disorientation of swinging beneath the branches of the tree, watching the world fall away as I was lifted off the ground. What did He see when He rose into its boughs? I recall other experiences with Him in the woods, and the sound of His body falling sharply down through the boughs. I remember some of His heiti, his praise names, particularly ones having to do with the Tree. I think about how the Tree is always nourished in blood, and what such an initiation would mean. I think about the runes and why it took this type of ordeal and sacrifice to win them. I might call to mind the rune poems and see how they too are connected to the Old Man. Maybe, if I am in a mood to do so and if, in the flow of my contemplation, it feels correct, I galdr the rune itself with the goal of being given insight into that moment, that time, that experience.

I read and think on Odin, and think about all the parts that went into suspending me in my tree. How was He suspended? Did the Tree itself grasp Him up? Did the branches pierce His flesh and hold Him true until He was empty of screaming and could be filled by something else? Or was that process too an ordeal to be surmounted, a tactical challenge to be met?

I might turn to prayers that I have written or collected that tie to that experience in some way, that bring to my heart's mind and senses Odin on the Tree. I might say them, and then return to the Edda passage, going over those lines again, rooting out connections to other things, all so I can find my way to Him. If emotion comes, I will sit with it and allow it its voice. That too can be a connection to Him.

The passage talks about the roots of the Tree. Images of ancient trees with huge, gnarled, tangled roots come to mind and I let them. I think about how when I was lowered to the ground again after my ordeal, after however long I hung suspended in the tree, my feet touched the ground and there was relief, release, and pain, such pain as the muscles in my lower back went into full, several-days-long spasm. I wonder if it hurt Odin just as much when He was released from the Tree as when He ascended it to be taken up. I think about all the things that can never be remotely comprehended save by initiatory experience and how it breaks one's world into a before and an after, how there's never any going back. I wonder what regrets He left at the Tree, or whether He didn't have them until later, or whether He had them at all. I wonder how He contextualized the experience that of necessity must have changed Him so in its aftermath. I pray to be opened up to understanding, to greater connection to Him, knowing that it will change my life, and I contemplate how far I might go in my devotions to ready myself and make this possible. I think about how far He went. I return to some of my personal prayers that I've written for Him at various times, as well as my spontaneous utterances in the moment, and I offer these up to Him again, moving away from the Runatal text and back again and again and again.

Having this particular text memorized adds another layer to the experience of engaging physically with a written text. The text is already present in my memory, but I involve my sensorium (sight, touch, sound if I choose to read aloud) when I'm looking at a book and that adds another layer of both engagement and meaning. Being a language person with more than a smattering of Old Norse, I might also ponder the syntax and grammar of the original as well to see what can be gleaned there. We all bring different experiences and skills to the table in our devotional life, and I think it's good to use what you have to begin these practices.

I could go on from here, line by line with the Edda, or with any other text, but I think the process is relatively clear. The important thing isn't being well-read in lore, the important thing is to read lore keeping always the ultimate goal in mind: veneration of the Gods, developing a devotional relationship with the Gods, calling Them into the seat of the heart, developing greater understanding of that place in which one dances in relationship with Them. If you're going to use lore, understand that it is not an end in itself. It's a map, and as with any map, there is a goal external to the process.

Issues with the Lore?

We're blessed to have the fragments of the lore that we have. They may not be in themselves sacred, but they contain doorways to the sacred if we know how to read them. But, and this is a big caveat, it's painfully easy to mistake engagement with the lore as engagement with our Gods and to allow it to take the place of actual devotion—though one *may* engage devotionally through the medium of the lore, as I've described above. But then the purpose isn't the lore itself; the lore is a means to draw closer in devotion to the Gods. Having a reified scripture can damage a tradition. Religion isn't an intellectual exercise. There are protocols and practices to be learned because it is necessary to meet the Holy on properly prepared ground, especially the ground of our hearts and minds. When "god" is an idea and not an experienced, shattering Presence, the mystery is stripped from one's religion, and it becomes a game, a brittle carapace. With so many of us having converted from monotheisms, from religions centered around a deeply reified sacred text or texts, it's important to challenge and push ourselves out of our comfort zones. We prioritize the written word in a way that our ancestors never, ever did. We look to the written word to define our experiences instead of allowing our experiences to inspire our written word.

Moreover, we should be getting the interpretation of our lore not from scholars but from our shamans, spirit workers, clergy, and specialists, from those steeped in the deepest mysteries of our traditions, not from those who would analyze the holy out of those traditions. Doing the latter damages not only the community and those devoted to their Gods, but sterilizes the tradition as a whole. If one is properly steeped in one's tradition, the lore can lead one to insights that lie beneath the surface. For instance, the story of Thor killing his goats so a peasant family that was offering hospitality to the Gods might eat well, and then restoring those goats the next day provides a trail that can be followed when one is contemplating how to do proper sacrifice (e.g., make sure the bones of the animal are not broken, which rules out using a gun). The story of Odin hanging on the Tree and winning the runes provides a blueprint for one of our esoteric traditions. The story of Freya winning Brisingamen points to connections, deep and powerful, between the Duergar and the Vanir, and to the link between creativity and abundance otherwise only hinted at in our stories. It's not enough to read the lore or to memorize it. One must steep oneself in the cosmology so that one has the necessary keys to decode and interpret. General lore thumping is all the more frustrating because it's a further corruption of the holy. Yes, the stories are fundamental, but *not* the text itself, rather what is important is what the text alludes to.

Story is always alive. Reifying lore is no different than Christians mistaking the Bible for the Word. It's the Word that creates, not the book. Of course, this is also a symptom of our converts having been raised in a monotheistic, modern culture that wants quick, clearly organized, rigid answers. Mystery is never, ever easy and simple. It's painful, often bloody, confusing, messy, and bigger than we can ever imagine. Most importantly of all, it has to be experienced to be understood; otherwise it's just useless trivia. I think there's a difficulty in Heathenry, and in our world in general, with mistaking knowledge of the lore for experience. I also think wanting those rigid categories becomes a dangerous crutch. It further conditions the mind to keep the holy terror at bay, but the holy terror is what mystery is made of. It is the essential conduit to our Gods. The lore contains accounts of the holy, so they contain the holy even if in imperfect form. They're doors into that world that underlies this one. Truly comprehending our sacred stories prepares one for being dropped into mystery.

All of us need to be steeped in our cosmology, starting with the Poetic Edda. This means not just having read them, but having meditated upon, discussed, and analyzed them. That cosmology needs to shape the fabric of our minds. The Eddas were written down two hundred years after conversion by a Christian. They're not in themselves sacred writ, but they are what we have of the stories of our Gods and invite us into the cosmology and contain, even such as they are, hints at our mysteries. This all came up when I was teaching my apprentices the basics of our fire mysteries. In my tradition (and this much I can say publicly), that starts with learning how to make fire from flint and steel. Part of this connects us to our ancestors, but part of being a good fire worker isn't just being able to pull off the technique, but rather consciously reenacting the cosmological moment of creation, when the world of fire and the world of ice met. One reaffirms and recreates that through the headspace one is in while doing the technique. When you're making fire with flint and steel, you're bringing together opposing forces, recreating that moment. Flint hits steel and sparks, and *boom*, it's the action, not either of the tools themselves. I think of the beginning of Goethe's *Faust*: *In Anfang war die Tat* . . . , "In the beginning was the deed." The interplay of opposing forces, so often repeated in our cosmology as a theme, is in turn a necessary consequence of polytheism: multiple Forces with different desires, agendas, preferences, and They're going to be in conflict and crash into each other, and that's not a bad thing but, on the contrary, a tremendously, terrifyingly creative thing. These are mysteries. Our whole cosmology is contained in starting a fire, which is why it's the first mystery.

Going into our spiritual work, our devotion, our practices with an awareness that unites the stories we have read with an understanding of the sacral interplay of forces (and Forces) in our world, is the point of the lore. The lore must never, ever be mistaken, however, for experience of the mysteries, nor for the Gods Themselves.

How to Set Up a Shrine

A particularly good place to start with one's devotions is setting aside space that is specific to the Gods and ancestors. Generally, it's good to have an ancestor shrine and then a shrine for one's Gods. (We have to work with the space we have, so this might take a bit of creativity. Some people like portable shrines, using decorated boxes, elaborate handmade prayer books, and the like; others prefer to have shelves or a table, and there are any number of variations on this.)

First, it's important to understand exactly what one is doing when one commits to setting up and maintaining a shrine. (That's the corollary, the oh-so-important corollary: it's not enough to set one up and be done with it. A shrine must be regularly maintained.) Understanding this will then dictate the how and what and where. Likewise, the nature of the God or Goddess being honored on the shrine will dictate its composition and the offerings made.

In setting up a shrine, we are giving our Gods a concrete place in our homes, hearts, and lives. It becomes Their space, a conduit for Them, and a place where we can go to make offerings, pray (though of course one can and should pray anywhere and everywhere), and contemplate Them. It is a visible reminder of, but also, more importantly, an invitation and welcome to the Holy Powers. It's also a sign of a life ordered around devotion and piety. So there's a lot going on when one sets up a shrine. Most importantly, it is space for the Gods we are honoring.

Proper shrine maintenance can transform one's devotional life. We are, as I've said before in numerous places, creatures of the sensorium.

We experience our world, including our devotional world, through sight, sound, touch, taste, and smell. Plato wrote about beauty being a thing that had the power to elevate the soul, to bring one into a greater awareness of the Good, and that is true. It also helps prepare the soil of our hearts and minds in a way that creates a fertile environment for devotion. Prepping a shrine is an act of love. We bring those things to the shrine that speak to us of beauty, that speak to us of the relationship we're building with the Deity in question, and I've often found that one's shrines will reflect the state of one's devotional and spiritual life.

Of course, starting out in devotion, one may not have a sense of the relationship yet. Like any relationship, those with our Gods require careful tending. They need time to grow and strengthen, to flower. They require our time, attention, and consistency. The Havamal (verses 41, 44) counsels us to travel often to our friends' homes and exchange gifts regularly, because doing so strengthens and nourishes the friendship. This is good advice in building a relationship with the Gods too. So if you are new to this, where does one begin?

Understand that this is a commitment. While I consider it one of the essentials of devotional life, or close to it, it's not something to do without consideration. Better not to begin a shrine than to have one and allow it to become dusty and ill-cared-for. Once you've decided to take this step, however, the first thing you want to do is find a good spot in your home. This can be a special table, a windowsill, a shelf, or even a box. (I have one shrine, part of my ancestor shrine, not for a Deity, that is in a box. It's elaborately decorated inside and has little compartments, and I open it when I honor those particular spirits.) What is important is that it be consciously dedicated space that will not otherwise be disturbed. I will give one warning: shrines grow. Partly this is a natural outgrowth of the relationship with the Gods deepening over time; partly I find that when one honors a God, as that relationship develops, one might be "introduced" or pushed to begin honoring other members of that God's divine family. I began keeping a shrine to Loki, and a year or so later, was suddenly moved to begin honoring Sigyn. They now share a shrine. Common sense, and where that fails, divination can sort out whether or not a second or third shrine is required, or the Deities in question may share one.

Once you've figured out the where, then comes the process of figuring out the what and how. I usually suggest that one begin with an image of the Deity in question: a prayer card, a statue, an icon for instance. Some people prefer aniconic emblems, and if this resonates more, then it's perfectly fine. Make the shrine beautiful. This space will change and evolve as your relationship with the Powers changes and grows. This is good, natural, and necessary. I always feel sad when I see shrines that are bare and sterile. This is space set aside for the Gods. We should make it lush, welcoming, and lovely, and how one does that is completely dependent on one's creativity. I usually try to have a selection of shrine cloths, candles, things that remind me of the Gods, and images. I like my icons and statues and such. I feel they help me grow closer in my mind and heart to the Gods. Anything that reminds me of that Deity and brings Their presence to mind is good and useful. One is limited only by the breadth of one's creative vision.

Finally, there is always the question of offerings. The most common are flowers, incense, water, alcohol, food, candles, and lots and lots of prayer. When I make offerings, be it incense, flowers, or anything else, they usually go on the shrine. (I may dispose of them later by burying them, throwing them into the river behind my home, or burning them, depending on divination and/or the Deity in question). As with the structure of the shrine itself, one is limited in the kinds of offerings one might make only by one's imagination. Offerings don't have to be financially lavish. It is possible to give according to one's means, and everyone can at least give water. What is most important is consistent attention. Go to the shrine often, pray, sit, and meditate on the Gods. Build the relationship by investing in it. Everything else is a corollary to that.

On Prayer

One of the most powerful tools we have for connecting with our Gods and ancestors is prayer. To dismiss prayer as a powerful and effective practice is to cripple our devotional lives and our relationship with our Gods. Over the years, I've seen many Pagans and even polytheists dismiss prayer as something Christian. Well, it's not. The earliest recorded prayers date from Sumer, written to the God Nanna and the Goddess Inanna by the priestess Enhenduanna. We have surviving prayers from Greece, Rome, and Egypt, to name but a few polytheistic cultures. Polytheists prayed. It's one of the fundamentals of practical religion. Why are we so eager to render ourselves mute before our Gods?

Prayer does not mean that one does nothing else. If there is more that one is able to do on a practical level, then it goes without saying that one should do that. I'm reminded of the Benedictine motto: *ora et labora* (pray and work). It's not an either/or situation. In fact, prayer can help us acquire a mindset of attention and gratitude toward the Gods and ancestors that has the power to motivate us more than anything else in creating change on a practical level, in addressing the challenges of our lives and world. Furthermore, having a consistent prayer practice to the Gods and ancestors is one of the best ways to maintain devotional clarity, to keep the lines of communication open, to strengthen those devotional relationships, and to grow in faith, devotion, and grace. To pray is to approach the Gods as petitioners, to give thanks, to express our love and adoration, and a thousand other things. It provides Them with an opportunity to act in our lives and in our world. It provides us with an opportunity to accept, again and again, Their grace.

We are tasked with learning how to pray effectively. While set, formulaic prayers can be enormously powerful, it's not enough to just say words. Proper prayer is a matter of preparing our minds and hearts. Our hearts need to be receptive to our Gods. Our minds need to be committed and focused on this process. It's one of the key devotional disciplines that no one seems to talk about anymore. As we pray, we learn how to do so more effectively. It is not in the capacity of any human being to compel the Gods. But we can reach out to Them, we can ask, and most of all we can trust that we have been heard. Prayer is powerful in part because it allows us to stand in perfect, active alignment with our Holy Powers. The more we do that consciously, the more we are changed and perhaps even elevated by the process. Because it allows us to stand consciously in that alignment, it is a potent protection against all that is inimical to our Gods and Their ways. It reminds us, purifies us, realigns us again and again into our devotion. Every time we pray, we recommit ourselves to our traditions and our Gods and to living in ways that cultivate piety.

Remove purification, sacrifice, devotion, and prayer and what do you have? Certainly not a religion and that's something to keep in mind if you meet Heathens who are anti-prayer, anti-devotion, and really, if we come right down to it, anti-Gods. Ours is a community in the midst of growth and theological flux. It is not monolithic, and theological arguments abound. That is good and healthy, but it's important to understand what is really at stake in some of these debates: not just the future of our traditions, but our integrity before our Gods. We should act accordingly. There is no greater tool that we have than our capacity to reach out to the Gods and ancestors via prayer. It is *the* most fundamental aspect of religious practice.

A very wise woman once told me that her deepest prayer, every day, was this: "Oh my Gods, Whom I love beyond breath, because I love You, teach me how to love You." I didn't realize it then, but what she'd told me was the seedling at the very core of devotion: because I love You, teach me how to love You; everything flows from there. That love becomes a weight, a power in the heart, mind, and spirit that one cannot ignore. It shifts and eddies and flows around every sharp-edged corner of our doubt, of our pain, of our weakness, of our pride, of our longing, and it shifts us, carefully smoothing away the flinty edges of that internal scream that calls out to the Gods with all its might and fights Them just as fiercely. It brings warmth to the coldness of spiritual desolation. It brings illumination to our unknowing. It carefully adjusts and reorients us until the entire world inside and out is transformed. It is the weight of longing that pulls one down into devotion and sustains one through it all. It is not a feeling so much as a goad, a champion, a driving force. Make me new again, oh my Gods, that I might be always remade in You, that with each faltering, fumbling step I might please You and open myself ever more to Your understanding, Your mysteries, Your presence. It is a rendering sometimes sweet, sometimes purest agony.

Giving Too Much

One will inevitably encounter within the community Heathens urging one not to give too much to the Gods (as if this were even possible). They'll quote stanza 145 of the Havamal—"better not to give than to give too much"—completely out of context, urging a paucity of devotion. That passage occurs during the section of the Havamal referred as the Runatal. It describes Odin hanging on Yggdrasil to win the runes and then goes on to offer advice on negotiating and working with the runes. That passage specifically and quite clearly refers only to working with rune spirits. It has nothing to do with pious offerings to the Gods and ancestors, nothing at all. It is, quite simply, not possible for us to "give too much" in light of the many blessings we have been given. So give freely, proudly, and without hesitation. Give within your means. One doesn't have to be ostentatious in offerings. Neither our Gods nor our ancestors want us to become bankrupt! It is always possible to offer regularly even if one's means only allow for prayers and offerings of water. These are good offerings if they are the best one can give. Remember, our tradition has been effectively broken for a thousand years. We are making up for all the generations that could not or would not give rightly and properly to the Gods, the land, the dead. The best advice I've ever seen on this matter was offered by Sarah Kate Istra Winter, author of *Kharis*:

So, give.

Give to your gods.

Give Them everything you can.

Give Them tangible offerings.

Give when you are feeling enraptured by Their presence.

Give when you are not feeling Their presence at all.

Give when you need, and give to show gratitude, and give for no reason at all.

Give big, as big as you can, as often as you can.

Give together with others who know your gods, and be inspired by the gifts of others.

Give alone, just you and Them, where no one else will see.[5]

There are many different ways of engaging with the Gods and ancestors, and many relationships that can evolve out of that engagement, but regardless, the necessities of devotion are the same. Our tools in this journey are simple ones: prayer, meditation, service, compassion, strength, discipline, and courage. But what wonders they reveal if applied assiduously! There is a wonderful quote by medieval Christian mystic Meister Eckhart that beautifully sums up the spiritual journey: "Be ready. Be aware. God is a thousand, thousand times more ready to give than we are to receive." I would add that the Gods, in my experience, are amazing opportunists. If we but give Them the smallest opening, They will surge forth, filling our hearts and minds with Their presence and love. Perseverance, reverence, and devotion are the keys on this royal road of wisdom. Holiness is nothing more than the ongoing discipline of spiritual mindfulness, and to that we can all aspire.

CHAPTER 11

HOLY TIDES

L ike any other religion, Heathenry has its holy days. Generally these holidays, called *holy tides*, follow the cycle of the seasons and the natural year. This is because people's lives in preindustrial civilizations depended for survival on the rhythms of the earth—ploughing, planting, and harvesting. The most important holidays fall on the solstices and the equinoxes. At least for Anglo-Saxon Heathens, the entire year was broken up into ten months, each defined by either agricultural or holy work to be done during that time. Celebrations were usually held on the eve of the holiday in question.

It is entirely likely that there were many other holy days interspersed among those listed here. Regional cultus meant that the various Gods were honored differently across northern Europe. In some places, Odin might have primacy, but in others it might be Frigga or Tyr or Frey or another of the Holy Powers. It also means that as a community developed their own collective relationship with the Gods and ancestors, they likewise would have developed unique and individual ways of celebrating throughout the year.

We simply don't have a complete account of the Heathen holy tides in any of the surviving material. Christian writers had little motivation to record the holidays of polytheists, and what we do have was generally written after Christianization and is thus more than a little biased. Today, while most of these holidays are celebrated across denominations, each tradition and each Kindred may in fact have additional holy tides that they maintain. This is good and natural and an organic development of modern cultus. That being said, let's start this chapter with what is probably *the* most important of the universal holidays: Yule.

Yule

According to Branston,[1] "the last month of the old year and the first of the new were together called Giuli (Yule)." The most sacred and important of all Heathen holy celebrations falls within this span of time and is called *Modraniht*, or Mothers' Night—a celebration honoring the tribal Goddesses and one's powerful Dísir. As in ancient times, this rite is usually held on the Winter Solstice. Many modern Christmas customs, such as the giving of gifts and the raising of a tree, were actually remnants of earlier Heathen practices.

Yule is a celebration replete with feasting and gift-giving, and it is one of the holidays during which traditional sacrifices to the Gods are made, such as the sonargöltr (the sacrificial Yule pig). It is a time when Woden is said to ride freely through the skies at the head of the Wild Hunt, ever ready to gather the souls of the unwary. It is also a time when the veil between the realms of the living and the dead is thin and strong communication may be made with one's ancestors. In addition to blóting to the Gods (usually Woden, Thunor, Frigga, Frey), at least one day of celebration should be devoted to the ancestors.

Yule is a liminal time of great power. The twelve days of Yule celebration (December 25 through January 6) are more powerful than any other time of year. It is a time for resolution of old debts and a laying of new wyrd, a time when fate may consciously be turned. The most elaborate feasts and high symbel are held throughout Yuletide, and it is a time of frith and mighty oath-taking. Oaths taken during this period are among the most binding and holiest of all utterances. Work—particularly that associated with Frigga, such as spinning and weaving—would cease during this holy time and the last sheaves of hay left in the fields were given in offering to Woden's horse, Sleipnir, to honor (and likely pacify) the Wild Hunt. Gifts were traditionally exchanged throughout the holiday season. The figure of Santa Claus evolved from Odin as Julfaðr and Óski or Wish-Giver.

Yule is also a time to pay special attention to one's ancestors. It's a good time to clean the ancestor shrine, tell their stories, and set out a special meal for them. My own Lithuanian ancestors get a traditional porridge made of a variety of grains (I've never actually found a recipe for this, only descriptions, so I make do) to which I add dried fruits, nuts, and honey. It's a time to celebrate family, living and dead, and hope for a blessed spring. It marks the time after which little by little, slowly but surely, the light returns, and for a people who endured harsh winters, bundled together in their longhouses, like many of our ancestors, it was a time of potentiality and renewal.

For Anglo-Saxon Heathens, Yule was also a time for making a traditional drink of blessing and welcome called Wassail. This could be given in offering and enjoyed with one's family and guests. Here is my favorite recipe. It's supposedly a traditional English recipe. It was so strong I was tipsy just from the fumes while cooking it, so beware!

Traditional Wassail

> *Two large bottles of dry English cider*
> *200 ml dark rum*
> *Half a cup of sugar*
> *One bar of dark chocolate*
> *2 vanilla pods split*

1 tablespoon pink peppercorns

4 star anise

3 sticks of cinnamon

2 teaspoons cardamom pods

2 teaspoons cloves

1 orange and 1 lemon zest expressed

(Serves ten people.)

Put the cider and the spices (in a mulling ball) and cinnamon sticks in a pot and bring to a boil.

Once it comes to a boil, add the sugar, rum, vanilla, and zests and simmer for 15 minutes.

Remove from heat and break up the chocolate. Whisk it in until it's melted and thick and dark.

Drink.

Wish everyone a happy Yule.

Charming of the Plough

The next month—roughly our February—was called Solmonath: Sun Month. This was a time when the land was blessed and offerings made (usually bread or pastry) to ready it for planting in the months to come. Ploughs and field implements would also be blessed, a ritual that survived into the Christian era. Today, because the majority of Heathens no longer depend on the land for their livelihood, this holiday has been expanded to include any implement of work or creativity, including laptops, cars, and business ledgers. It's a time to honor our ability not only to support ourselves by right means, but also the means by which we leave our mark in the world. It's a time to celebrate the renewal of the creative spark—in the land and in our minds and hearts.

It can seem odd, when we don't live in direct dependence on the land quite so obviously as our ancestors did, to think about blessing the land in February, and truth be told, this holy tide can be combined with Ostara or performed later in the season. It makes more sense to do this when the land is ready for planting, right? Still, regardless of when one chooses to celebrate this holy tide, a wonderful way to do so is to make offerings to the Goddess Jorð or Erda, Mother Earth. She sustains us, and without Her bounty, tended by our farmers, we would know only hunger and famine. Even though many of us today are separated from that cycle of survival, it's worth remembering. Traditionally (as mentioned in the Aecerbot, an eleventh-century Anglo-Saxon poem) bread, honey, and milk were given to the land in offering. It's a good thing, on a chilly February day, to express our gratitude toward the land, the Goddess of that land, and Her bounty.

Ostara/Eostre

Solmonath is followed by Hreðe and Eostre (March and April, respectively), both named after Goddesses. The holy tide that falls during this time is also called *Eostre* or *Ostara*. Modern Heathens usually celebrate Ostara on or around the Spring Equinox. It may also be celebrated at the first full moon after the equinox. Many contemporary Easter customs and symbols, such as decorating eggs and the folk image of the "Easter Bunny" (both symbols of fertility), come from the Heathen holiday. Unsurprisingly, just as the Charming of the Plough honors those tools that work the land, so Ostara honors the fecundity of the land itself, the quickening of the seed within the dark earth, and the coming of spring.

Eostre/Ostara is a time of renewal and rebirth. It's an excellent time to embark upon new projects. It's also a good time for cleaning and cleansing—perhaps the real reason behind "spring cleaning"! Ostara is a time to bid goodbye to winter. The name of this holy tide comes from the Goddess of spring and the dawn, called Ostara or

Eostre (I'm not actually sure whether these are regional names for the same Goddess, or whether we're dealing with different Goddesses, but either way, invoking Them with respect is key).

Having been born in March, I have a particular affection for the Goddess Hreðe, though we really don't know very much more about Her than Her name and that She is associated with the chilly winds of March. Here is a prayer that might be helpful in coming to honor Her.

31 Adorations to Hreðe

I adore You, Victorious One.
I adore You, Famous One.
I adore You, Goddess of the lion winds of March.
I adore You, Herald of spring.
I adore You, Untamed.
I adore You, Proud.
I adore You, Never forgotten.
I adore You, Friend of Eostre.
I adore You, Who will not be bound.
I adore You, Who can never be captured.
I adore You, Friend of the winds.
I adore You, Racer.
I adore You, Dancer.
I adore You, Laughing Whirlwind.
I adore You, Fierce One.
I adore You, Irresistible One.
I adore You, Warrior.
I adore You, Friend of children.
I adore You, Friend of farmers.
I adore You, Who steals away the chill of the land.
I adore You, Who delights in wild places.
I adore You, Patron of those born in the sign of Aries.
I adore You, Who opens the way.
I adore You, Far-sighted One.

I adore You, Implacable One.
I adore You, Never Still.
I adore You, Goddess of gaiety.
I adore You, Goddess of raw, chilly places.
I adore You, Who delights in Her solitude.
I adore You, Who delights in freedom.
I adore You, Who delights in the seasons
and never-ending inevitability of change.
Hail to You, Hreðe. Hail, Goddess of the whirlwind. Hail,
Goddess of March, Who prepares the way for Ostara's blessings.

And here is a prayer in a similar vein for the Goddess Eostre (or Ostara).

28 Adorations to Eostre

I adore You, Goddess of spring.
I adore You, Goddess of the wet and fertile field.
I adore You, Ever-brightening Dawn.
I adore You, Who hides Your mysteries in liminal places.
I adore You, Rebirth.
I adore You, Renewal.
I adore You, Aching tug of awakening hungers.
I adore You, Goddess of adolescence.
I adore You, Goddess of bursting bloom.
I adore You, Goddess of the new season.
I adore You, Goddess of New Growth.
I adore You, Who awakens the womb of the earth.
I adore You, Who brings fertility.
I adore You, Laughing dawnlight.
I adore You, Who looses the hare.
I adore You, Who quickens the belly.
I adore you. Who fills the egg with life.
I adore You, Holder of all potentiality.

I adore You, Who opens the passage from winter to summer.
I adore You, Whose gentle caress causes winter to yield its sway.
I adore You, Who sweeps away the cold with a kiss of light.
I adore You, Alluring One.
I adore You, Who delights in the rising cock.
I adore You, Who delights in the wet cunt.
I adore You, Goddess of playful delight.
I adore You, Friend of Mani.
I adore You, Friend of Sunna.
I adore You, Eostre.
May You be hailed at this time, as cold turns to
warmth, darkness to light, winter to summer,
fallow land to fertile growth. Hail, Eostre.

I also often find it lovely to honor the moon God Mani and the sun Goddess Sunna on Ostara. It is, after all, a time when Their power is in the ascendant, and we are balanced between Their blessings. I often suspect that our ancestors must have paid these two Deities far more respect and heed than we do today, since they lived a largely agricultural existence for which the blessing of Mani and Sunna would have been paramount.

28 Adorations to Mani

I adore You, Sweet Incantation of Night.
I adore You, Hati's Fetter.
I adore You, Son of the Keeper of Time.
I adore You, Delight of Mundilfari's House.
I adore You, Brother of Sunna.
I adore You, Nephew of Nott.
I adore You, Kin to Sinthgunt.
I adore You, Lustrous Illuminator.
I adore You, Beloved of Unn.
I adore You, Singer of Odd little Rhymes.

I adore You, Intoxicator.
I adore You, Of the thirteen turnings.
I adore You, Bearer of the gleaming scimitar.
I adore You, Who sometimes shields his face.
I adore You, Ancient Splendor.
I adore You, Protector of Children.
I adore You, Solitary Singer.
I adore You, Keeper of Cycles.
I adore You, Master of Tides.
I adore You, Friend of Álfar dark and light.
I adore You, Who inspires longing.
I adore You, God of Camellias.
I adore You, Who makes the heart ache.
I adore You, Protector of the Mad.
I adore You, Beautiful as Alabaster.
I adore You, Gleaming Pearl in the body of Night.
I adore You, Master of the Abacus.
I adore You, Golden One and Beautiful.
My Adoration, I hail You. Sweetest God, ancient
and beautiful. Be ever praised, Mani.

Walpurgisnacht/Beltaine

The month of May, according to the old Anglo-Saxon calendar, was called *Thrimilci*, because this month was traditionally a time of plenty, when the cows could be milked three times a day and, in contrast to the leaner time of winter, food and milk were plentiful. Walpurgisnacht is generally celebrated on April 30. Traditionally it was seen as a time when witches ride and dangerous beings gather to feast. The Goddess Holda is strongly associated with this feast, as is Freya. Charms and prayers for the protection of livestock and the fields would be offered, and bonfires kindled atop mountains to honor these mighty beings.

Walpurgis was also a time of courtship and romance, and it is in this way that it survives among modern Heathens—unsurprising, if we remember that Freya is a Goddess of both witchcraft and attraction. This holiday is a fitting time to honor romantic partners and friends—all the loves in one's life. It's a time to celebrate the flowering of relationships and to pray for fertility, not necessarily of body but of those relationships in general. Offerings may be left for Vaettir and Etins, to ward off ill luck, but gifts may also be given to loved ones and friends. This is a joyous holiday, and its symbols are those of fertility and sexuality: wreaths of flowers, bonfires, and of course, the maypole—a phallic symbol if ever there was one. Of course, the maypole may also be a stand-in for the World Tree—the axis of power that supports all life.

Either way, Walpurgis is a celebration of life, plenty, and passion. It's a seasonal festival all about fertility and fire, abundance, and rampant, unadulterated, unapologetic creativity. It's about the burning in the loins, and the earth's seasonal orgasm that brings a flood of life into being as spring turns to summer and the land yields its bounty to the blazing beauty of the sun. It's not just about sex, but about loosing creativity and readying the land for summer growth, the explosion of life that comes with the turning of the season. It's a very good day to make offerings to Freya and celebrate the ones you love.

Litha

This leads us into our next holy tide: Midsummer. The months of June and July were called *Litha*, which may mean "moon,"[2] and Midsummer was celebrated on the Summer Solstice. It is second only to Yule in being the most important holiday, regardless of denomination, to Heathens both ancient and modern. First and foremost, it is a celebration of summer and of the luck and wealth of the folk. Thanks are given for health and prosperity, and prayers offered for continued might in the coming year. Traditional rites, just as at Yule, would often include the sacrifice of a pig to the God Frey, in gratitude for the community's abundance and good fortune.

Midsummer is a fire festival, and bonfires were an integral part of ancient celebration. Offerings, including the remnants of the sacrificial pig, were tossed into the fire as gifts to the Gods. This holiday is a time when Heathens celebrate the rebirth of their faith, their connection as folk, and their connection to the Gods of their ancestors.

Every time we gather together to celebrate, every time we pour out libations, make offerings, sacrifices, celebrate the many mysteries of our Gods, we are remaking the fabric of our world, millimeter by millimeter. We are taking back ideological space ceded with the dominance of monotheism. We are doing a good thing for our Gods and for ourselves. Keep that in mind as you celebrate this season. Every time we pour out an offering to the Gods, every time we mindfully keep these holy tides, we're restoring and rebuilding our traditions, giving Them back what should be Theirs, and returning to ourselves the potential for all the blessings They can bring. It's good and holy work.

Hlaefmaest

At the end of July, usually on the full moon or sometimes the very last day of July (I tend to personally celebrate it on July 31), modern Heathens celebrate the harvest. (August was referred to as *Weodmonath*: month of weeds. No holy tides falls during this time.) This is really a modern practice drawn from a number of harvest festivals celebrated in pre-Christian England and Germany. There was no one, large, universal harvest celebration at this time, but smaller, regional celebrations were common. According to the agricultural calendar, this was the time when the fields would be threshed and grain harvested. It was also the time when folk would begin putting away stores for the winter months. Sometimes this holiday is referred to as *Freyfaxi*, and sometimes *Lammas*, which literally translates as "loaf-mass." Rites celebrated at this time generally honor the bounty of the harvest. Offerings are given to the Gods and Vaettir, partly in thanks and partly in the hopes of a healthy and safe winter. Traditions include making bread fashioned in the shape of a man, for both feasting and offering. Modern Heathens often connect this particular feast to the story of Loki cropping Sif's hair, connecting the shearing of Her hair to the act of harvesting grain.

One simple way to keep this holy tide is to make bread from scratch as an offering, giving some to the Gods and sharing some with your friends and family. In this way, we're connecting to the work of hands and heart that formed so much of our ancestors' (particularly our female ancestors') lives. We're bringing together all these disparate elements and blessings (grain, milk, eggs, etc.) and transforming them into nourishment for our families. While it would be nice if we had huge citywide processions, there were gorgeous temples and multiple sacrifices, and celebrations loud and joyous all around, it still matters and it still counts if we keep these sacred days quietly. It is still a joy to the Gods. It is still a time of remembrance and celebration for us.

Bread is such a powerful thing. It represents everything good and holy, everything that nourishes life, and it can even be used in esoteric cleansings.

This is my Lithuanian grandmother's favorite recipe.

> 8–9 cups flour
> 1 cup sugar
> 1 teaspoon salt
> 3 packages dry, active yeast
> 1½ cups milk
> 1 cup (two sticks) butter
> ½ cup water
> 2 eggs

In a large bowl combine two cups of flour, the sugar, salt, and yeast.

In a medium saucepan heat the milk, butter, and water until very warm. The butter doesn't have to melt all the way.

With a mixer at low speed gradually pour the liquid into the dry ingredients. Increase speed to medium and beat for two minutes. Stir in the additional flour and the eggs to make a soft dough. At this point you may add a cup or two of raisins, if you like. I prefer to use golden raisins.

Turn the dough out onto a lightly floured surface and knead until smooth and elastic, about ten minutes. Shape into a ball and put in a greased bowl, turning all over to coat the dough completely. (I use butter to grease the bowl.) Cover with a dry towel and let rise in a warm place until doubled, about an hour.

Punch down the dough. Cut it into thirds or halves, cover, and let it rise 15 minutes. Put the sections of dough into greased pans and let them rise for 1½ hours.

Bake the loaves at 350°F for 35 minutes.

Be sure to share the bread with your Gods and ancestors.

Haligmonath

The month of September was called *Haligmonath* or "holy month." It is another harvest holiday, generally celebrated at the Autumnal Equinox. It is akin to a Heathen Thanksgiving, continuing the theme of giving thanks for the bounty of the harvest. It is the last great feast before the winter months. This was also the month of offerings of all types. Folk would make offerings in thanks for luck, health, and wealth experienced during the previous year, but also to ensure a fruitful harvest in the year to come. These offerings were a way of giving something back to the Gods, of recognizing and honoring all that we receive from Their hands. The process of celebrating the holy tides and making offerings makes each and every person a partner in the unfolding cycle of their wyrd. It is at this holiday that Heathens celebrate their part in that cycle of life.

For many of us, September, and specifically the Autumnal Equinox, begins a rather intense ritual season leading up to Yule. While we should be honoring our ancestors year-round, as autumn approaches, it often feels like they are suddenly very, very present and the whole world becomes about them. As the weather starts turning chilly, we also edge into the time of the Wild Hunt, sacred to Odin, and between the equinox and Yule, November brings us Veterans Day and a chance to honor the military dead, important for many Heathens. That's what is important to our honored dead: that we remember them. The Autumnal Equinox is a good time to start.

Winternights/Winterfyllith

The month of October was called *Winterfyllith*. It was a time when Heathens made offerings to their dead and remembered their ancestors in feasting, stories, and sacred rites. Modern Heathens generally celebrate Winternights as a day of the dead. The Dísir and Álfar are given offerings, usually a complete feast. Their stories are told, they are hailed in fainings, and it is generally seen, like the Celtic celebration of Samhain, as a time when the veil between the world of the living and the world of the dead is thin. Ancestral veneration is a foundational tenet of Heathenry, and the ancestors provide strength, luck, and blessings to the folk. This holiday is a time to repay those gifts with offerings, rituals, and mindful attention to the dead. For those seeking specific wisdom from their ancestors, there is no better time to facilitate communication.

Winternights also heralds the arrival of winter. Many Heathens choose to hail Deities associated with the winter months at this time, such as Skaði and Ullr. This holiday begins a cycle of introspection and reflection culminating in the twelve nights of Yule. It is a time to make amends for any ill actions committed, wrap up unfinished projects, and take stock of one's choices and actions the preceding year.

The month of November is called *Blótmonath*: "blood month." Though no holidays fall during this month, it was a time when the surplus livestock were butchered in preparation for the winter. Today it is not uncommon to hold fainings and blótar to Woden, Frey, and Thor during this time. Additionally, Veterans Day falls in November, and it is nearly a universal day of remembrance for modern Heathens. Fainings are held to honor the Einherjar, warriors who have fallen in battle and thus earned their place in Valhalla in Odin's army. Ancestors who have served in the military, living relatives who serve, as well as loved ones left behind, are all named and honored. Memorial Day is another day of remembrance observed as a holy day in the Heathen community.

Military service is considered a great honor among modern Heathens, and veterans are highly respected for their courage and sacrifice. All of us had ancestors who were warriors and soldiers or we would not be here. Regardless of how we may feel about their wars and conflicts, it's important to remember the men and women themselves and their sacrifices. If you can, this is a good time to go talk to the veterans in your family. Record their stories. Buy them coffee. Listen. Pay attention to the weight they carry and the dead that walk with them too. See if there's anything you can do to help your local VFW. Go and learn their stories.

In addition to the major holy tides, many Heathens celebrate feast days of heroes and heroines celebrated in Heathen history and lore. Figures such as Penda, the last great Heathen king of Mercia, and Queen Sigrid the proud, who refused a marriage proposal from Olaf Tryggvason (a figure loathed by modern Heathens for his attempts to convert the folk to Christianity by any means necessary, resulting in numerous Heathen martyrs), are often honored for their deeds, as well as for the inspiration they give to modern Heathens. The format of the rites celebrated on the holy tides does not differ considerably from the basic faining, symbel, or blót. It is the intent and the nature of the prayers made and offerings given that determines the difference.

Many Heathens avoid holding Winternights around Halloween, largely because Wiccans and other Pagans hold their rite of Samhain at that time, but I have always found it to be a powerful time of year and, perhaps also because it honors my Celtic ancestors, prefer to hold my Winternights celebration from October 29 through November 1. I also like the idea of being festive about the dead. Maybe that's not what secular Halloween is about now, but I still enjoy it and I like to think my ancestors do too. There is a time for intense grief, and a time to be somber in our reflections, but sometimes it's okay to celebrate them with joy too. There can be such tremendous joy in devotion, both to the Gods and one's ancestors. I've had rituals for Winternights and/or Samhain that went to both extremes: a communal sharing of grief for our beloved dead and at other times a raucous celebration of their lives. Sometimes I don't know what it's going to be, which way it's going to go, until the rituals are about to begin. So much depends on the hearts of those participating, their losses, their griefs, where they are with their ancestors and their ancestors with them, and what they're willing to share. In a way that's the true magic of ritual work: you can and should prep and plan, but then when you're in sacred space and the ritual unfolds, so much depends on what everyone brings to it. It's beautiful, often unexpected, weaving together so many threads of experience into a shared and powerful whole. Then all of that is given to the Gods or the dead. Good rituals are warmth and light to the spirit. They enchant and sustain and help us not only to honor the Holy Powers well, but to remember ourselves somewhere in the bargain. If you can't think of any other way to celebrate, go and visit the graves of your beloved dead: family, friends, mentors, anyone who mattered to you in life. Let them know they still matter in death.

In addition to those days noted here, you may wish to celebrate birth and/or death days of certain ancestors, martyrs, or heroes. Don't be constrained by this list. Traditions evolve and develop as those that practice them have devotional experience with the Gods. They grow through personal gnosis, and through love, piety, and respect.

CHAPTER NOTES

Introduction

1. Though many Fellowship of Isis Iseums and Lyceums are Wiccan, the organization as a whole is not a Wiccan organization.

2. Though some Heathens might disagree, I tend to use Odin, Oðinn, and Woden interchangeably.

3. It's commonly believed that to wear the valknot is to dedicate oneself irrevocably as a living sacrifice to Odin, to be claimed at His will and at the time of His choosing.

4. There is an ongoing debate in Heathen circles about whether Heathen clergy should be trained in counseling. Some prefer to restrict the role of the Heathen priest to ceremonial, sacrificial, and ritual performance. Others, like myself, favor a more service-oriented approach in which counseling forms a very definite basis.

5. Former Catholic priest Matthew Fox was defrocked in 1989 for "consorting with Witches," because of his long-standing professional association with modern Witch Starhawk. The controversy surrounding his book *Coming of the Cosmic Christ* and his stance in favor of creation spirituality had much to do with his dismissal. He was later accepted into the Episcopalian priesthood.

6. While syncretization is one thing, it is important to guard against cultural misappropriation or "strip-mining." Worship of

our Gods and Goddesses evolved in specific cultural contexts. Their sacred stories and symbols reflect this. Out of respect, learn about the culture in which worship of our Gods initially evolved. Guard against transposing twentieth-century ethics onto ancient cultural markers. Strive to meet the God or Goddess on His or Her own ground. It is respectful to the Deity and the tradition. Don't mix and match.

Chapter 1

1. Tacitus, *Germania* 9, trans. Mattingly, p. 109.

2. Hulsman, §1.1 "The Viking Age."

3. See, e.g., Thomas DuBois, *Nordic Religions in the Viking Age* (University of Pennsylvania Press, 1999).

4. Jones and Pennick, p. 156.

5. Olaf Tryggvason ruled Norway 995–999. His name is reviled among modern Heathens for the violence and cruelty with which he forced conversion on his people.

6. Wodening, *Hammer of the Gods,* p. 10.

7. Some historical accounts give 999, but 1000 is the most commonly accepted date.

8. Utiseta—a common Nordic system of divination, meditation, and wisdom-seeking wherein the seeker would isolate him- or herself literally underneath a cloak or animal skin for a given period of time.

9. John Lindow, a respected scholar in the field of Norse mythology, commented in his book *Norse Mythology* (2001) that "there was a revival of 'belief in the aesir' some years ago in Iceland, which seemed to have to do at least in part with tax breaks for organized religion, although partying is also important. That revival had its counterpart in Norway, where a group of students announced

themselves to be believers in the aesir. In celebration, they drank some beer and sacrificed a sausage," p. 38. This is not an uncommon attitude among modern scholars.

10. 2001 Asatru Folk Assembly online article, "Hitlerism v. Odinism," *http://archive.li/qEOIh*, accessed 9/4/2018.

11. Hulsman, §1.3.

12. *Asatru* means "faith in the Gods" and is one of the largest branches of Heathenry. Its practitioners draw largely from Icelandic sources for religious inspiration.

13. Tribal law or custom.

14. A rooftree issue is any issue that belongs in the realm of one's home, does not affect the community, and is, to be frank, none of the community's business.

15. The problem isn't atheists per se. If someone wants to attend a ritual and behaves respectfully, that's fine. The problem is that atheists come into our communities and demand leadership positions, while refusing to accommodate the traditions or respect devotion. Instead, they attempt to twist the religion to their own lowest common denominator. This isn't a problem only in polytheistic traditions, but is happening in various monotheisms as well.

16. Polytheisms tend to have more traditional values, sexual ethics, and much more of a focus on devotional piety than any generic Paganism. They also tend to encompass mystery cultus, which is exclusionary by its very nature, having solid lineages, protocols, and strict ways of doing things. They are not generally religions in which "anything goes" spiritually or morally.

Chapter 2

1. The best Eddic sources for Heathen cosmology are the Völuspá, Grimnismal, and Vafðrudnismal.

2. H. R. Ellis Davidson, *Gods and Myths of Northern Europe,* p. 199.

3. Snorri Sturluson, *Poetic Edda,* "Völuspá," trans. Taylor and Auden, pp. 147–48.

4. Lindow p. 254, from Völuspá.

5. Right away we're confronted with the issue of cosmogonic time. Essentially, at this point in our narrative, we're dealing with time-less moments. Temporality as such is not yet a player in our tale. It doesn't exist. It's not a factor in these first initial unfoldings of creation. To quote Edward Butler (who had the dubious pleasure of reading my initial draft), "Platonists were of the opinion that the sequence of events in a mythic narrative should be understood as a kind of stacking of timeless moments upon one another, so that instead of a linear unfolding of events, we get a kind of layer cake effect in each moment, which is a cross section. Part of what a cosmogony is doing is founding and grounding time itself. The first moments have to be timeless because time isn't yet. But things that happen when time isn't can't have happened 'then,' 'before,' or 'now.' They have to be happening now." (Private mail with E. Butler on March 8, 2015). It's crucial to understand that while we may be forced by the constraints of language to use qualifying adverbs, to position our narrative temporally, in reality temporality did not yet exist, was not yet a factor.

6. Simek, p. 303.

7. Stanzas 26, 30.

8. Simek, p. 73.

9. This comes up again in the story of Odhroerhir as well. The creative force is lethal until it has been purified through the act of creation. The poisonous mead of inspiration was created from the crushed body and soul of Kvasir and brought death and misery to anyone it touched. Only through the alchemy of Odin and

Gunnloð's union could it be purified through the bodies of two shamans and rendered safe for consumption through grace.

10. "The sons of Bor slew Ymir the jotun; and where he fell there spurted forth so much blood from out of his wounds, that by means of it they drowned all the tribe of the Rim-thurs . . . " (translation mine).

11. While the identification of Loki as Loður is not universally accepted, there is skaldic evidence for this attribution both in Völuspá 18 and Þrymlur I–III 21.

12. Perhaps this is one of the real cosmological meanings behind Ragnarok before Christians got their hands on it. This conception of Ragnarok also allows for the Gods to recreate and restore Themselves.

13. Of course, the question of the difference between a Jotun and a God is a curious one. The Jötnar were the primal divine race. Until the moment Odin and His brothers decided to create the worlds, the beings that sprang from Ymir's body were Jötnar. At no point in the surviving creation story is there a single moment where suddenly some of them are transformed from Jotun to Ás, unless it be the moment that Odin and His brothers decided to slaughter Their ancient kinsman Ymir to create the worlds. That is the only defining period in the creation epic where differentiation occurs. Suddenly these three Gods decide to act in a way that transforms everything that comes after. If *Aesir* refers specifically to a clan of Powers focused in some way on creating and maintaining cosmic order—and there is enough in the surviving myths that scholars like Dumézil certainly thought so—then membership in this clan might be somewhat mutable, all Aesir having begun as Jötnar perhaps? We likewise know that there are other clans of Gods like the Vanir, whose cosmological focus is different. Perhaps it is such cosmological foci, however enduring or transitory, that ultimately determine membership in these divine clans. (See further

my article "The Demonization of Loki in Modern Heathenry" in *Walking the Worlds,* volume 4, issue 2, Summer 2018, pp. 4–19.)

14. This of course makes the Jötnar in general and Loki (whom Dumézil, in *Loki*, describes as the "unquiet thought") in particular essential to the proper functioning of divine order. And if we accept, as the skalds did, that Loki and Loður are the same being, then it is Loki who forms the bridge between these two states of being: undifferentiated potentiality/chaos and divinely crafted order. Perhaps this is why it is Loður who gives good hue, which implies a healthy circulatory system, the pumping of the heart, the flow of blood and warmth, the God who is able to move between both states investing us with potentiality (i.e., chaos), carefully contained in ordered flesh, while unordered bodily chaos brings death for us. Like Ymir, we bleed out, but contained within the order the Gods have decreed, it brings health and ongoing life and the potential to affect our world and to remake it at times according to our will.

15. Just as excluding Loki may lead to entropy and rigidity.

16. "And this is my belief, that he Odin and his brothers must be ruler/controller of heaven and earth."

Chapter 3

1. Sun Tzu IV.1.

2. Simek points out that Grimm was sceptical of this, as the name of wild moss (*Polytrichum aureum*) in Old Norse translates as "Sif's hair."

3. Private e-mail correspondence.

4. Snorri Sturluson, *Prose Edda,* trans. Young, p. 59.

5. Snorri Sturluson, *Poetic Edda,* trans. Hollander, p. 150.

6. Simek, pp. 71–72.

7. In Anglo-Saxon and Germanic healing theory, sudden pain in the bones and joints, arthritis, and rheumatism were often said to be caused by poisoned darts shot into the patient by unseen beings common to the natural world. This was also used to describe certain types of magical attack.

8. Along with Bald's Leechbok, the Lacnunga forms the largest surviving body of Anglo-Saxon healing lore.

9. In Nordic lore, the dead—particularly strong female ancestors—are known to grant healing wisdom and advice.

10. According to the Poetic Edda, Her handmaidens are Hlíf ("Protection"), Blíð ("Blith"), and Fríð ("Right Order, Peace").

11. Simek, p. 309.

12. Snorri Sturluson, *Poetic Edda*, "Völuspá," trans. Hollander.

13. Simek, p. 191.

14. Ynglinga Saga, Chapter 8.

15. Tacitus, Chapter 40, trans. Mattingly.

16. Simek, p. 105.

17. The pig was a holy animal to the Germanic folk, representing both battle prowess and fertile abundance. Freya shares this attribute with Her brother Frey.

18. Multiple private correspondences.

19. Simek, p. 260.

20. Because alcohol plays such an important role in Heathen religious rites, many Heathens home brew beer and especially mead.

21. Wodening, *Hammer of the Gods*, p. 88.

22. *Marklander: A Journal of Nordic Heathenry* #75 (Vol. X, No. 3).

23. Snorri Sturluson, *Prose Edda*, trans. Young, p. 61.

24. Aecerbot, a blessing of the fields, is one of the few surviving Anglo-Saxon charms/prayers wherein an actual Heathen Deity is openly invoked. (Trans. from Albert C. Baugh and Kemp Malone, *The Literary History of England: Vol 1: The Middle Ages [to 1500]*, 2nd ed. [London: Routledge & Kegan Paul, 1967], p. 41.)

25. Not to be confused with the male God Fjorgynn, father of Frigga.

26. Simek, p. 229.

Chapter 4

1. I have provided the Anglo-Saxon names, where known or reconstructed, in parentheses following the better known Norse appellations. I tend to use Norse and Anglo-Saxon names, especially for Odin, pretty interchangeably but this is a personal decision. There's no hard-and-fast rule here.

2. Krasskova, p. 24.

3. A comprehensive list of His heiti, or bynames, may be found online at *en.wikipedia.org* (Accessed 9/5/2018.)

4. Personal correspondence with Wulfgaest, Heah Aeweweard of the Ealdriht.

5. From the Old Norse verb *gala,* "to croak or to crow."

6. H. R. Ellis Davidson, *Gods and Myths of Northern Europe*, p. 70.

7. Modern Heathen lore is comprised of the Elder Edda; Younger Edda; Icelandic Sagas; Anglo-Saxon Healing Texts; law codes and histories; and current anthropological, archaeological, and historical analysis.

8. Snorri Sturluson, *Poetic Edda,* trans. Larrington, p. 34.

9. Trans. D. L. Ashliman (*http://www.pitt.edu/~dash/merseburg.html, accessed 9/5/2018*).

10. The Lacnunga manuscript, in Pollington, *Leechcraft,* p. 217.

11. Snorri Sturluson, *Poetic Edda,* trans. Larrington, p. 35.

12. Such as when He summons the seeress forth in the Völuspá and commands her to scry the future for Him.

13. Branston, *Gods of the North,* p. 112.

14. Jan de Vries, *Altgermanische Religionsgeschichte* (Berlin: de Gruyter, 1970), Vol. II, §360.

15. "Teiwas—His Law and Order in Middle Earth" by Dan Halloran (*http://mirror.macintosharchive.org/ca.cdn.preterhuman. net/texts/religion.occult.new_age/Asatru/Community_Resources/ Dan%20O%27Halloran/Teutonic%20Culture%20-%20The%20 Development%20of%20the%20Folk/3.%20Germanic%20Law. htm*). (Accessed 9/5/2018.)

16. Simek, p. 227.

17. Simek, pp. 135–36.

18. Dumézil speculates that Heimdall is a God of long life, symbolized by His birth of nine mothers; however, He just as likely may be connected to the concept of reincarnation and rebirth.

19. I have heard it speculated that Loki and Heimdall are inextricably connected, because of Their complementary powers: Loki possesses the destructive power of fire, the catalytic power of unexpected change; Heimdall, fire's nourishing power, its warmth and life-giving properties, and balanced, guided change.

20. Within Neoweanglia Maethel, Heimdall is the patron of the School of Theodish Studies, the Contemplatives Guild.

21. Wodening, *Hammer of the Gods,* p. 81.

22. H. R. Ellis Davidson, *Gods and Myths of Northern Europe,* p. 168.

23. "The Demonization of Loki in Modern Norse Paganism," *Walking the Worlds* 4.2 (Summer 2018).

24. Sheffield, p. 35.

25. Simek, p. 195.

26. Wodening, *Hammer of the Gods*, p. 79.

27. Simek, p. 276.

28. Simek, p. 201.

29. The section on Weyland was graciously provided by K. C. Hulsman.

Chapter 5

1. Snorri Sturluson, *Poetic Edda,* trans. Larrington, pp. 3–27.

2. Bauschatz, p. 6.

3. Snorri Sturluson, *Poetic Edda,* Grimnismal, trans. Larrington, pp. 87–106.

4. Bauschatz, p. 13.

5. This is one of the fundamental cosmological concepts of any shamanic tradition; see Dubois, pp. 122–38.

6. The old Norse concept of personal prosperity, luck, and might passed from one generation to the next. Like orlog, it could be affected by a person's choices and actions.

7. In Norse theology, one's Hamingja, or luck, is said to form part of the soul matrix.

8. Bauschatz, p. 21.

9. Ibid.

10. Bauschatz, p. 23.

Chapter 6

1. The Norse word is given first, followed by the Anglo-Saxon, where it is known.

2. Wodening, *Hammer of the Gods*, p. 52.

3. Thorsson, *Runelore*, p. 168.

4. Wodening, *Hammer of the Gods*, p. 55.

5. On one occasion I had trouble with a meddlesome dead aunt who was fretful about my religion. I told her point-blank that if she wants to be honored in my house, she will respect my religious choice, and I pointed her toward some more enlightened relatives who could explain things to her. Just because a person is dead does not mean he or she is all-knowing. If an ancestor is causing problems, he or she can be uninvited.

6. Some folk will use an Anglo-Saxon term: wight or wights. Please note that this has nothing to do with race. Wight is in fact pronounced to rhyme with "wit," and simply means "spirit" or "living being."

7. A good book on ritual purity in ancient Greece is *Miasma: Pollution and Purification in Early Greek Religion* by Robert Parker (Oxford: Clarendon Press, 1983). I've had pushback from Heathens and other polytheists for using a term that is specific to Hellenic polytheism, but the word *miasma* exists in English and is perfectly serviceable to express a concept of spiritual pollution common to nearly all polytheisms in one form or another. If Heathenry did not have a concept of pollution and cleansing, it would be quite unusual among the family of Indo-European religious traditions to which it belongs. We know the Norse and Germanic tribes had clear ideas of the holy, and where there is a sense of the holy, there is likewise a sense of pollution as a matter of course. Norse words pertaining to holiness and pollution include *helgan* (f), "sanctity"; *helga* (v), "to appropriate land by performing sacred rites, to hallow to a deity, to proclaim the sanctity of a meeting"; *saurr* (m), "mud, dirt, excrement (defilement?)"; *saurga* (v), "to dirty, defile, pollute"; *saurgan* (f), "pollution, defilement"; *saur-lifi* (n), "lewdness, fornication, lechery." The opposite of *saur-lifi* is *hreinlifi*, which means "chastity." *Hreinn*

is the opposite of *saurr*. It means "clean, bright, clear, pure, sincere." (As a noun the same word means "reindeer," interestingly enough.) *Hrein-hjartaðr* (a) means "pure of heart"; hrein-látr (a) "clean, chaste"; *hrein-leikr* (m), "cleanliness, chastity"; *hrein-liga* (adv), "cleanly, with purity." We also have *hreinsa* (v); "to make clean, to cleanse, to purge, to clear," and *hreinsan* (f), "cleansing." So when Heathens complain that this is not relevant to Heathen practice, I strongly suggest they think again. It's not just in the lore, but in the very language our ancestors spoke. (Thanks to D. Loptson for help in hunting down these etymologies.)

8. A brief Google search on the term *miasma* brings up multiple references to the house of Atreus, in which misfortune follows misfortune because of heinous crimes and the slaughter of children. That's massive miasma on a level beyond what I'm discussing in this chapter.

9. I wrote about this at the time, and a commenter pointed out that the movie wasn't about Heathen Gods, i.e., the Norse Gods specifically, as if that mattered. I strongly believe that if we are present, it diminishes us to allow any Deity to be shown disrespect and I do not believe that our Gods, those we claim as "ours," would necessarily protect us from any ill consequences of such blindness and bad manners.

Chapter 7

1. The Havamal is part of the Poetic Edda. In it, Odin offers wise counsel on how to live a good and honorable life.

2. Elder Eric Wodening wrote a very important book titled *We are Our Deeds: The Elder Heathenry, Its Ethic and Thew*, an invaluable resource.

3. Wodening, *Hammer of the Gods*, pp. 41–43.

4. In fact, according to pre-Christian Germanic ethics, taking up the blood feud to avenge the murder of a relative might be considered a means of restoring the frith.

5. For Platonists, evils were the privation of something good, like health, substance, etc., a separation from the Good. For some philosophers like Kant, evil was rather a matter of human nature. A more thorough discussion, outside the scope of my piece here, of philosophical viewpoints on evil may be found here: *plato.stanford.edu/entries/concept-evil/*.

6. I like to tell people, when the subject of ancestral debt comes up, that the pain and suffering, joys and victories, the deeds good and bad of our ancestors don't just go away. There is no "away." Like a stone thrown across a still lake, some choices have repercussions that ripple outward down the generations.

7. Sadly, in a culture formed from generations of monotheism, industrialization, secularism, pop culture, and modernity we cannot look for examples of anything approximating virtue—unless we're looking for negative examples.

8. I firmly believe that the true battle of Ragnarok is not Gods against other Holy Powers like the Jötnar, but Gods joined across pantheons against this force, which seeks only to unmake all that the Gods have crafted.

9. It is significant that the words *cultus* and *cultivation* share the same root. In Latin, it's actually the same word: *colo, colere, colui, cultus, -a, -um.*

Chapter 8

1. Simek, pp. 271–272.

2. The Bragafull, over which vows and sacred oaths were made. This has survived in the modern Heathen practice of symbel, in which a horn filled with alcohol is passed around three times: once to

honor the Gods, once to honor ancestors, and once to make sacred vows or boasts. A vow taken over the horn is especially sacred within Heathen tradition.

3. "Hakon the Good's Saga," from Heimskringla by Snorri Sturluson. The excerpt here is taken from a version published by the Norroena Society, London, in 1907, which may be found online at *www.sacred-texts.com/neu/heim/05hakon.htm.* (Accessed 9/6/2018.)

4. From the Sigdrifumal in the Poetic Edda, my paraphrase.

5. Available in Edred Thorsson's *Futhark.*

6. Available in Swain Wodening's *Hammer of the Gods.*

7. Krasskova 2004, p. 18.

Chapter 9

1. Murphy, p. 149 and 67, respectively.

2. The most common example being the Goddess (and saint) Brigid.

3. Chickering, lines 491–95 and 615–630.

4. Pollington, *The Meadhall,* p. 47.

5. Tacitus, *History* 4.61, 65. Numerous works have examined the role of women in symbel and within the warband, most notably *Weahltheow and the Valkyrie Tradition* by Helen D'Amico and *Lady with a Mead Cup* by Michael Enright.

6. *The Whisperings of Woden* by Galina Krasskova (Global Book Publishers, 2004).

7. Pollington, *The Meadhall,* p. 54.

8. Ibid.

9. Snorri Sturluson, *Poetic Edda,* trans. Larrington, p. 24.

10. Pollington, *The Meadhall,* p. 53.

Chapter 10

1. Mickaharic, pp. 16–17.

2. Thanks to Jason Barnes, Frey's-man and goði, for this bath recipe.

3. For the Protestant attitudes dominant in American secular culture see Janet R. Jakobsen and Ann Pellegrini, *Love the Sin: Sexual Regulation and the Limits of Religious Tolerance* (Boston: Beacon Press, 2004) and the volume *Secularisms* (Durham: Duke University Press, 2008) edited by the same authors. For the impact of Vatican II on the devotional life of the Church and the absence of Mary see Charlene Spretnak, *Missing Mary: The Queen of Heaven and Her Re-Emergence in the Modern Church* (New York: Palgrave Macmillan, 2004); Marina Warner, *Alone of All Her Sex: The Myth and the Cult of the Virgin Mary* (Oxford: Oxford University Press, 2013); and for the focus of the Protestant Reformation, Eamon Duffy, *The Stripping of the Altars: Traditional Religion in England, c.1400–c.1580*, 2nd ed. (New Haven: Yale University Press, 2005).

4. Havamal 138-139, trans. Larrington.

5. Quoted with permission from S. K. I. Winter.

Chapter 11

1. Branston, *Lost Gods of England,* p. 51.

2. Ibid., p. 52.

GLOSSARY

Aesir [*Eye´ seer*]: The primary tribe of Gods, often associated with wisdom, order, justice, and knowledge. Odin, Thor, and Frigga were numbered among the Aesir. The word *Ás* itself means "God."

Álfar [*Owl´ far*]: Male ancestors. This word may also be used to indicate elves or inhabitants of Alfheim.

Beot [*Bay oat*]: An oath or vow taken over the horn in symbel.

Blót [*Bloat*]: A ritual involving the sacrifice of a sacred animal to the Gods. Some Heathens use this word to indicate any ritual done to honor the Gods wherein a horn is passed among participants.

Bursar: Another word for Jötnar.

Cultus: From the Latin *colo, colere, colui, cultus,* the word means to nourish, cultivate, care for, or tend. It is used in a religious sense to refer to the rites and rituals common to a particular Deity. The English word *cult* comes from cultus but the original Latin carries no negative meaning.

Dísir [*Dee´ seer*]: Powerful female ancestors. The singular is *Dís*.

Ealu bora: [*ay´ ah loo boor´ ah*]: The Anglo-Saxon word for the woman who carries the horn in symbel.

Etin: Another word for a Jotun.

Faining: A basic ritual honoring the Gods that does *not* include the sacrifice of an animal.

Frith: Right order, security, and peace enjoyed while among one's own folk, where all are adhering to the same social and ethical codes.

Frithstead: A sanctuary or place where sacred rites are performed. This does not necessarily indicate any type of freestanding structure.

Fulls: The various rounds of drink passed in formal symbel.

Futhark: The runes.

Fylgja: A guardian spirit, often associated with one's family line or tribe. It is also part of the soul matrix and may refer to a guardian ancestor.

Galdr: A type of magical chant. The word comes from the Old Norse *gala* which means to caw or crow. It is a dissonant chant used in rune magic.

Gefrain [*Yeh ' frane*]: Reputation.

Gielp [*yee elp*]: A boast made over the horn in symbel.

Ginnungagap: The primal void from which all life evolved.

Goði or Gyðia: The word means priest, *goði* being the masculine form, gyðia the feminine. It is also used to represent part of the soul matrix, referring to the part of the soul always in communication with the Gods, what some might call the Higher Self, though Heathens would not use such new age terminology. The words may be anglicized as *godhi* and *gythia* respectively.

Hamingja [*Ha ' ming yah*]: One's personal luck.

Heiti [*Hay ' tee*]: Praise names or bynames.

Holmgang: The practice of ritual combat or dueling in medieval Scandinavian cultures. It was a means of settling disagreements and legal disputes.

Holy tides: Holy days.

Howe: A burial mound.

Husel: A sacred meal, usually involving the sharing of meat from ritual sacrifice. Anglo-Saxon Christians adopted the term to refer to the Eucharist. It may also be spelled housel.

Innangarð [*In an garth*]: The sacred enclosure of one's community and society bounded by thew.

Jötnar [*Yot nar*]: Beings of chaos often at war with the Gods.

Kenning: A word-knot or figurative expression used in Norse poetry to refer to something. For instance "bane of wood" for fire or "feast of raven's" for warrior.

Maegen [*May ´ gen*]: One's personal might, vitality, and life force.

Maethel [*May ´ thel* or *math ´ el*]: A regional group of households, individuals, and Kindreds united by hold oath to a Lord.

Nornir: The three weavers of fate and destiny who lay the strands of wyrd for each individual. Their names are Urd/Urð/Urða, Verdandi/Verðande, and Skuld/Skulda.

Orlog: One's individual strand of wyrd.

Recels: Bundles or herbs that may be lit on fire, the smoke then being used to cleanse a person, place or thing.

Rooftree: Under one's own roof. When something is referred to as a "rooftree issue" it means that it is not subject to the dictates of tribal thew, but a matter of personal choice, within an individual household, and as such, cannot be gainsaid by a tribal elder without a violation of one's freedom of conscience.

Runemal: Rune work, specifically rune magic.

Scop [*Shope*]: Bard.

Seiðr: Sorcery, magic.

Shild/Scyld [*Shild*]: Debt or obligation of honor.

Skald: Old Norse word for poet. The Anglo-Saxon analogue is "scop" (pronounded shope).

Sonargöltr: The boar traditionally sacrificed at Yule in pre-Christian Heathen practice.

Spae: Reading the threads of wyrd, a type of divination or seership.

Symbel [Anglo Saxon: *Sim ' bell*, Norse: *Some ' bell*]: The most sacred of Heathen rites.

Symbelgerefa [*Sim ' bel yer ef ah*]: Host or hostess of symbel.

Thew: Custom, observance, tribal/community law.

Thing: In the Icelandic sagas a gathering at which legal disputes would be resolved and laws determined; legal assembly

Thyle [*Thill*]: Lawspeaker; one who has an exceptional understanding of lore, thew, and ritual practice. The Thyle has the responsibility to ensure that improper oaths and boasts are not accepted in symbel, thereby protecting the tribal luck.

Utgarð [*Oot ' garth*]: Those places that lie outside of the community and outside of thew.

Vaettir [*Vy ' teer*, often mispronounced "*veht ' teer*"]: Land spirits often associated with natural places or phenomena. Certain types of Vaettir inhabit houses and homes as well. The singular is Vaet [pronounced *Vight*]. Some English-speaking Heathens use the word *wight* instead. This does not in any way indicate a racial bias, but is a corruption of the original Norse term.

Valkyrie: The Norse word for the woman who bears the horn during symbel; also, fierce female warrior beings who ride in Odin's battle retinue, choosing those who will die and join Odin in Valhalla.

Vanir [*Vahn ' neer*]: One of the tribes of Gods often associated with fertility, abundance, wealth, and sexual pleasure. Frey, Freya, and Njorðr are numbered among the Vanir.

Vitki: A rune worker and magician.

Weonde [*Weh' on deh*]: A song of hallowing chanted before Anglo-Saxon style Heathen rites. It blesses and hallows the space. The song is chanted as fire is carried clockwise about the space.

Wergild: A legally determined financial settlement in Germanic and Anglo-Saxon law for a murdered kinsman.

Wyrd [*Weird*]: Fate, causality, and consequence; that which governs every person's life.

Yggdrasil [*Eeg' drah seel*]: The World Tree; Odin hung for nine days and nights on this Tree to win the runes. The word means "Steed of Yggr." Yggr is a byname of Odin, and the Tree is referred to as His steed because it was the means by which He gained the ability to travel between worlds.

BIBLIOGRAPHY

Adalsteinsson, Jón. *Under the Cloak: A Pagan Ritual Turning Point in the Conversion of Iceland.* Ed. Jakob S. Jónsson. Trans. Terry Gunnell. Reykjavik: University of Iceland Press, 1999.

Bauschatz, Paul. *The Well and the Tree: World and Time in Early Germanic Culture.* Amherst, MA: University of Massachusetts Press, 1982.

Blain, Jenny. *Wights and Ancestors.* Wiltshire: Wyrd's Well Press, 2000.

Branston, Brian. *Gods of the North.* New York: Thames and Hudson, 1980.

———. *The Lost Gods of England.* London: Thames and Hudson, Inc., 1974.

Brink, Stefan, and Lisa Collinson. *Theorizing Old Norse Myth.* Turnhout: Brepols, 2017.

Chickering, Howell D., trans. *Beowulf.* New York: Anchor Books, 1989.

Cook, Robert, trans. *Njál's Saga.* London: Penguin Books, 2001.

Crossley-Holland, Kevin. *The Norse Myths.* New York: Pantheon Books, 1980.

Davidson, Hilda R. Ellis. *Gods and Myths of Northern Europe.* Harmondsworth: Penguin, 1964.

———. "Hostile Magic in the Icelandic Sagas." In *The Witch Figure: Folklore Essays by a Group of Scholars in England Honouring the 75th Birthday of Katharine M. Briggs*, ed. Venetia Newall. Boston: Shambala, 1988.

———. *Pagan Scandinavia.* London: Thames & Hudson, 1967.

Dubois, Thomas. *Nordic Religions in the Viking Age*. Philadelphia: University of Pennsylvania Press, 1999.

Eliade, Mircea. *Shamanism: Archaic Techniques of Ecstasy*. Trans. William Trask. Princeton, NJ: Princeton University Press, 1964.

Enright, Michael. *The Lady with a Mead Cup: Ritual, Prophecy, and Lordship in the European Warband from La Tene to the Viking Age*. Dublin: Four Courts Press, 1996.

Glosecki, Stephen. *Shamanism and Old English Poetry*. New York: Garland Publishing, 1989.

Gundarsson, Kveldulf. *Teutonic Religion*. St. Paul, MN: Llewellyn Publications, 1993.

Hastrup, Kirsten. *Culture and History in Medieval Iceland: An Anthropological Analysis of Structure and Change*. Oxford: Oxford University Press, 1985.

——. *A Place Apart: An Anthropological Study of the Icelandic World*. Oxford: Clarendon Press, 1998.

Herbert, Kathleen. *Peace-Weavers and Shield-Maidens*. Wiltshire: Anglo-Saxon Books, 1997.

Hulsman, K. C. *Heathen Magicoreligious Practices: From the Ancient Past Through the Reconstructed Present*. Arlington: University of Texas Press, 2004.

Jesch, Judith. *Women in the Viking Age*. Woodbridge, Suffolk: Boydell Press, 1991.

Johnston, George, trans. *The Saga of Gisli the Outlaw*. Ed. Peter Foote. Toronto: University of Toronto Press, 1963.

Jones, Prudence, and Nigel Pennick. *A History of Pagan Europe*. New York: Routledge, 2003.

Krasskova, Galina. *Devotional Polytheism*. New York: Sanngetall Press, 2015.

——. *He is Frenzy*. New York: Sanngetall Press, 2013.

——. *Honoring the Ancestors*. New York: Sanngetall Press, 2015.

——. *Northern Tradition for the Solitary Practitioner*. Franklin Lakes, NJ: New Page Books, 2008.

———. *Runes: Theory and Practice*. Franklin Lakes, NJ: New Page Books, 2009.

———. *Sigdrifa's Prayer: An Exploration and Exegesis*. Hubbardston, MA: Asphodel Press, 2007.

———. *Sigyn: Our Lady of the Staying Power*. Hubbardston, MA: Asphodel Press, 2009.

———. *Transgressing Faith*. New York: Sanngetall Press, 2013.

———. *The Whisperings of Woden*. New York: Global Book Publishers, 2004.

Kvideland, Reimund, and Henning Sehmsdorf, eds. *Nordic Folklore*. Bloomington, IN: Indiana University Press, 1990.

Larrington, Carolyne, Judy Quinn, Brittany Schorn. *A Handbook to Eddic Poetry*. Cambridge, UK: Cambridge University Press, 2016.

Lewis, I. M. *Ecstatic Religion: A Study of Shamanism and Spirit Possession*. New York: Penguin, 1971.

Lindow, John. *Norse Mythology*. Oxford: Oxford University Press, 2001.

Lord, Garman. "The Ásatrú Movement." *Marklander* 61 (2002): 8–10.

———. *A Short History of Anglo-Saxon Theodism*. Watertown, NY: Theod Press, 1994.

———. "Tomorrow's Reawakening." *Marklander* 58 (2002): 10–11.

McQueen, Gert. "A Short History of Anglo-Saxon Theodism." Watertown, NY: Theod Press, 1994.

Mickaharic, Draja. *Spiritual Cleansing*. York Beach, ME: Weiser Books, 1982.

Miller, William. *Bloodtaking and Peacemaking: Feud, Law, and Society in Saga Iceland*. Chicago: University of Chicago Press, 1990.

Murphy, Ronald. *The Heliand*. New York: Oxford University Press, 1992.

Olsen, Karin E. *Conceptualizing the Enemy in Early Northwest Europe*. Turnhout: Brepols, 2016.

Owen, Gale. *Rites and Religions of the Anglo-Saxons*. New York: Barnes and Noble, 1981.

Pálsson, Hermann, trans. *Eyrbyggja Saga*. London: Penguin, 1989.

Pálsson, Viðar. *Language of Power: Feasting and Gift-Giving in Medieval Iceland and its Sagas*. Ithaca, N.Y. Cornell University Press, 2016.

Pollington, Stephen. *Leechcraft: Early English Charms, Plantlore and Healing*. Trowbridge: Anglo-Saxon Books, 2000.

———. *The Meadhall*. Norfolk, England: Anglo-Saxon Books, 2003.

Reicher, Sophie. *Spiritual Protection: A Safety Manual for Energy Workers, Healers, and Psychics*. Pompton Plains, N.J. New Page Books, 2010.

Ross, Margaret Clunies, ed. *The Pre-Christian Religions of the North*. Turnhout: Brepols, 2018.

Scudder, Bernard, Andrew Wawn, Keneva Kunz, Terry Gunnell, Ruth C. Ellison, Martin S. Regal, Katrina C. Attwood, George Clark, and Anthony Maxwell, trans. *Sagas of the Icelanders*. New York: Viking Press, 1997.

Sheffield, Ann Gróa. *Frey, God of the World*. Meadville, Penn. Medoburg Kindred, 2003.

Simek, Rudolf. *Dictionary of Northern Mythology*. Cambridge, England: D. S. Brewer, 1993.

Strmiska, Michael. "Ásatrú in Iceland: the Rebirth of Nordic Paganism?" *Nova Religio* 4.1 (2000): 106–132.

———. "The Evils of Christianization: A Pagan Perspective on European History." Conference on Perspectives on Evil and Human Wickedness, Prague, Czech Republic, March 2002.

Sturluson, Snorri. *The Heimskringla*. Trans. A. H. Smith. New York: Dover, 1990.

———. *The Poetic Edda*. Trans. W.H. Auden and Paul Taylor. London: Faber and Faber, 1969.

———. *The Poetic Edda*. Trans. Henry Bellows. New York: American Scandinavian Foundation, 1926.

————. *The Poetic Edda*. Trans. Lee Hollander. Austin: University of Texas Press, 1994.

————. *The Poetic Edda*. Trans. Carolyne Larrington. Oxford: Oxford University Press, 1996.

————. *The Prose Edda*. Trans. Jean Young. Berkeley: University of California Press, 1954.

Tacitus, Cornelius. *Germania*. Trans. J. B. Rives. Oxford: Clarendon Press, 1999.

Thorsson, Edred. *Futhark*. York Beach, Maine: Samuel Weiser, 1984.

————. *Runelore*. York Beach, Maine: Samuel Weiser, 1987.

Turco, Jeffrey. *New Norse Studies: Essays on the Literature and Culture of Medieval Scandinavia*. Ithaca, N.Y. Cornell University Press, 2015.

Turville-Petre, Gabriel. *Myth and Religion in the North: The Religion of Ancient Scandinavia*. London: Weidenfeld & Nicholson, 1964.

Tzu, Sun. *The Art of War*. Trans. Thomas Cleary. Boston: Shambhala Publications, 1988.

Wallis, Robert. *Shamans/Neo-Shamans: Ecstasy, Alternative Archaeologies and Contemporary Pagans*. New York: Routledge, 2003.

Ward, Christy. "Women and Magic in the Sagas: Seiðr and Spá." *www.vikinganswerlady.com/* (Accessed 9/6/2018).

Watts, Edward. *The Final Pagan Generation*. Berkeley: University of California Press, 2015.

Wodening, Eric. "Knowest How to Blót." *https://archive.li/vh1e7* (Accessed 9/6/2018).

————. *The Rites of Heathendom*. San Leandro, Calif.: Café Press, 2003.

————. *The Threefold Initiation of Woden*. New York: Theod, n.d.

————. *We Are Our Deeds: The Elder Heathenry, Its Ethic and Thew*. New York: Theod Press, 1998. (Reprint White Marsh Press, 2011.)

Wodening, Swain. "Anglo-Saxon Witchcraft." *Marklander* 66 (2003): 9–11.

————. *Hammer of the Gods*. Little Elm: Imprint Books, 2003.

SUGGESTED READING

Heathens pride themselves on being well read both about their faith and the historical period in which it originally evolved. Many even go so far as to study the ancient languages—Old Norse, Old English, and Gothic—as well as modern Icelandic and German. Studying the lore is one of the primary devotional practices in modern Heathenry and even minute points of controversy are discussed avidly. Following is a basic list of suggested resources to help the newcomer become fairly well versed in Heathen lore. This is *far* from a complete list, but the books named are essential and will provide a thorough foundation from which the reader may branch out.

The Poetic Edda by Snorri Sturluson

This is the "holy" book of modern Heathens. There are numerous translations available, and it is generally advisable to read at least three or four different versions. The most commonly available are those translated by Carolyne Larrington (Oxford University Press) and Lee Hollander (Texas University Press). Older translations by Henry Bellows (American Scandinavian Foundation) and Olive Bray (AMS Press) are generally considered preferable, but they are more difficult to find as the volumes are out of print. Online specialty bookshops such as *AbeBooks.com* are a godsend for Heathens, and it is possible to find out-of-print books at a fairly reasonable price.

The Prose Edda by Snorri Sturluson

This is a prose retelling of the tales found in the Poetic Edda and is also a "must read." The two most popular versions are by Jean Young (University of California Press) and Anthony Faulkes (Everyman Library). American Scandinavian Society published a translation by Arthur Brodeur, which is considered one of the superior translations.

Norse Myths by Kevin Crossley-Holland (Pantheon Books, 1980)

An entertaining retelling of the Eddic tales, it is rather like CliffsNotes to the Eddas. An excellent and very approachable book that should grace the shelves of any beginner's library.

Teutonic Religion by Kveldulf Gundarsson (Llewellyn, 1993)

This was one of the very first books written on modern Heathenry, and it was very influential within Asatru. The author is an elder within the Troth and contributed widely to the source material available on their website (*www.thetroth.org*). The book is a solid reference that discusses every aspect of Heathen practice and custom.

Gods and Myths of Northern Europe by H. R. Ellis Davidson (Penguin Books, 1990)

This is one of the first books generally recommended to newcomers. It is a scholarly work discussing the Norse Gods and the culture in which They were originally worshipped. It's an invaluable companion to the Eddas, and the reader will come away with a firm understanding of each of the Gods, though it should be kept in mind that the author was not a practicing Heathen.

The Road to Hel by H. R. Ellis Davidson (Greenwood Press, 1968)

The Road to Hel discusses the concept of death and the afterlife in Heathen cosmology. Funeral customs, the soul parts, and the various possible destinations in the afterlife are covered in detail. This is the seminal work on the topic and, along with the following book listed, invaluable. Sadly, it is out of print and very difficult to find, but it's worth scouring libraries and asking among local Heathens for copies.

The Well and the Tree by Paul Bauschatz (University of Massachusetts Press, 1982)

Bauschatz examines the concept of wyrd within Heathen cosmological thought, the role of Urda's Well, Yggdrasil, and the idea of layering fate. This is an exceptional book and, as far as I know, the only scholarly work on the subject. Sadly, it is out of print, but worth the trouble of tracking down. Like *Road to Hel*, this book is invaluable for a thorough understanding of wyrd, orlog, and fate within Heathenry. Modern Heathens owe this scholar a great debt for this work alone.

Beowulf

A great deal of knowledge about Anglo-Saxon holy customs can be gleaned from *Beowulf*. There are numerous translations available. Of particular interest are the dual text versions by Seamus Heaney (W.W. Norton & Company, 2000) and Howell Chickering Jr. (Anchor Books, 1977).

Dictionary of Northern Mythology by Rudolf Simek (D. S. Brewer, 2000)

This is a wonderful compendium for any Heathen or scholar. Simek has compiled an exhaustive dictionary of Heathen terms encompassing heroes, Gods, names, and concepts found throughout the lore. This book is an invaluable reference and the most thorough currently available. It covers the entire history of Germanic culture and religion, and I would suggest making it one's first purchase after the Eddas.

Rites and Religions of the Anglo-Saxons by Gale Owen (Barnes & Noble Books, 1981)

This book examines Anglo-Saxon pre-Christian religion and culture. Though very basic, it is useful for developing an understanding of the historical roots of modern Anglo-Saxon Heathenry.

The Lost Gods of England by Brian Branston (Oxford University Press, 1974)

A fascinating volume that examines surviving Christian texts for clues to Anglo-Saxon Heathen worship, Branston has given us a valuable resource for modern Anglo-Saxon Heathens. Because England converted earlier than any other Germanic country, much of its cosmology and lore were lost. Branston attempts a valuable reconstruction from the surviving fragments and does much to enhance our understanding of the English Gods.

Gods of the North by Brian Branston
(Thames & Hudson Press, 1980)

Branston examines Eddic cosmology and discusses each of the main Gods and Goddesses in turn, examining the folklore and beliefs surrounding Them. It's a valuable resource—equal, in my opinion, to H. R. Ellis Davidson's *Gods and Myths of Northern Europe*.

The Sagas of the Icelanders, edited by Örnólfr Thorsson (Viking Press, 2000)

A collection of several influential Icelandic Sagas including *Egil's Saga*. While entertaining stories in their own right, modern Heathens look to these sagas for clues to pre-Christian religious practices. Additionally, one should read the following sagas:

Eyrbyggja Saga, translated by Hermann Pálsson (Penguin Books, 1989). Replete with magic, treachery, cunning, and political maneuvering, *Eyrbyggja Saga* provides a unique glimpse into the social structure, political climate, and surviving folk practices in Iceland shortly after its conversion.

Njal's Saga, translated by Robert Cook (Penguin Books, 2001). One of the most famous sagas, this tale of murder and blood feud chronicles the era of transition from Heathenry to Christianity in Iceland.

The Anglo-Saxon World: An Anthology, translated by Kevin Crossley-Holland (Oxford University Press, 1982)

A compendium of the major Anglo-Saxon texts. Though the majority are overtly Christian, they provide many clues to folk practices and Heathen cultural mores and are valuable resources for that purpose.

Myth and Religion of the North by E. O. G. Turville-Petre (Greenwood Press, 1964)

This book examines the religion, Gods, and culture of pre-Christian Northern Europe, offering an examination of the lore, beliefs, and practices of the Arch-Heathens that dramatically increases understanding of the nature of the Gods. It stands with *Road to Hel* and *The Well and the Tree* as an essential volume for thorough understanding of Heathen lore.

The Whisperings of Woden by Galina Krasskova (Global Book Publishers, 2004)

This was the first Heathen devotional to be published specifically for the God Woden. It offers meditations and devotional prayers to help the votary develop a relationship with this God. The prayers and exercises given may be adapted for any God or Goddess and provide a more personal means of honoring the Gods than usually presented in lore-based sources.

We Are Our Deeds by Eric Wodening (Theod Press, 1998)

This slender volume examines Heathen ethics, thew, and the concept of good and evil within Heathenry, both ancient and modern. While not necessarily "easy" reading, it is essential to any understanding of modern Heathen values.

Further resources may be found in the bibliography.

INDEX

ABOUT THE AUTHOR

Galina Krasskova has been a priest of Odin and Loki since the early nineties. Originally ordained in the Fellowship of Isis in 1995, Krasskova also attended the oldest interfaith seminary in the United States, the New Seminary, where she was ordained in 2000 and where she later worked as dean of second year students for the academic year of 2011–2012. Beyond this, she took vows as a Heathen gythia in 1996 and again in 2004. She is currently the head of *Comitatus pilae cruentae* and a member of the Starry Bull tradition.

Krasskova holds a diploma from the New Seminary (2000), a BA in cultural studies with a concentration in religious studies from Empire State College (2007), an MA in religious studies from New York University (2009), and an MA in Medieval Studies from Fordham University (2019). She has also completed extensive graduate coursework in the classics. She is currently pursuing a PhD in theology at Fordham. Krasskova has written a number of academic articles and presented at various academic conferences. She taught Latin at Fordham University for over a decade as part of her graduate training.

Krasskova's published books run the gamut from introductory texts on the Northern Tradition to runes, prayer, and devotional practices. She is also the managing editor of *Walking the Worlds: A Biannual Journal of Polytheism and Spiritwork* (ISSN 2474-3135). While very busy with teaching and school, she occasionally lectures around the country on topics of interest to contemporary Heathenry and polytheisms. She maintains a blog at *krasskova.wordpress.com* and may be contacted via that site.

TO OUR READERS